Reads well, is packed with useful content and will certainly be a valuable addition to the bookshelves of "ordinary people" and counselors/therapists too. Congratulations you have hit the proverbial nail on the head, an excellent book.

Margaret Newman, psychologist, co-author of best selling *Really Relating*, author of best selling *Stepfamily Life* as well as the co-founder of the prestigious Jansen Newman Institute, a leading tertiary education centre in counselling and human change.

~~~

Physical health can be so dependent on one's emotional well being and understanding one can help improve the other. This book will give you insights into why you think and react the way you do and how that impacts on both your relationships with others and also with yourself. Implementation of this knowledge will increase emotional health which can improve your overall physical well being.
          Dr. Richard Schloeffel M.B., B.S., F.R.A.C.G.P.

~~~

Gail Pemberton has written an excellent guidebook to relationships that blends an easy reading style and down-to-earth examples with a strong underlying basis in sound psychological theory.

This gives her book, unlike other books in this genre, a high level of coherence and integrity. This guide will not have you "flying by the seat of your pants" but rather, an understanding of "how" to do relationships better, and the "why" of her recommendations and suggestions. I believe that you will "do" relationships better as a result of reading this book, and you will also deepen your awareness and understanding of relationships.

Gail Pemberton's deep humanism and inherent spirituality underlies and supports her words, and this gives it a resonance that is unmistakeable.
          Michael Le Page PhD, Psychologist

~~~

I certainly understand a lot more about the unconscious mind from reading your book and it is simply fascinating! Loving the insights and getting a lot from it on both a personal and professional level.
          Karlee Fox MApp Psychotherapy

~~~

If you only buy one book on relationships, this is it. **Andrew MacDonald**

I wish I could have got my hands on the information in this book 16 years ago when my marriage dissolved. Instead it has taken hundreds of books and umpteen years of self development, therapy and personal growth. You Can Live With Anyone, well almost *will save you a lot of heartache and hard slog if like me, you are a "repeat offender" in the relationship stakes. This book saves us from continually creating the same person in a variety of different forms over and over again from our subconscious patterns, behaviours and thoughts. Thank you for getting the message out there*

Anna Stone

~~~

While it may be unorthodox to endorse your mother's book, we think some of our success can be attributed to her offering us sound and healthy psychological advice.

Some of the most difficult relationships in life can be those that we have with our family. Everybody experiences situations of conflict at some stage, whether it be in the office or at home. I think our family has always been able to resolve these easily, because we understand and use the principles that underpin this book.

Mum has put her heart and soul into researching and developing the fascinating and interesting information in this book. We know it makes profound improvements in our lives.

Rex Pemberton, (Youngest Australian to climb the world's seven summits and second youngest in the world in 2007) and **Caroline Pemberton** (Miss World Australia 2007)

~~~

A rich readable and above all useful work **Adrian van den Bok**
(Psychotherapist, supervisor, lecturer and coach)

~~~

As a G.P I am very aware of the interaction of mind and body in producing human distress and disease. Building resilience is an important technique in trying to minimize the problems associated with emotional turmoil. I am delighted to recommend Gail's very thoughtful, informative and practical book as a guide to helping people understand their stress and then take steps to decrease it. These steps may involve simply understanding what is happening or perhaps, changing oneself or maybe seeking further help due to an increased recognition of the need for such help. Many people start with their general medical practitioner.   **Dr F Black G.P.**

YOU CAN LIVE WITH ANYONE, WELL ALMOST

A Transformational Guide to Relationships

To my family for their unfailing support, my husband for his constant love who has truly helped me grow and my three amazing children who continue to inspire me to follow my dreams as I see their courage, determination and desire to make the world a better place.

And for everyone out there who is working to improve themselves and their relationships.

YOU CAN LIVE WITH ANYONE, WELL ALMOST

A Transformational
Guide to Relationships

Gail Pemberton

2008

Copyright © Gail Pemberton 2008

All rights reserved. No part of this book may be reproduced or transmitted in any form or by any means, electronic or mechanical, including photocopying, recording or by any information storage and retrieval system without prior permission in writing from the author.

National Library of Australia Cataloguing-in-Publication entry

Pemberton, Gail (Marie Russell), 1950- .

You can live with anyone, well almost: a transformational guide to relationships.

1st ed.
Bibliography.
ISBN 9780646474236 (pbk).

1. Interpersonal relations. 2. Interpersonal conflict — Prevention. 3. Mental suggestion. I. Title.

158.2

For further information please contact www.buythatbook.com.au

Cover design by Whalen Image Solutions
Typeset in 11/16 Palatino and Verdana
Printed in Australia by Corporate Documentation Management Pty Ltd

CONTENTS

Acknowledgements		ix
Introduction		1
1	Understanding the Power of your Unconscious	6
2	How the Unconscious is Programmed	33
3	Identifying the Problems in Relationships	56
4	The Secret Self	77
5	Projection	100
6	Triggers	124
7	Taking Responsibility	140
8	Living with the Most Important Person in your Life, You	170
9	Identifying our Needs	192
10	Power and Control	222
11	The Effect of our Background on Healthy and Unhealthy Relationships	263
12	What our Difficult Relationships Cost Us	291
13	Choices	315
14	Self-acceptance	334
15	The Spirituality of our Relationships	355
	Appendix	377
	Bibliography	381

ACKNOWLEDGEMENTS

There are so many people to acknowledge and thank for their invaluable input into this book.

When the idea first came to me to write down the insights I was gaining I thought I was being presumptuous. When I voiced this concern to my friend, Gai Hoole, she was quite pragmatic telling me, I was but a messenger to get this information out to the world, so start writing. Throughout this journey she unfailingly gave me her support and encouragement, as did Laura Riddell who was the first person to read it and give me her feedback. Ideas have come from many wonderful people: Viki Wright who edited the first part of the manuscript, Michele Stewart, one of my peers, who gave me wonderful critical comment which helped refine the material as did Bonnie Blaau, Marika Robinson, Misako and Julian Fairfield.

However, I could not have done without the support of my family. My father, whose opinion was difficult to hear but valuable in changing my somewhat overbearing tone at times, my daughter Caroline who gave me good advice about talking to a younger audience and, last but not least my husband Jon, whom I nagged to read it for his systematic appraisal of whether he could understand it and whether it made sense.

Perhaps most importantly I need to thank my many clients whose stories I have often drawn upon, changing names and situations so they are unrecognisable, but who have taught me so much. Also, David Jansen and Margaret Newman who set up the Jansen Newman Institute and whose course changed my life, enabling me to find my passion. Last but not least my many teachers, whose inspiration I have drawn on.

Without you all this book would not be before you now. Thank you.

INTRODUCTION

Is this audacious title: *You Can Live with Anyone, Well Almost* over the top, ridiculous or preposterous? It is a contentious and inflammable claim, and as you have just picked up this book the idea of being able to live with anyone or get on well with everyone, probably conjures up a picture of the person you find most difficult in your life right now. Perhaps the immediate reaction to the idea of harmonious interactions with that difficult other might be, "I don't think so" or, "I couldn't live with my mother-in-law and I don't think you could if you knew her…"

If you are skeptical about the idea of being able to get on with anyone, you may well wonder about the "well almost" in the title *You Can Live with Anyone, Well Almost*. Let me clarify that. It would be foolhardy to try to include some people in your circle of family, friends, colleagues and acquaintances. Axe murderers spring to mind, why would you take the risk? On a more serious note people that fall into the "well almost" category would be those that have marked personality problems and would almost certainly need specialised attention. Unfortunately, however much we may like to, we can't lump everyone we find difficult into that basket. Even though it would make our life a lot easier. Firstly, we have to look fairly and squarely at the part we play in the relationship difficulties we are having. But the good news is, that after you have undertaken the journey that this book will take you on, you will be well equipped to make that decision and then take appropriate action with that impossible other.

In undertaking this exciting trip you will realise that it is not about changing others, it is about changing you and the way you react to others. This is infinitely easier to do than trying to modify the behavioural patterns of others, who think that you are being the impossible one.

Friction is an inevitable part of living together and life without friction would probably be pretty dull. Often the more intimate and connected the relationship, the greater the potential for fireworks. Rather than to be feared, fireworks signal passion and energy, they are often the life in a relationship, a sign of vitality. This book is about understanding the friction, becoming aware of where it comes from and how it works, so it does not run rampant through your life destroying your relationships. You will have control over the tensions, rather than them controlling you and your reactions.

Look at it another way. Before a diamond is polished it is an opaque lump, not particularly special. That uncut diamond needs friction to become a gemstone. Our difficult relationships are the friction turning us, as unpolished diamonds into glittering gems, reflecting all the colours of the spectrum. We actually need friction to reveal our true beauty. The problem is, the friction is never comfortable and we try hard to avoid it. *You Can Live with Anyone, Well Almost* aims to make that polishing process less painful so we emerge as the gemstone, which is the essence of who we really are.

Fear, our need to keep safe to survive and our conditioning as children, have largely worked to suppress our true essence. If we had no fear, our relationships could flourish and grow and there would be room for us all with our particular idiosyncrasies. On this voyage of self-discovery, we have to be prepared to delve within ourselves, have the courage to face fears and have the endurance to follow through and apply our learning. We all have the resources within us right now to do this and we can make it work. That doesn't mean that there won't be any more challenging, teeth-grinding relationship dilemmas to resolve. However, hopefully we'll perceive them as challenges and hunt for the clues to resolutions in the damaging patterns, rather than either; continue discontentedly or, even initiate destructive conflict that festers for years. Sometimes having looked and learnt from the clues we may conclude we just have to walk away from some relationships. This book will enable you to recognise which is the most appropriate course of action for you.

What I learnt on my own journey of self-discovery was that it wasn't about changing others, as I always wanted to do, it was about learning why I thought the way I did, and understanding how my own unique programming had influenced the way I choose to see things. Have you any idea of how your own conditioning or programming affects the way you see things? Reading this book, we will learn what makes us tick and how our personal thoughts and belief systems have evolved. Often we avoid learning and getting to know ourselves as it can be painful, but it's much more painful not knowing. The good news is that when we do the work of finding out about ourselves, we don't continue to set up the same destructive patterns time and time again. Once we start on this journey the rewards come quickly giving us renewed zest and energy. As we learn about ourselves our life force grows. Self-knowledge inevitably increases as does love, courage and creativity, which reduces fear, conflict and hostility. As we become more self-aware change comes easily.

You Can Live with Anyone, Well Almost will enable you to become your own therapist. You will learn how to read your own body reactions to feelings and events, which will give you raw and vital clues to what is being experienced and felt deep down in your unconscious. You'll meet your secret self, a part of yourself that initially you probably would rather not know and yet, you will come to value as the key to many of your relationship difficulties. You will learn to analyse these signs and appreciate the extreme lengths you go to, that we all go to, to disguise what you do not want to think about or know. But when you truly begin to know yourself, you not only become stronger, but also more compassionate and loving. We will also examine what healthy relationships look like and what you need to experience a fulfilling interchange.

My experience as a therapist over many years has shown me that many people are unaware of what is an unhealthy cycle. An abusive cycle can, and usually does continue through generations. A child learns what his or her caretakers shows them and as such, automatically assumes that it is the norm, because he has no other yardstick to measure with or no other experience. This work will help you to identify unhealthy patterns that may have been set up in some of your relationships and give you knowledge and choice.

On this inward journey of self-awareness you cannot lose, you can only gain. Self-awareness becomes an integral part of our lives and brings its own gifts, since we never stop learning and growing. It builds our self worth and contentment as well as showing us that relationships are the gateway to spirituality.

I wanted to write this book for many reasons, but primarily because my own voyage of self-discovery has had a huge effect for the better on my life, and I think my family's life, so I wanted to share this information with you. I started to understand that the friction, anger, and resentment I was experiencing was about me and not others that I wanted to blame. Slowly I realised that there was lots to gain by exploring what had caused me anger, frustration, and pain.

I also discovered in my work that while there are lots of self-development books on the market I found nothing that demystified psychology by being a simple A to Z of why we behave as we do. Based on sound psychological principles and also on our fundamental need to be safe, I wanted to lift the veil on the mysteries of therapy in a way that you can immediately translate into a new and better reality.

1 UNDERSTANDING THE POWER OF YOUR UNCONSCIOUS

Are you irritated? Exasperated? Annoyed with certain people and their behaviour? Or just plain despairing and not knowing what to do next? Of course you don't want to live with these people. They are rude, inconsiderate, selfish, frustrating, arrogant – and the list goes on. It seems that life gives us plenty of chances to be irritated, exasperated, or annoyed by others. For many of us it is an everyday occurrence. Right up front I want to put you out of your misery and give you this gem of information that it took me seven years to discover.

The jewel is that everything you find so impossible in that difficult other person, and in all those others that make your life hell, is not about them at all. It is actually all about YOU. Yes, you. This can be difficult to accept, but unfortunately, the buck stops with you. All the problems you are experiencing are all about you. Does this annoy you? Are you disappointed? Are you

> *Unfortunately we can't blame others it's about you, not them.*

surprised? I was certainly annoyed to discover that what gets on my nerves about others is really all about me. After all, if we could prove that the root of our problems was the wrongdoing of others, it would allow us to keep blaming others and avoid change, essentially a much easier option. Believe me, I tried to blame others, but eventually concluded that it was not a healthy option. At least, not if I wanted to keep those dear to me in my life. I also discovered why my problems had so much to do with me.

It seems that so much of what goes wrong in our relationships comes down to how we think of ourselves, how much self-confidence and self-worth we have, as well as, the expectations that we have of others. This is why the following information about how we develop is vital because it is a cornerstone for understanding why our relationships go wrong. Let's start with the first fact, which is that we are the centre of our own universe.

How we think about ourselves affects all our relationships.

BORN SELF-ABSORBED

We are all born self-absorbed. This is our instinctive survival mechanism and it is hard wired into each and every one of us, without it we would die. Part of our healthy development as children is to be egocentric until about the age of seven. This is not acceptable to many parents, who are concerned that their offspring will grow up to be selfish brats, lacking all consideration, unless they are promptly taught to think of others. Consequently, from an early age we learn that it is not acceptable to be too self-absorbed and as such, self-love is firmly discouraged. When young children love themselves they have no sense of self-discipline, so we will not think twice about giving them exactly what they want, when they want it. The result: a spoilt child – which is not what a parent or society aspires to.

From a very early age we are taught that our behaviour needs modifying and, whilst we know we are the most important person alive, others are busily telling us that we are not. Our first conflicts happen very early. Now, as sensible adults we understand that we need to learn self-discipline, but what is also happening is that in our parents' desire for us *not* to turn out to be self-indulgent egotists, we are also learning some extremely important but covert messages. The most common message is, that unless we modify our behaviour, we learn that we are not particularly loveable.

Furthermore, in our desire to get our needs quickly met we learn that many of them are socially unacceptable, which can lead us to believe that our needs are not valid. Inadvertently, this often results in us believing that we are not particularly valuable and we doubt our own worth. Consequently, we absorb that the self-confidence that we were born with, when we only had to open our mouths and scream to get our needs met, is slowly being eroded. Self-love and self-liking are entwined with being valued and getting our needs met as children.

As young children we learn that to be loved, most of the time we need to be the way others want us to be. Many of us, as children, learned to submerge our needs to a greater or lesser extent if they did not please our caregivers. The degree to which this happens is different for all of us, and depends on the level of our caregivers' understanding and knowledge.

Unfortunately, those with little knowledge of childhood development or who had stern parents themselves, will often be harsher and with a lesser understanding of a child's needs. Lack of acceptance severely impacts on our self-development. Unless a balance is struck, a child's self-liking and self-worth slowly dissipates. The parenting job is very difficult. It is a juggling act to meet children's needs as well as teaching self-discipline.

Let's look at how easy it is to modify children's behaviour. It all starts with our brain and mostly with our unconscious. I appreciate that this may sound extraordinary but did you know that *the unconscious influences virtually everything we do?* It seems that not many of us do and most of us have very little conception of what the unconscious really is.

The unconscious operates on multiple levels, and this chapter explores how that occurs and the impact it has on relationships. With understanding, you will be able to see with more clarity what is going on around you. Before we talk about it in more detail, let's look at a simple example of how the unconscious can be impacted. This may be quite simplistic but it will help us to grasp how powerful the unconscious is.

> Maria is in the kitchen chopping vegetables for the evening meal. Her son Tom, is five years old and comes rushing in with muddy feet on the kitchen floor she scrubbed that morning. She is angry and shouts at him, waving a hand that holds the long sharp knife. She is unaware that she is even holding the knife. She has had another argument with his father and the muddy floor is the last straw for her.

> What did Tom see? He saw his mother threatening him with a long sharp knife. Before, watching children's cartoons on TV, he had seen his favourite character stabbed by a monster with a knife. Being so young and impressionable it is quite possible that he will carry the awful thought that his mother could be so displeased with him that she might kill him. There is often conflict between his Mum and Dad. Maria is hot tempered and Tom has seen her brandish knives before when she has been in the kitchen arguing with his father, and once she even threw a saucepan lid at Tom. The thought that Mum could kill him if she became really cross flits through Tom's mind, but it is too confusing and painful to contemplate so it sinks out of his awareness into his unconscious.
>
> Later in therapy, or in reflection, he may realise that he has never felt very safe around his mother, but never consciously understood or acknowledged that. His fear seems irrational but maybe justifiable. At some level he internalised that women are dangerous and they can't be fully trusted.

INFLUENCING VIRTUALLY EVERYTHING WE DO

Lets look at some facts about the unconscious. The terms unconscious or nonconscious, are becoming increasingly mainstream as psychologists realise that a significant amount of sophisticated mental processes take place out of the conscious mind. Timothy Wilson in his book *Strangers to Ourselves, Discovering the Adaptive Unconscious,* says that our five senses are taking in more than 11 million pieces of information at any given moment. This is an incredible thought. Scientists have determined that by counting the receptor cells, each sense organ has the nerves that go from these cells to the brain. Our eyes alone receive and send over 10 million signals to our brains each second. Yet, the most liberal estimate of how people are able to consciously process this, is a mere 40 pieces of information per second. So, what happens to the other 10,999,960 pieces of information? It is processed out of conscious awareness. It would be a terrible waste of a magnificent design if this incredible sensory acuity, when not consciously able to use the information, were not able to function – because we were consciously processing all this.

> Our unconscious is the gateway to efficiency and competency, once we become skilled in a particular area.

Wilson goes on to explain that our minds operate most efficiently by relegating much of our high level thinking to the unconscious, in much the same way as you would put a modern airliner on automatic pilot. Or, when you use your computer to send an email, you have no conscious idea of what is going on behind your screen in order to send that email to the other side of the world, or even next door.

The modern view of the unconscious is that it is a collection of modules that operates out of our awareness while doing other things. This enables us to breathe without thinking about it whilst eating. So, our unconscious enables efficient functioning. Your unconscious will be able to judge if you are about to do something dangerous, like step in front of a car while daydreaming as you walk down the street. It will enable you to recall the name of the high school teacher who was fantastic, but until you thought about it, was not in your conscious memory. Likewise, the unconscious is hard at work when you are reading a book and realise that your thoughts are a million miles away.

Our unconscious is automatically processing so much of what we do. Take driving a car. Remember when first learning to drive a car how much there was to think about, now for the majority of us we get into a car and we are "in the zone". Like athletes, when we become unconsciously skilled as opposed to consciously skilled, we can operate at our optimum.

The defining feature of the unconscious is our ability to operate on automatic pilot, which has five key characteristics. It is nonconscious, fast, unintentional, uncontrollable and effortless. All valuable in the appropriate place. For example, we are able to learn so much out of conscious awareness, like children when we learnt our mother tongue. We were not aware of learning it – it went into our implicit memory. This implicit memory (which we cover in more detail later), is one of the most important functions of the unconscious and it computes information more quickly and more effectively than our conscious minds.

The unconscious is designed to scan the environment. It detects patterns easily, but does not unlearn very well. It is a rigid, inflexible inferencemaker. It develops early and continues to guide our behaviour into adulthood, says Wilson, and it will categorise and stereotype others. This process seems innate and it seems we are prewired to fit people into categories. However, the big disadvantage is that being set in its habits, our unconscious is slow to respond to new and contradictory information and this is where many of our problems with others arise.

So, if the unconscious wields such influence, what part does the conscious mind play? The chart opposite gives us some idea of the different functions both parts of the brain play.

The adaptive unconscious versus consciousness

Adaptive unconscious	Consciousness
Multiple systems	Single system
On-line pattern detector	After the fact check and balancer
Concerned with the here-and-now	Taking the long view
Automatic (fast, unintentional uncontrollable, effortless)	Controlled (slow, intentional, controllable, effortful)
Rigid	Flexible
Precocious	Slower to develop
Sensitive to negative information	Sensitive to positive information

(Prof. Timothy Wilson in *Strangers to Ourselves, Discovering the Adaptive Unconscious*, 2002, Harvard College.)

Most of us like to think it's our conscious mind that drives us. In one sense it seems quite terrifying that our unconscious plays such an enormous part that for the most part we are largely unaware of, and yet on the other hand is such a magnificent instrument working for us behind the scenes. Before we go on to explore the unconscious more let's orientate ourselves by taking a brief look at the functions of the conscious and subconscious parts of our brains. We now know that our brain is an amazing instrument, quite the most brilliant ever discovered. It can perform quick nonconscious analysis of vast amounts of information.

THE CONSCIOUS MIND

The conscious mind is the newest part of our brain and the most recently evolved, it is called the cerebral cortex. The cerebral cortex is thought to be more developed in humans than in any other species on the planet. It is the part that thinks, feels and acts in the present, it is in the now. It understands time. The conscious mind evaluates, judges and observes, it looks and sees. This part of our brain perceives and analyses what is going on and makes decisions. We use it to think things through: plan, anticipate and to organise information and ideas. This part of us is inherently logical and wants a rational explanation for everything.

> *The conscious mind analyses and evaluates. It is also good at criticism, both of ourselves and others.*

The conscious mind is orderly and wants to analyse the cause and effect of ideas, thoughts and actions. The power of criticism comes from this part of the brain. The conscious mind is usually used as the gauge in intelligence tests and is the part of the brain that we generally think of as who we are, our lives tend to be dominated by it, as it rarely shuts up. If you pause for a moment and concentrate on being present, right here in the now, can you shut your thoughts down for a few seconds? Just be aware of your body, your breathing and any sounds that you may hear around you. Be aware but try not to let any thoughts intrude on your awareness. If they come in, merely observe them and remain focused on your breath and your body. What is your body feeling, right here, right now? Observe, don't think, don't analyse. For people who haven't tried meditation this is often a really difficult exercise. The power of the conscious mind is so strong that it wants us continually to be thinking some thought or another. Many of us actually feel guilt if we stop the thinking process for a few moments.

THE SUBCONSCIOUS

The next layer of our mind is the subconscious. There is a difference between the unconscious and the subconscious. Nowadays the words are used interchangeably, but there are actually four different levels of consciousness: the conscious, the subconscious, the unconscious, which is what we are primarily going to talk about, and the very deep level of unconscious, that perhaps we may never access. For the purposes of this book, I am going to refer to the unconscious as being at a deeper level than the subconscious.

The subconscious using a dictionary definition is, "being present in the consciousness, and capable of being the subject of, or involving mental activity, but not fully perceived and recognised by the mind, or completely and clearly present to the attention." For example, you are walking down the street, past a bookshop, going about your business. That night you happen to dream of the bookshop, and of a particular book in the window. The next day going past the bookshop, you look and see that indeed the book that you had dreamt of, is in the window. You are very surprised because the previous day you had not consciously been aware of looking at the window as you passed, yet your subconscious absorbed that information. The subconscious is not the same powerhouse as the unconscious, however, you could think of the subconscious as being the messenger or link that plies between the levels of consciousness and unconsciousness.

THE UNCONSCIOUS MIND

Most of the time we are quite unaware of our unconscious which, as we know, is an extraordinary complex part of the mind. Anatomically, it is part of the brain stem and limbic system and the oldest part of the brain. The unconscious is present in all vertebrates. It oversees all our vital functions including reproduction and self-preservation. Furthermore, it is also the source of physical action and emotions. Scientists can physically manipulate this part of the brain to create spontaneous outbursts of fear and aggression. The most important function of the unconscious is to keep us safe.

In his book, *Getting the love you want*, Harville Hendrix describes the unconscious mind well when he says, "The only thing your old brain seems to care about is whether a particular person is someone to: 1) nurture, 2) be nurtured by, 3) have sex with, 4) run away from, 5) submit to, or 6) attack. Subtleties such as, "this is my neighbour," "my cousin," "my mother," or "my wife" slide right on by." In many ways our unconscious mind is very primitive.

The unconscious is the seat of our memories, our experiences and indeed all we have learned. It is like a large filing cabinet of all our past information. In certain circumstances, it can also undertake most of the functions of the conscious mind, with one important exception, the power of criticism and evaluation.

NO POWER OF CRITICISM

For example, imagine being asked to hold a fountain pen. As you hold it, you are told that it will become hotter and hotter. At this point, your conscious mind is likely to be saying what a load of rubbish, fountain pens don't get hot. It immediately evaluates the situation. It has drawn on past experience of pens, stored in the unconscious, and knows that fountain pens do not get hot.

However, if you were to propose to someone in a hypnotic trance, where the conscious mind and its power of criticism has been bypassed, that the pen was getting hotter, the pen would indeed appear to be heating up. (When someone is in a hypnotic trance they are awake and aware, yet deeply and completely relaxed.) The power of criticism and evaluation is very much part of the conscious mind, and absent in the unconscious. Because the unconscious mind is unable to evaluate a situation logically and rationally, it accepts whatever is fed into it as "truth." Our unconscious mind does not know the difference between what is true and what we think is true. Whilst in a hypnotic state, we are programming the unconscious mind to accept this idea of a hot fountain pen as being part of our reality. This is a really

> *Our unconscious does not differentiate between what is the truth and what we think is true, but may not be.*

important fact to grasp, as the power of the unconscious mind will become clear as we go on.

The dictionary definition of the unconscious is "the part of the mind whose content is not normally accessible to consciousness but which is found to affect behaviour." This could be explained as the storehouse of feelings, memories and impulses, which is not directly available to the conscious mind, yet strongly influences our every action. We also know that in the unconscious there are often links between the cause of strong reactions in daily life and past difficulties. So negative feelings and memories that we may have tried to bury or forget in the unconscious are active, and have an influence on how we make choices and live our lives.

Another way of thinking about the unconscious is to think of it as a deep pond. We can see the surface of the pond, so that is accessible to our conscious, but have little if any awareness of what is below the surface. Usually our happy experiences and memories sit on the surface of the water, while the fearful memories and experiences sink to the bottom of the pond, which is murky and obscure. If, however, people have suffered major trauma or abuse they may not be able to feel much at all, not even the good things. It all sinks to the bottom, leaving people with deadened emotional responses.

Like cleaning out a cupboard, we have to look at everything in the cupboard in order to decide what we want to keep and what we want to chuck out. It's the same with the unconscious, we need to become aware of our old feelings of fear, guilt and shame. We need to do the work of reclaiming these portions of our psyche so they no longer exercise murky power. We need to take a deep breath and dive down to the bottom of the pond and look at what is down there. The work won't be done in one duck dive. It will take a number of dives, but it will be worthwhile. If we do the work we will never be afraid of what is under the water again, because we will have a greater level of awareness. Usually there is no monster lurking there, but some destructive beliefs and habits, left over from times when they helped to make our lives more manageable and served a useful purpose. Like protecting Tom from dreadful thoughts of his mother with a knife. Retrieving these now unhelpful beliefs from the secret self depths, we are uncovering more of who we are, and are in a much better position to be able to deal with whatever emerges.

THE UNKNOWN POWER OF THE UNCONSCIOUS

It is probably an understatement to say that most of us don't understand the power of the unconscious and we barely acknowledge its existence at all because it represents that part of us that is unknown. So how do we talk about what we don't really know or understand? A very common way is to deny its existence, or just pay it lip service and ignore it. The most common way is not to talk about it at all. To a rational and logical mind it is much easier to ignore. When other people are in difficulties but we can't see any logical reason for why they feel as they do, it is probably safe to assume that something is being triggered in their unconscious that is making them feel unsafe and fearful.

> *The main function of the unconscious is to keep us safe.*

Remember, the primary job of the unconscious is to keep us safe, and it does that by activating our flight or fight mechanism. At a conscious level we may not have any idea of what is going on, but we know we feel uncomfortable and need to react. We do that in lots of different ways. We pick an argument, blame someone else, or maybe avoid the situation by switching on the TV, having a drink or withdrawing. More about these avoidance mechanisms in chapter 6. However, it is those reactions that are so important to observe within ourselves. They give us vital clues about what is happening. They are the signposts pointing out the direction of the old belief systems we have absorbed. To track them down we need to be very aware.

Sigmund Freud, pioneer of modern psychotherapy, not only said that most of us spend our adult lives acting upon the hungers, drives, insecurities and anxieties that we created when we were small, but also made extensive use of the term unconscious in his treatment philosophy of psychoanalysis. The power of the unconscious underpinned his work and he referred to it as a sort of garbage bin for all the emotions that we did not really want to deal with. The idea that a large portion of the mind was unconscious was Freud's greatest insight.

Freud was very interested in the work of the great hypnotist Franz Mesmer, born in 1734, and his skill in curing patients using hypnosis and the power of the unconscious. Nearly two centuries later Milton Erikson, the father of modern hypnosis, took Mesmer and Freud's work further still. Erikson's vast body of work was based largely on the belief that if the conscious does not intervene, the unconscious will ensure that the person does what is best for him or herself. He did not always need to put people into a trance or under hypnosis, he believed the power of suggestion was enough. He would try to bypass the conscious mind and make suggestions directly to the unconscious. He believed that if he could help free the unconscious from domination by the conscious, he would be more effective in preventing people's self-destructive behaviour. The conscious mind, in his view, learns a great deal about what we can't do, rather than what we can. His patients' unconscious, he believed, contained positive forces waiting for liberation. It is a good way of looking at it. The unconscious is a storehouse of unexplored treasures. Following the clues can lead you to your own inner wealth.

THE POWER OF THE UNCONSCIOUS

It is an extraordinary thought that the unconscious has such power and such impact on our behaviour. Almost without our awareness it categorises and stereotypes people. Then it doesn't really want to change its initial assessment. Perhaps more frightening is the idea that, we may have a conscious mindset that is in conflict with an unconscious one. Because the unconscious plays such a major executive role in our mental lives by collecting, interpreting and evaluating information, it can set goals in motion, quickly and efficiently, says Wilson. The danger is that, are we conscious of what our unconscious agenda is? Is it different to our conscious agenda? Speed and efficiency may come at a cost that our conscious minds may think is too high. For example, we may take an unconscious dislike to our boss, and it would behove our

> *Our unconscious behaviour may sabotage our conscious goals.*

conscious mind to analyse all the information available in order to make an informed opinion about both our boss and a subsequent course of action.

Many of our chronic dispositions, traits and temperaments, are part of the adaptive unconscious, says Wilson. (To distinguish between the different levels of the unconscious, Wilson uses the term the adaptive unconscious, where I have simply called it the unconscious.) "The adaptive unconscious is more likely to influence people's uncontrolled, implicit responses, whereas the constructed self is more likely to influence people's deliberative, explicit responses. For example, the quick, spontaneous decision of whether to argue with a coworker is likely to be under the control of one's nonconscious needs for power and affiliation. A more thoughtful decision about whether to invite a coworker over for dinner is more likely to be under the control of one's conscious, self-attributed motives," says Wilson.

Returning to the idea that our unconscious goals may differ from our conscious desires, I am reminded of a mature aged student at university, who was diligently doing all the necessary research for completing her assignments. Yet when it came to actually writing, she had enormous difficulty. Under hypnosis she discovered that as a small child a teacher had said, "don't get too smart young lady, it won't do you any good" and subsequently she had never progressed academically to her full capability. At some level her unconscious had stepped in to protect her, to keep her safe. Perhaps when we believe we are highly motivated to do something yet never quite get around to doing it, it is possible that at an unconscious level there is another agenda at play.

The power of the unconscious can also be seen in the example below. However, when we have little awareness of its influence it can sabotage us dramatically, which is hardly conducive to positive outcomes. The conscious and the unconscious, although different in so many ways, are constantly exchanging and interpreting information. It is easy to understand how important it is to try to bring the unconscious into consciousness as the first step to empowering ourselves.

> John drives his father mad. James suspects that John is heavily using drugs. When John gets a job, he only seems to hold it for about a month and then he is either retrenched, fired, or he leaves because he can't stand it any longer. James remonstrates him saying, "This just won't do, John. You have to get something and stick to it. Here you are now 22, still living at home, still no job, no career, no qualifications, owing us that money for your car, and not even able to pay your mother any board. It has to stop. You don't even keep your room tidy, and you never lift a finger around here to mow the lawn or wash the car. Your mother still does your washing. I wish I knew how you manage to go out and get drunk on a Friday and Saturday night, while complaining you never have any money. When I was your age I was working nearly 60 hours a week, because your mother and I wanted to get married. I had no one to rely on except myself, and I made a good fist of it. I don't know what is wrong with you? I think we must be far too soft and it has to stop."
>
> John wishes his Dad would get off his back. "You're always nagging and criticising me. Whatever I do will never be good enough. It isn't my fault I can't get a job. It was

different when you were young, there was employment. You are forever telling me how wonderful you are with all that you've achieved. You never bloody well let me forget it. I'm not like you and never will be. Nor would I ever want to be. It's your bloody generation that that has stuffed it up for my generation and we can't get work. If I could work it would be different, I'd be out of here so fast."

Dad's frequent criticism of John when he was very young had a serious impact. John's unconscious didn't register the words, but it registered the message, that he was bad. The unconscious tends to deal in ideas and images. It "sees" pictures rather than hear words. It hears the melody not the lyrics. It registers the nonverbal message. Wilson postulates that the unconscious brain may be more sensitive to negative information than the conscious self and we all know how sensitive most of us are to criticism at a conscious level.

At some level John internalised that he was bad, and many years later, he is acting out an unconscious belief that he has absorbed. This message can take many forms. John may be passive aggressive and taking revenge on his Dad by living at home doing nothing or being so doped up, he's not really aware. At a conscious level he thinks he would like to have a satisfying job, but deep down he believes he won't or can't get it right, and that is what transpires. He may not realise that this belief is now becoming a self-fulfilling prophesy. For John to move on in his life he will need to actively challenge this belief by trying hard to have a different outcome.

HOW THE UNCONSCIOUS PROCESSES BELIEFS

Our unconscious perceives criticism as a threat to our safety because it has no powers of reasoning or rationality. So in the case of John he has absorbed the "truth," that he is inadequate and is acting it out. Using drugs helps him to numb the pain of the realisation that he is not good enough, if he ever thinks that far. Usually he submerges the unpalatable truth by using drugs as soon as he feels the slightest anxiety. Until he can consciously look at the discomfort he's feeling, John will not progress. Meanwhile, the drug habit becomes more entrenched, making the whole cycle even more difficult to break.

It doesn't really matter that we are criticising the behaviour and not the person, the unconscious will not make that distinction. For every criticism made about us, it takes a great amount of praise to counteract the negative comment.

BECOME YOUR OWN THERAPIST AND EXPLORE THE UNCONSCIOUS

To maximise the benefits of reading this book, get yourself a workbook, a nice fat exercise book will do fine, and take the time to do the exercises that are presented throughout it. By the end of the book you will have a diary showing you how far you have come, and all the things you understand and appreciate about yourself.

How do we find out what lies in our unconscious? We can't directly observe our unconscious, we need to become good observers of our behaviour. Wilson believes that it is difficult to know our unconscious by looking inward, he believes that it is better to deduce the nature of our hidden minds by looking outward at our behaviour, how others react to us and coming up with a good narrative about how we got to be the way we are.

There are undoubtedly many different ways of gaining insight into our unconscious, perhaps for most people the best-known route to the unconscious is dreaming. Many people keep dream journals and by observing patterns and symbols are able to get glimpses into their unconscious. At this point it would be useful if you jot down any unforgettable recurring dreams that you may have had over the years, with examination their meaning could become clear. Dreams are undoubtedly a helpful way of adding to the information you have about yourself, however you can do a lot more by reading your personal signposts. When you know what to look for you, can become your own therapist. The way to change our unconscious inclinations is to change our behaviour, which might sound and can be difficult. When you understand your behaviour it becomes much easier to change.

This book will act as a guide to help point out the signposts. Then you will notice your own signs, and as you gain awareness there will be plenty. This requires you to watch and listen to yourself carefully and objectively in order to understand what motivates your behaviour. Sometimes we will be dredging the bottom of our deep pond, pulling up the old beliefs. At other times we will be observing other's infuriating behaviours and asking ourselves:

Your journey

- Could I possibly do something similar?
- Why does this irritate me so much?
- What can it tell me about myself?
- Who did a similar thing when I was a child?

Gradually, the answers fall into place. As you progress on this journey, and you recognise the signs, you will be amazed at the depth of your powers of absorption and adaptability.

Without realising it, we try to resolve in our relationships, unresolved issues that started in early childhood. The perplexing part about it is, that we have little conscious awareness that we even had such issues.

> Miriam was an unhappy child in high school. She had moved from Scotland to New Zealand at age eleven and started a new school in a different culture. Physically she was an early developer, and consequently was much bigger than most of the kids in her year. To add to her embarrassment she had a broad Scottish accent, so she was the butt of lots of jokes and ridicule. Being sensitive, she hid in the toilets during lunch breaks. As she got older her refuge was the library. She had absorbed a belief that people did not want to be her friend. As an adult Miriam was convinced that she couldn't make or keep friends, and it became a self-fulfilling prophecy. She is too shy to make anything more than very indirect overtures in case she is rebuffed. This means that people find her distant and

> consequently do not make the effort to get through her natural reserve. So Miriam, age 30, feels she has no friends, which has a huge impact on her emotional health. She sought counselling for the problem.

When a belief is firmly embedded in our unconscious we believe it is the truth. Unless we question the belief we live our lives governed by it, without being aware of its power. If we challenge the belief we may realise that it is irrational but still find it very difficult to break. In fact it takes constant vigilance, self-monitoring and re-education before we can break free of its hold. In Miriam's case, she was convinced that she couldn't make friends because she never had. It was very hard for her to change this pattern, because unwittingly she sabotaged all her attempts by not persisting and not realising the strength of her fear of rejection. Her unconscious belief overruled her highly intelligent, rational, logical mind. Her persistence in becoming aware of her unconscious programming and facing it, is now enabling her to build a social life for the first time, but it is not easy. At the first sign of a rebuff she wants to retreat into her shell.

MORE ABOUT THE UNCONSCIOUS

Not only is your unconscious this amazingly fast processor of information, albeit at times not necessarily accurate, it is also the well from which your greatest creativity and ideas are generated. As Carl Jung put it in his book *The Practice of Psychotherapy*: "the unconscious is not just evil by nature, it is also the source of the highest good: not only dark but also light, not only bestial, semi-human and demonic but also superhuman, spiritual and, in the classical sense of the word, *divine*." Gradually, as parts of your unconscious become conscious and you become wiser about yourself, you will come to marvel at your own depths and ability to survive. There are parts of the unconscious that will always remain just that, unconscious and therefore inaccessible. No one knows the depth of the well of the unconscious, but each of us can become familiar with the accessible unconscious.

This is an example of how subtly the unconscious can work.

> Barbara, is a mother-in-law from hell who constantly wants her daughter-in-law Sue to be different. Brought up, immersed in the belief absorbed from her mother, that a women's job is to look after the physical needs of her husband and if she doesn't, she could suffer verbal abuse. Barbara never saw this abusive behaviour by her grandfather, but she certainly absorbed the lesson her mother had learned first hand: Look after your man and you should be safe.
>
> What Barbara also absorbed was that she had her father's approval when she was helping her mother. As a child she really only felt she belonged when she was doing something useful. Then both her mother and father would praise her. When she tidied the house, helped cook the meals, or did the ironing, she was able to bask in her mother's love. This reinforced the programming that a women's role is to look after the household. Not only did it come from her maternal grandparents' attitude, it was also prevalent in her paternal grandparents, and was indeed part of the older generation's stereotyping of roles.

> Barbara had not realised that as she criticised Sue, how deeply ingrained her own unconscious programming was, and how she was carrying that through and trying to exert control on a different generation. Her desire to change things came from her own deeply ingrained and unquestioned fear, that if you don't look after your man you'll find yourself in trouble. Alongside that was a belief that men weren't capable of looking after themselves. If she had asked herself, why am I finding Mark's situation difficult, instead of blaming Sue, it is possible that a lot of poison would not have polluted and permanently tainted the relationship. At some stage she could have casually talked to them both about how roles today are different from her generation. She could then have ascertained how Mark felt about the situation. It could be argued that in her concern she was trying to do the right thing by her son. In fact, not only was she alienating herself, but she was also assuming that Mark was still a little boy and not capable of sorting out his own domestic situation, if he found it unsatisfactory.

Meanwhile, back to the story of the Maria in the kitchen. What was she really thinking as she chastised Tom while brandishing a knife? Perhaps she was thinking about the argument with her husband and her anger transferred to Tom. Maybe he was "bad" because she unconsciously identified him with his father, who always seemed at loggerheads with her. We can never know exactly how unconscious conflicts will entangle an entire family. Maria had no conscious awareness of the impact of her actions on Tom, and if she had she would probably have been horrified. That is why an understanding of how your unconscious works is so important, and can have such far-reaching effects. Let's look at another example.

> Leon is two and his mother is heavily pregnant. One night while he is asleep, she is hospitalised due to complications. Leon has little awareness of what is going on as he is taken to his grandmother's house in the middle of the night. He certainly becomes aware that his world is far from right the next morning when he awakes, in a strange room with no mum or dad around. Later Leon always felt considerable anxiety when he was around his grandmother, even as a much older child, because unconsciously he associated her with fear and uncertainty. He was not able to identify exactly what it was that disturbed him, but came to recognise that at an unconscious level, it had something to do with not feeling safe around her. At a deeper level again there was a fear of abandonment, which had been compounded by many other small incidents that only emerged with therapy.

Often our seemingly irrational feelings and behaviour around a person may in fact have little to do with the other person, but much more to do with our unconscious. We can be triggered by someone which precipitates a feeling of discomfort or anxiety, which you may not be consciously aware of until you stop and try and think: does this person remind me of someone else in some small way, or has a similar situation in the past felt like this? When we have no rational justification for our decision, it is worth stopping and trying to analyse it. When we have an instant very strong emotional reaction to somebody, or something somebody says, then we know it is coming from the unconscious. In its more primitive way the unconscious is waving a warning flag, "this might be dangerous, watch out." Hopefully, our rational mind will come in and ask, what is this all about? What is going on here? As you become aware that your thinking could be irrational and there is no logical reason for why you feel like this, become aware that this reaction could be a warning flag, or maybe a linking piece of your inner jigsaw. Try to explore exactly what it is that you do not like.

We know that the unconscious has no power to critically evaluate a situation, that it works on gut instinct to keep us safe. Most of us could cope quite well if that was the only impact of the unconscious. However, its power is much more complex and entangled. This is because it does not differentiate between truth and what we think is true, and when we are very young this gives our caregivers enormous power to influence us.

As we end this chapter spend a little time reflecting and using your workbook answer the following:

Your journey

- Can you think of incidents in your life when your reaction to a situation or a person seemed illogical and reactive.
- Can you think of someone you have taken an instant dislike to?
- In light of the above information can you formulate some possible reasons for your thoughts and feelings. If you can't don't worry about it. Just note down the different experiences.

2 HOW THE UNCONSCIOUS IS PROGRAMMED

We are starting to get some appreciation of how factors, that for the most part were outside our awareness, can influence our relationships. Now let's look at how the unconscious gets programmed and how that programming becomes part of the biology of our brain. Firstly, to the programming.

Although the programming continues all through our lives, the blueprint of part of our personality is laid down in childhood through the unconscious. We know that the unconscious has no powers of evaluation, so it will absorb information that then becomes "fact." However, the "fact" is often the way others "think" we should be. The unconscious largely dictates how we behave, until we do the work we are doing now, which is uncovering our programming and deciding what is useful and what could be profitably chucked out. Doing this allows us to start to reprogram some of our unconscious.

In reading this chapter, think of your own childhood rather than wearing the parent's hat if you are a parent. As parents, we will never get it completely right and we don't need to beat ourselves up for that. As we learn, we will do things differently.

HOW WE ARE SOCIALISED AND PROGRAMMED

Earlier we learned that when we are born our survival mechanism is hardwired into us and is extraordinarily strong. We yell and cry when we are hungry, if our nappy is wet or dirty, if we are too hot or cold, or if we have pain. We will yell until we get something done. We want what we want, and have no concept of not getting what we need. As we get bigger we are taught that we can't always have whatever we want, whenever we want it. It is necessary for us to become socialised, and our caregivers do that. Our instinctual drive may be to eat the whole bar of chocolate and not leave any for others, or take what we want regardless of others. However, slowly we are taught that it is not OK to take what we want without thinking of others. If socialisation did not take place, the survival and harmony of humankind would be threatened.

Eric Berne in his book *Games People Play* says, "Parents, deliberately or unaware, teach their children from birth how to behave, think, feel and perceive." As we grow and continue to become more socialised, our parents or caregivers continue to write on the pages of the book of our life. They often write the same messages on us that were written on their own books of life. All families have rules, written or unwritten.

The overt rules are those we are told when our parents want to modify our behaviour. The unwritten rules are covert, we absorb these by observation. The basic purpose of these rules is to control the way people in the family relate, as long as everyone plays by the rules, the family is kept in balance and some sort of harmony. Each new member joining the family is taught the rules. As children we learned the rules generally in one of three ways. One way is by basking in parents praise when we behaved appropriately, another was experiencing the anxiety and discomfort when a rule was broken: "Just wait, Daddy will deal with you when he gets home." The third way by experiencing a parent's anxiety: "Just look at what you've done, how will I cope? I can't stand it." The anxiety may take many forms, but basically it is fear. The end result is that breaking the family rules when you are young leaves you feeling powerless and vulnerable. Breaking those same rules as an older child, adolescent or adult may, on the other hand, leave you feeling strong and empowered as you are breaking out of the parental mould.

> *The unconscious messages we absorbed in childhood play out in all our relationships until we gain awareness.*

In *Family Ties that Bind*, Dr Ronald Richardson says, "The balancing and counterbalancing that goes on in our families of origin affects us for our whole lives, even if we never have any contact with family members after adolescence. Next to our biological drives, it is the single most powerful influence on us. No one escapes its impact." The messages we absorbed in our unconscious as children continue to play out in our relationships, until we bring them into consciousness and decide whether to change them.

We are generally not consciously aware of how we cope with our feelings of vulnerability and fear when we break the accepted rules, but one thing is certain, we adapt. We go to great lengths to avoid feeling fear. We may not be aware of what form our fear will take, and that is a predicament for the unconscious. Do we fight or take flight? The fear of the unknown is worse than a specific fear. Most adults and most children will do anything to avoid this anxiety, even if it means creating other uncomfortable feelings. Rather than feel fear, they may show signs of paranoia, depression or obsessive compulsions. The fear goes to the bottom of our murky pond, out of sight and out of mind, but nevertheless, controlling our life to some degree.

Tom's unconscious fear of the knife in his mother's hand (page 30), contributed to his sense of anxiety around women and being out of control. The original fear that she could kill him, had sunk out of sight, into the depths of Tom's unconscious.

As very young children the person in control is the person who can make you feel this anxiety, this fear, and parents soon learn to use this to control their children. The most effective way of controlling children is to withdraw love, or threaten to withdraw love. This plays on the universal fear that we all have when young, the fear of abandonment. Unless we have actively looked at this or done therapy, this fear is still present to a greater or lesser degree, all through our lives, although most of us would deny it. Losing our partner, children, job, friends and anything we hold dear is all a manifestation of the fear of abandonment. As children, the fear of abandonment creates enough anxiety to change our behaviour.

We have all watched a parent tell a child it is time to go home and the child says "no" and won't move. The parent could just pick up the child and cart him off, but instead she uses psychological force. She walks away and says, "OK you stay, I'm going." Soon the child follows. Using the fear of abandonment is psychological abuse and it controls the child's personality. As children are so vulnerable and need their parents, they will suppress the parts of themselves that the parents find objectionable, rather than feel that fear. Instinctively, children know they can't survive on their own. This is how we learn it is dangerous to be ourselves. The greater the level of abuse, the less and less the real child will be present, and the "deadened" adapted child comes into view.

The parents, perhaps unknowingly, could have thought it was normal disciplining behaviour. However, it may have traumatised a sensitive child. Her parents may also have made every decision for her, telling her, they knew best and if she did as she was told, they would look after her. Over the years the child lost confidence in being able to make her own decisions. The average parent, thinking they are doing the best they can for their child, would no doubt be horrified to learn this.

As a result, our fears and weaknesses unconsciously shape the way we operate in our environment, we adapt. In this way, our personalities develop. But not only do our personalities develop, so does our brain and the way it functions.

THE IMPACT OF OUR PROGRAMMING ON OUR BRAINS

New technology is enabling science to better understand how the brain works. There have been revolutionary advances in scanning equipment, that enable us to more accurately see how the brain reacts to different stimuli. We are learning the ways mental processes are created by the activity of neurons firing in the brain, says Dan Siegel, in his book *Parenting from the Inside Out*. We now know, that experience physically shapes our brain by altering connections among the neurons of our brains. Furthermore, this process goes on throughout life and the ramifications are enormous. It means, that each and every one of us has the means to change our brains, by changing our perceptions of our experiences. We also know that the mind develops as the brain responds to on-going experience. So, because you are born with a particular genetic encoding, it doesn't stay that way. Your experiences are continually influencing the growth of your brain.

In our early years of life our genetic information influences how neurons become connected, shaping the emerging circuitry of the brain but experience changes the neural connections by using memory. "Memory is the way experience shapes the neuronal connections, the present and future patterns of neuronal firing are altered in particular ways. If you've never heard of the Golden Gate Bridge, then reading those words will elicit a different response in you than in someone who lives in San Francisco and can easily visualise the bridge and generate sensations, emotions and other associations with that bridge," says Siegel.

Implicit and explicit memory

The two major forms of memory, implicit and explicit, are quite different. The infant has the neural circuitry available to develop functional forms for implicit memory, (emotional, behavioural, perceptual and bodily modalities). This form of memory is available from birth, and probably even before. Implicit memory also includes the way the brain creates summaries of experiences, in the form of mental modes.

Explicit memory utilises basic implicit memory encoding mechanisms, but in addition, processes this information through an integrative region called the hippocampus. It is dependent on the maturation of that region of the brain after the first year and a half of life. Explicit memory is not fully available until then. With the development of the hippocampus, the mind is now able to make connections between the disparate elements of implicit memory, and create a contextual mapping of integrated neural representations of experience. This is the fundamental basis of factual and then, autobiographical forms of explicit memory," Siegel explains.

So as a pre-verbal young child, our experiences are encoded in implicit memory. This is memory that goes directly into the unconscious. Let's take an example. Imagine for the very first time you put your feet into a pool of cool water, your brain is making new synaptic connections which will add to your store of experiences. This occurs anytime we do something new, the experience is stored for later retrieval and use. All of our firsts, good and bad, that happen in our lives lay down new connections. This builds a type of model of how we view life. This model then serves as a perspective, or state of mind, that will directly influence how we look at the world and how we respond in the future. It becomes a type of lens and it is formed very largely outside our conscious awareness.

Memory encoding

We know from the scientific studies how memory is encoded, that it is shaped by our experience. The difficulty comes from how we perceive the events, as that, shapes how we process the experience. For example, going back to the first time we experienced putting our feet into a pool of cool water, did we judge that incident as good, bad or indifferent? The consequences of our perception is that our encoded memory of it, will be however we judged it: good, bad, or indifferent.

So what was your perception of putting your feet into the cool water?

- If delightful – it becomes a good memory
- Who was with you?
- Are they good people, trustworthy people?
- The experience, the people and circumstances become encoded as being beneficial. This is then stored in the unconscious and out of general awareness unless recalled. Perhaps fragments of the experience are recalled, not necessarily the event, but the feelings will be tucked away, and they will be comfortable and pleasant.

If however the experience of putting your feet in a pool of cool water was frightening or unpleasant it could be

- Encoded as a bad memory
- Who was with you?

- Are they trustworthy or are they bad that they allowed you to be exposed to this situation, or even introduced to the situation?
- Can you trust them or has doubt and mistrust been introduced?
- This will also be stored in the unconscious

You can understand how this relates to our programming as children. It means that all the experiences, all that we were taught as children has largely been laid down in implicit memory, in the unconscious and much of how we look at life today, is through those "lens". However what many of us are unaware of and don't want to hear, is that most of the patterning and programming laid down in early childhood remains largely untouched and in active operation, until such time as we do this type of work. Putting that another way, imagine driving a 20, 30 or 40 year old car, or perhaps even older, depending on your age. That is what so many of us are doing psychologically, and this is translated into the neurophysiology of our brains.

Until we become aware of our programming most of us are driving the equivalent of vintage cars psychologically.

Our beliefs and attitudes are activated in certain ways, triggered by our childhood experiences and function very quickly to shape our view of reality. All this programming directs to a very large extent how we will engage with the world around us, how we will think, what we will think and the resultant effect on our behaviour.

Furthermore, we know that, "emotion as a fundamental integrating process is an aspect of virtually every function of the human brain. As a collection of massive amounts of neural cells capable of firing in a chaotic fashion, the brain needs an integrating process to help it achieve some form of balance and self-regulation. Emotion is the process of integration that brings self-organisation to mind", says Siegel. "Emotion, meaning and social connection go hand-in-hand." When people feel our emotion or share our emotion we feel connected, met or heard, which enables us to feel good about ourselves and them. As Siegel puts it, "our emotions have been given resonance and reflection".

Emotional resonance

Much of what happens in relationships stems from emotional resonance. When we attune to each other's primary emotions, sadness, fear, anger, joy surprise, disgust and shame, there is connection or resonance. We feel understood. Even when we are physically separated from the other person we can continue to feel their energy. This energy becomes part of our memory of the other and so becomes part of us, says Siegel.

When a relationship goes sour or there is dissonance it is usually because our anxieties and fears are triggered at a deeper level. Even if we are not aware of it, we are extremely good at being able to read other's emotional states, our unconscious very quickly determines are they friend or foe. We do not necessary bring this information up to a conscious level, but it seems that our brains have the built in mechanism to help determine such matters in the form of mirror neurons.

Mirror neurons

Mirror neurons can detect the intention of another and may also serve to link the emotional expression of one to another. For example, if we see another cry we may feel like crying or even cry. When we see another angry, we may feel anger. The interesting thing is that these mirror neurons don't fire in reaction to any action seen in someone else. The behaviour must have an intent behind it. Waving our hands in front of someone will not activate these mirror neurons. So, as Siegel says, the brain is able to detect the intention of another person. While we may have intuitively grasped that, it is a different matter that science is now able to back it up.

These mirror neurons give us further hints at how our brains have evolved to be profoundly relational. Our emotional well-being relies on the interconnections with others. We even learn how others are feeling by putting ourselves in their shoes or by checking how our own body/mind responds. We are already aware in our ability to have survived this far, that we have the ability to read each other's external expressions, as signs of internal states. We also know that our emotional understanding of others, is directly linked to our awareness and understanding of ourselves, and as we learn more about ourselves we will understand others much better.

So with a better understanding of how our brain works, lets try and identify some of our own early programming.

RULES WE ARE TAUGHT AS CHILDREN

In order to socialise children and make our own lives easier as parents, we teach the "should" of "good" behaviour. Some of the most common rules we are all taught are given below. They are not necessarily all obvious or actually said, but are nonetheless covert messages we receive. Many of them will be unconsciously given, with parents largely unaware of what is conveyed. Often they will be the same messages that they repeatedly heard themselves as children. Many of the sayings sound like something from the Victorian era, although in reality they will go back as far as time. Parents have always tried to control their offspring, the reasoning being, to help make them better people and have happy, easier lives.

Don't	How many times have we either said that as parents, or heard it as a child.
Don't be you	Perhaps the more covert message is, behave how I want you to behave. How you are is not OK, or doing exactly what you want, is not OK.
Don't exist	Again similar to that old adage, children should be seen but not heard.
Don't feel **Don't cry**	"It will go away soon, it's nothing". This is a dismissal or minimisation of what you are feeling. Or, "Be a man, men don't show their feelings."
Don't be close	"Go away, I haven't got time now." "I don't want to know what's going on for you." "I haven't got time for a cuddle." "Boys don't need hugs and kisses."

Don't be separate	Usually another covert message. "You can't do it without me. It's dangerous to be independent." This links in with the next one.
Don't grow up	"Be dependent on me and I'll look after you." What this is really saying is, you can't be trusted to be independent and make your own decisions. It is also a way of the caregiver saying, "Don't leave me," or
Don't trust	The world is a dangerous place and covertly the message is, "I'm the only one you can really trust."
Don't think	Again a similar underlying message, undermining a child's ability to work things out. Trying to prevent mistakes that are an inevitable part of the learning process. The subliminal message is, "I will do the thinking for you."
Don't be well/sane	Secretly the child is being told, "I would prefer you to be feeble because then you will need me, and I can be important." Deep down this adult has an unhealthy need to be needed, and would rather a sickly child than an independent healthy individual.
Don't be a child	This is the opposite type of message. It is really saying, "Grow up quickly, be independent, and don't bother me."
Don't be important	"You cannot be in the limelight." The fear may be that the child becomes narcissistic, or it may be that if the child is important, it may detract attention from the parent who wants that important position.

Don't make it	Similar in vein again, to the one above. A child will often threaten a parent emotionally by being more successful than the parent is or was, so the message is, "Don't succeed, or don't exceed what I have achieved."
Don't enjoy	This seems to be very common. When children are really enjoying themselves parents will often try to damp it down, perhaps thinking the child will get over excited and then, as parents, they will reap the consequences. The message conveyed is that "It is wrong to get too much pleasure."
Don't be sexual	Particularly seems to be applied to girls, probably because parents fear unwanted pregnancies. A common threat for boys was to be threatened with blindness if they played with their genitalia.
Don't ask	"If you ask, you will not get." You should be grateful for what you have without asking for more, the typical Oliver Twist message.
Don't be lazy	"Do something."
Don't belong	Covertly, "If you belong to another group you will not belong to me."

Not only will we absorb a number of these type of rules, but parents will be trying to instill some drivers, or the same motivational type rules, that they have had instilled in them.

The most common drivers that parents instill in their children will be:

Please others	Do as you are told
Think of others	Be strong
Work hard	Be perfect
Hurry up	We know best

The combination of all the above should cover just about all instructions normally given to us in childhood. However, just to make certain that we learn all the correct messages, the famous psychotherapist Virginia Satir, with her Universal Should List, nicely summarises it all and covers any that are missing:

> **"Rules for being a good Person**
> I must always be:
> Right
> Clean
> Bright
> Sane
> Good
> Observant
> Healthy
> No matter what the cost of situation
> For
> Everyone counts more than I
> And
> Who am I to ask for anything for myself?"

Yes, perhaps it is all taken to an extreme but the point is so important. A substantial number of these rules will be etched into the fabric of our being and are still driving us, influencing not only our thoughts about ourselves and others, but also our behaviour.

- Write down those that resonate for you. It is unlikely to be all of them, but the more you think about them the more you could realise the impact of their power in your life right now. Because these thoughts are largely unconscious, we are often unaware of their operation. They are not all bad and do not need to be instantly jettisoned, but it is the degree to which they rule our lives that we need to be aware of. To modify or jettison those that are not helpful is going to take vigilant hard work, it will not be an overnight miracle for most of us. However, each one of them should be carefully looked at and considered to see how they impact your life. Being ruled by any one of these conditions is not conducive to happiness or emotional wellbeing.

- What impact do you think they have in your life right now?

NOT ALL BAD NEWS

These rules and "shoulds" are not all bad news. As Eric Berne says, although the unconscious and the rules we have absorbed as children largely govern our life and, "Liberation from these influences is no easy matter, since they are deeply ingrained and are necessary during the first two or three decades of life for biological and social survival...children do have some discretion as to which parts of their parents' teachings they will accept...because the adaptation was a series of decisions, albeit largely unconscious, they can be undone, since decisions are reversible under favourable circumstances."

BEING SET UP FOR FAILURE

We can't change what we are unaware of, however, it is important and useful to examine the rules and drivers carefully. Even the drivers, those phrases designed to drive us on, such as work hard, think of others and the multitude of others we hear as children and whilst seemingly innocuous, are setting us up for failure. This is because we cannot always fulfil them and when we fail we castigate ourselves, and judge ourselves as failures. So the negative self-talk continues

If our self-talk is negative and critical it is unhelpful and erodes our self-confidence. It is old thinking left over from being a child, scared of getting it wrong.

with its vicious cycle, etching itself ever more deeply into the fabric of our being. Self-talk is the mind telling us what to do and think. It generally keeps up an incessant chatter, which is the only way it knows of fighting to protect us from emotional pain. Unfortunately, its thoughts are often obsessive, repetitive and compulsive, which only adds to our discomfort. Have a listen right now and hear what it is saying.

Your journey

- Can you write it down?

- How does it feel to write it down?

- What feelings are coming up? Can you just observe those feelings without judging them, For example, telling yourself you shouldn't feel like that, or that you should be doing something different? Continually operating under an injunction like "try harder" sets us up for continual self-criticism. Remind yourself that it is far healthier and more encouraging to acknowledge what you have achieved, rather than dwell on what you haven't.

As children we learn through our actions. We are continually absorbing and exploring. Jean Piaget, who was the first scientist to make systematic studies of how children learn, says in his book *Handbook of Child Psychology*, that it is through actively turning to look or listen, through following and repeating, through exploring by touch, handling and manipulating, through striving to walk and talk, through dramatic play and the mastery of every sort of new activity and skill, that a child continually enlarges and organises in order to fit in physically and socially.

Because children are so active and curious, it is easy to understand how a busy mother always coping with the demands of her children, and often a number of children, gets exasperated and will do things she would not consciously choose to do. As a consequence, young children can absorb a totally different message from what the mother actually intended. This is not meant to lay a guilt trip on parents, as said earlier, there is no such thing as perfect parenting. However, the more we can be aware and take notice of what our children are saying the easier it is for them to grow up as happy responsible adults. It is in the disrespecting of our children's emotions that great damage is inflicted. Everyone needs to be able to express him or herself. Alice Miller in *The Drama of Being a Child* says, "Every human beings central need is to express herself, to show herself to the world as she really is, in word, in gesture, in behaviour, in art, in every genuine expression, beginning with the baby's cry." When children's expressions are not heard or invalidated, they slowly learn that it is not safe to express themselves and the need goes into the unconscious to emerge at a later date, usually as adults.

> Charlotte, age 2, wants an ice cream and throws a tantrum when she doesn't get one. The tantrum in the shopping center has lots of people all turning around to look at the cause of the noise, and her mum, to alleviate her own anxiety and in an attempt to stop the noise, quickly gives Charlotte a short sharp slap. The mother's anxiety may be related to the fact that she considers Charlotte to be misbehaving and she is fearful that other shoppers may look at her and think, she is a bad mother having such an unruly child. In all probability the mother's own programming as a child was, "Don't ask, be good." From Charlotte's perspective, after a few more such incidents, she unconsciously internalises that message, "Don't ask. It is not safe to ask." It may seem trivial and meaningless at

> the time, particularly if you are a parent, but the impact on the child can be far-reaching.

Inevitably, all children experience the unpredictability of their parents' love. At some level they are aware that they are always on "probation." They are always looking to prove themselves, to please those who care for them. In order to do that, they learn to adapt. At a very young age, children's reasoning skills are not developed and their learning is still almost entirely action based. Young children's minds work in a similar way to the unconscious, with no powers of evaluation or judgment. Consequently, almost everything is swallowed and absorbed as "truth." It is hardly surprising that in the process of being socialised we all grow up thinking a large part of us is "bad."

As older children we realise that stealing is not OK, but we want the object and take it. If somebody finds out we lie about it. The action of stealing leaves a residual uncomfortable energy. To cover our discomfort we may rationalise our actions to ourselves. It takes energy to hold down the unpleasant feeling and out of our awareness, the energy gets trapped in the unconscious. So although we think we may have forgotten all about stealing the article the guilt makes itself felt. We may have bad dreams about having things stolen from us, or being caught.

As adults a common way to rid ourselves of the discomfort is to criticise and deride others caught stealing. Often we will be the most verbal and the most derogatory of the accusers.

This, hopefully, puts others off our scent, but the action then becomes part of the unconscious.

UNCONSCIOUS, UNMET CHILDHOOD NEEDS MOTIVATE OUR BEHAVIOUR

The way we were as children doesn't go away when we grow up, it remains a dynamic part of us motivating our current experiences. If we didn't get what we needed as children (and it is worth emphasising that none of us ever had or could have the perfect childhood), we continue to seek what we really need through our relationships. *So your unmet childhood needs for security and approval continue to haunt all your relationships, until they become conscious.* That is how unconscious desires, ideas and decisions, that we had no idea we had or were making, rule our lives. To a greater or lesser extent they dictate our everyday actions and interactions.

> *O*ur unmet childhood needs for security and approval will plague all our relationships until we become aware.

For example, if we absorbed a rule that it was not OK to ask, when we see other people asking for what they want and getting it, we may feel resentful or angry, but have no idea why or where the anger came from.

> Brent, Janice's husband, did not have this conditioning, and he feels comfortable asking for what he wants and, more often than not, gets it. At some level his behaviour continually grates on Janice, because her childhood programming made it not OK to ask. She would just hope

> people – particularly Brent – would notice and then offer, when he doesn't, she feels irritated. Over time this anger grows, until all she sees is his lack of consideration, which to her is totally inexcusable. Eventually, she exploded and accused Brent of selfishness. Brent was both amazed and angry. He felt his behaviour was quite appropriate, he did not realise that Janice wanted him to read her mind and give her what she wanted without having to ask for it.

In this story there is no right or wrong. The difference was the result of two completely different upbringings. However, it makes for much easier relationships if people can tell people what they want, without expecting them to mind read.

PHYSICAL DISCOMFORT

When we are in conflict with ourselves we often feel uncomfortable. At a conscious level we may not realise what is going on, but there is a vague feeling of anxiety or discomfort an unpleasant feeling. We try to get rid of the feeling and do this in many different ways. We may pick a fight and blame someone else, or we may reach for a cigarette, or a drink, or bury ourselves in our work and ignore the angry feeling. We all have many different strategies for not dealing with what we don't want to think about. In the chapter entitled Triggers, you will be invited to stop and think about your own personal strategies for avoiding the anxiety, whether it is reaching for the chocolate snack, the drink, the cigarette, or abusing the next driver on the road who cuts you off without thinking. A common strategy is to find someone to blame for the discomfort we are feeling. We are not aware of our reaction, until we stop and think about it. What is happening to me? Something is triggering me. The greater the discomfort we feel, the more energy we are using trying to deflect our attention away from looking at this inner conflict. Our unconscious is signalling that something is not safe and we don't really want to deal with it.

As we work on through the following chapters you will start to recognise more clearly the triggers that tell you your unconscious is alive and well, and possibly wreaking havoc in your life. Its power is awesome, yet most of us have little awareness of just what impact it has on our day-to-day lives. It can be reprogrammed, to some extent, when we change or moderate the life scripts that are not working for us. Firstly this takes awareness, then it takes perseverance and constant vigilance. However, by noticing the signposts you can become your own therapist.

3 IDENTIFYING THE PROBLEMS IN RELATIONSHIPS

There is another aspect of our unconscious that we need to be aware of because it just loves to throw a big spanner into our relationships. It is the need we all have to be right. It all comes back to the unconscious's need to be safe. We know that experience shapes our brain and the more we think a particular thought, the more truth that thought holds, because our unconscious reacts in a predictable way the more often it thinks a certain thing. So the more often we think we don't like the boss or our mother, the more we will find evidence to back up that thought, even though the facts may not stack up. Social psychology has taught us, that we will go to great lengths to view the world the way we want to view it. Just as we have a physical immune system to keep us healthy, we have a psychological immune system that works towards keeping our world the way we want to see it. So given that the unconscious "plays a

> *We all have a need to be right and we will try and see the world in a way that makes us right!*

major role in selecting, interpreting and evaluating information", it is no surprise that one of the rules it follows is, "Select, interpret, and evaluate information in ways that make me feel good", says Wilson. The ramification of this is that we are naturally programmed to make ourselves right and everyone else wrong. While this would be wonderful, it means we have to work extremely hard to convince others we are right, because they all think they are right.

> *Our belief systems are often not ours at all but those laid down by others.*

The conflict between the need to feel good about ourselves and the need to see others' viewpoints, is one of the major battlegrounds of the self. How this battle is waged and how it is won not only determines how we feel about ourselves, but also how successful our relationships are.

One last aspect we need to be aware of in our quest not to have our unconscious rule our lives, is to be aware that your belief systems are not really your own. Would you think that impossible, weird, or extraordinary? Actually, as an infant you absorbed your mother's unconscious belief systems. Bearing in mind that we have not developed a belief system when we are born, we unconsciously absorb our mother's or our principal caretaker's values without even being aware of it. The result of this means that again we absorb everything we learn as absolute truth. So, from the moment we are born, like a little sponge, we start absorbing our parents' belief systems and with no power of critical evaluation we accept everything as truth, that's partly how Father Christmas, the Tooth Fairy, the Easter Bunny, and other mythical figures continue to thrive. Likewise, how good and evil have such power over children.

With our unconscious always wanting us to be right, and with all our different childhood rules and life scripts at play as well as carrying others' belief systems, it is a miracle that we have any working relationships at all. In fact most of us carry on life with lots of successful relationships, it is only the very knotty ones that catch us. I think we could profitably pause for a moment, to reflect and congratulate ourselves on all the good interactions we have, while knowing we are on our way to many more.

So with this background knowledge, let's start to look at that problematic relationship that probably influenced you to pick up this book. As mentioned in the introduction, there are people that make it almost impossible to interact with in a healthy way. For example, you may unknowingly, and despite all the love in your heart, be involved with someone who has a personality or mental disorder. If that is the case and they have a clinically diagnosable disorder, they would challenge the patience of a saint, let alone mere mortals. It would probably be inadvisable and self-destructive to try to turn yourself inside out to make such a relationship work. However, if you know one party is severely handicapped and realise that this will never be a "normal" relationship, it becomes a different matter.

PEOPLE WE MAY NOT CHOOSE TO LIVE WITH

What sort of characteristics will people have that will make a relationship almost impossible to maintain? It is safe to say self-abusers (the most common categories being alcoholics and drug addicts), psychopaths, sociopaths, and sexual deviants need to be avoided. Exploitative relationships with people who take all that you can give and give nothing back are also far from ideal. These are associations where you persistently feel you are doing all the giving. You are compliant, flexible, understanding and accommodating, yet when you ask for similar consideration it is not forthcoming and you feel used. Many of us may already be in such relationships and in desperation are picking up this book. While the circumstances are far from ideal, you will gain knowledge both about yourself and the impossible other that will enable you to make decisions to enrich both your life, and the person you are trying to live with. You will have strategies to cope and make changes, but I wish I could say the changes will be easy. Unfortunately, there is no way to change the past but we can make the future easier as a result of the knowledge we are gaining.

A number of us may be interacting with people who have clinical and personality disorders. The most common personality disorders have names such as Dependent, Histrionic, Borderline Personality Disorder, Narcissistic, Antisocial, Avoidant, Paranoid, Schizoid, Schizotypal, or Obsessive Compulsive. Different types of depression would also be classified as disorders. In the appendix I have given a sketchy description of some of the disorders. If you feel that you are living with any of these, it is advisable to check it out further by doing some research on the internet or in the local library. Although most of us will have tendencies toward some of these traits, for it to be a diagnosable disorder the symptoms must be very pronounced and a number of criteria have to be met. Your local doctor or health clinic will be able to advise you and help is available to deal with such situations.

THE COST OF THE RELATIONSHIP

We have glanced at some of the major obstacles to a mutually satisfying relationship: personality disorders, alcohol or drug addictions, abusive and exploitative relationships. Perhaps you have already recognised aspects of the problem, or problems in the behaviour of the person you struggle to get along with/live with. Now conjure up that thorniest, trying relationship and start thinking in terms of what it is costing you.

Ask yourself the following questions and answer them in your workbook.

- Are you walking on eggshells all the time?

- How much anger, aggravation, nervousness, tension, anxiety, resentment, discomfort, unhappiness or fear does it cause you?

- On a scale of one to ten, one being low and ten high, what number would you give it? Is it a four out of ten: irritating, but not enough to loose sleep over? Is it an eight or nine: you are feeling really unhappy and suffering a great deal of anxiety and fear?

In the following table you may like to rank each category separately, and add any other words describing this relationship that spring to mind. This will show you clearly which category the relationship fits into, in terms of personal cost, and give you valuable pointers about where the problem comes from.

DIAGONISE THE LEVEL OF DISCOMFORT THE FEELING(S) CAUSE YOU

	1	2	3	4	5	6	7	8	9	10
Tension										
Discomfort										
Nervousness										
Resentment										
Anxiety										
Anger										
Unhappiness										
Fear										
Irritation										

When you have catagorised this information you may decide that if the feeling is low on the scale of one to ten, that you will discipline yourself to ignore the irritation. If it ranks highly the cost will undoubtedly be affecting your health and your general attitude to life, and it may finally be time to address the situation. Either way, by thinking about the problem objectively you are increasing your awareness of what the personal cost is to you, and as you read through the book, you will gain vital clues about why you experience these problems.

COMMUNICATION

The very nature of the word *relationship* implies that there are a minimum of two people involved. But if one of you is doing the tango and the other the foxtrot the dancing will not be smooth, and toes, as well as tempers will surely suffer. That is what happens in uncomfortable relationships. If neither one of you stops to discuss what is happening, tensions are obviously going to run high.

Communication, of course, is vital in this situation, but here we can hit the first problem. Are you able to sit down and talk about what you feel or is it just too difficult? Are you hoping that, if you say nothing the problem will just disappear? However, if you are able and prepared to sit down and talk, but the other person can't or say they would like to, but sit sideways to you, or keep getting up and walking away, or look anywhere except at you, then the problem escalates. For communication to work, it must flow like a figure eight. The energy and message leaves you and goes to the other person and they send their energy and message back to you. (∞ also represents the symbol for infinity) Ideally, communication is an endless process. Unfortunately, in many cases either we or the other person does not want to hear what is being said, and the relationship gradually starts to deteriorate and finally breaks down. The reason we don't want to hear is usually fear, and we will look at this more closely in Chapter 9.

GIVING AND TAKING

How does your communication flow in the difficult relationship? What part are you playing in the receiving and transmitting of messages? Are you keen to transmit or are you avoiding? Are you open to receiving or shying away? At this stage, it is important to become aware of the part you play in the interaction. If you are the one avoiding, Chapter 9 will help.

If you feel you are the one running the hotel and the "difficult other" drifts in, uses the facilities and drifts out without paying the bill, obviously you will feel anger, resentment, and bitterness. Some of us are much more willing to carry the load for longer than others, but eventually we all snap. Are you the giver or are you the taker? It is difficult to be honest when asking ourselves this question, but if you generally feel you are doing the majority of the giving, then you probably are, and it would be good to recognise that. If you can comfortably contemplate that question you are unlikely to be the taker, takers wouldn't ask the question.

The bad news is, if only one of you is willing to look at the problem there is nothing you can do about it. We cannot change others, only ourselves. If you are willing to explore the difficulties, and you are essentially the giver in the relationship but the diffident other does not want to participate, the cost of sustaining the communication and the association may be too high to be ultimately healthy. After reading this book and working hard and honestly with yourself, you may conclude that the relationship is not in your long-term best interest, but at least you will know that you gave it your best try and learned some important lessons. Unless we can figure out our part in the dynamic, we tend to repeat the same behaviour in numerous situations that contributed to the difficulties in the first place.

Many of us have been taught to be selfless as children, so we give and give until finally we cannot carry the load any more and the situation implodes. One aim of this book is to show you when enough is enough, where the fine line between being kind to others and being self-abusive is drawn.

DIFFERENT SCENARIOS

Here are some brief outlines of difficult relationships. Perhaps you identify with all or part of some of them. In your workbook, make a note of where your experience "fits" or has similarities. We will follow these examples throughout the following chapters, and watch how their relationships evolve or where they collapse.

> We have already met Janice and Brent on page 53. They are a couple in their mid thirties, and have been married for 13 years. At first their marriage was wonderful, nurturing and satisfying. They were great friends and had many of the same interests. Slowly things changed. Brent got more and more absorbed in his advertising career,

Janice's life seemed to revolve around their two children, and juggling everyone's demands with her part-time job and the housework. Not only did she feel exhausted but she also felt more and more excluded from Brent's life, which involved a fair amount of travelling and entertaining. To Janice, Brent's life looked fun and he seemed totally unaware of all she was doing to keep things ticking along. His shirts were washed and ironed, and dinner was waiting for him when he got home. Janice noticed that often the imaginary conversation she had with herself was saying, "I do so much for him, and he seems so ungrateful, never lifts a finger to do anything for me. Doesn't matter what I say, I just can't get through to him. He's totally absorbed in his work and when not working all he wants to do is have fun, play golf, watch TV and spend time with the kids. I do all the work around here. It's not fair. Can't he see how he's hurting me by pretending to hear what I'm saying but not doing anything about it? He just seems to ignore me."

Meanwhile Brent is saying to himself: "She's such a killjoy, never able to relax and have fun. She wants me to be at her beck and call as soon as I come home from work. I'm the one earning the money we live on, but it's not enough for her. She's always bringing up every little thing I've ever done wrong, never lets it go, has a memory like an elephant. She blames me for everything that goes badly in her life. Never thinks about all the good stuff I do for her all the time. Even the sex is going off, she's always too tired."

This marriage is starting to go off track, the resentment is building in both and there seems little joy. If at this stage both decided to take stock and work together to identify where the relationship is going wrong, it could be easily saved.

Neil has been working for Daniel for nearly two years and is at his wit's end. He is angry and frustrated. It doesn't seem to matter what he does, Daniel is never satisfied with his efforts. He seems to use any excuse to find fault, and even though Neil is working long hours of overtime to get the work done, which he doesn't get paid for, it is never enough. Unfortunately, Neil feels trapped by his work situation. He lives in the country and there are few jobs available that pay as well, and he needs the money for his mortgage. When he suggested to his wife that they sell up and buy a smaller house to reduce the mortgage, his wife got upset and quite aggressive.

Daniel is sick and tired of Neil's continual complaining. He pays top dollar and expects top value. He would like to get rid of Neil, but Neil is the only one in the local area that has the necessary technical expertise. The more Neil complains the more bitter and irritated Daniel becomes. He also feels stuck, and the arguments continue to escalate. He knows at some level that Neil playing victim triggers his aggression.

At this stage Daniel has no idea that he is as responsible as Neil for the situation they find themselves in. Both just want to blame the other. Unless the relationship is worked on, both parties seem destined to leave feeling hard done by and bitter. It has all the signs of becoming a lose/lose situation.

Sue (page 29) is a far cry from the daughter-in-law that Barbara hoped to have. She is sloppy, casual, and seems to have no go. She sits around most of the time doing as little as possible, and Barbara suspects that sometimes she uses recreational drugs. She does work part-time but the house is always a mess, and her son Mark often seems to do the cooking in the evening. He even has to iron his own shirts.

IDENTIFYING THE PROBLEMS IN RELATIONSHIPS

Mark really keeps the place together, and Barbara just cannot understand what on earth he sees in Sue. In the nicest way Barbara often says to Sue, "How lucky you are to have such a wonderful husband like Mark, but you know, my dear, it isn't wise to sit back and let him do so much of the work. These days, men quickly get fed up in their domestic situation, and then their eyes start to wander, and before you know it they have found themselves another woman. Mark likes a clean tidy house because that is how he was brought up. And you know with your make-up on and nicely dressed you can look lovely, it's so much more attractive than old jeans and baggy sweatshirts."

This makes Sue scream inside, but she merely nods and says nothing, thinking to herself, "You old cow, I bet you had to keep wearing make-up and have the house immaculate because without that no one could have stayed with you. It wouldn't matter what I did, you would always think that I'm not good enough for your precious son."

Both Sue and Barbara look poised to lose here. Barbara could lose contact with her son as perhaps unwittingly, she is forcing him to choose between his mother and his wife. Meanwhile Sue could lose a potential friend and support.

Tom is a medical specialist who works in a big metropolitan hospital. We met him as a small boy on page 9 and recently on page 36. His hours are extremely long and his job, particularly when operating, is very stressful. When he comes home all he wants is peace and quiet. His wife Cherie, however, seems to have no conception of this need. The house is usually messy and his four children, although happy, are running everywhere, generally causing chaos. He finds the whole situation extremely trying and has to resort to shouting, and sending children to their rooms, before he feels there is any sense of order or control in the household. It doesn't matter what he says to Cherie, nothing changes unless he loses his temper. She is far too easygoing, and sometimes seems to behave like a child herself, particularly when she's with the children.

For her part Cherie dreads Tom's arrival home. Unless the house is being run like an army camp, or probably more like a hospital, he is not happy. She feels she should move like a nurse, silently swishing along in rubber-soled shoes, dispensing what is needed in an orderly fashion, and the children should be quiet and just do what they are told. Cherie is not sure how the big excitable Labrador should behave, probably sit upright in his kennel outside and only wag his tail if he is spoken too. It is all becoming too much. Tom's need for control and his derogatory, abusive language is becoming more and more upsetting. Even the kids are starting to say, "Why does Daddy have to come home? Why doesn't he stay in the hospital?"

Without realizing it, Tom's level of stress and need for control is slowly eroding the family's trust in him, and at some level he can feel their withdrawal which only exacerbates his need for control. So a vicious cycle is being created and no one person is totally responsible. Unless open, honest communication and self-reflection takes place in this family system, which is far from ideal and detrimental for all parties, it will eventually break down.

Patrick and Rachael are both ambitious and have high-powered jobs, which demand long working hours and quite a lot of travel. Patrick heads up a department in a big bank with a large team of people reporting to him. Rachael is an advertising executive with a number of creative people reporting to her. Their relationship is struggling under the pressure of their careers. They have little time to spend with each other and by the time they have juggled the pressures of work, the gym, buying food, and doing some housework to keep their townhouse going, they are both exhausted and need time and space alone to regroup their energies for the next week. A new dilemma has arisen which has significantly increased the tension in the relationship: due to his work commitments Patrick is not able to take an annual holiday at the same time as Rachael. Consequently, Rachael is feeling rejected and that she does not count for much in Patrick's life, his job seems more important to him than her.

Unbeknownst to them, both are engaged in a power struggle for acknowledgment of whose job is the most important and demanding. On another level, both are trying to find personal validation through their work. Their self-confidence and feeling of self-worth comes from what they do, rather than who they are. (This is such a universally held belief and causes great angst when people, especially men, lose their jobs as economic rationalism bites ever more deeply.) Unconsciously, at an even deeper level, both want to know that they are more important than the other's job. That is, Patrick wants to believe he is more important to Rachael than her career, and his career advancement is the more important to their long-term future.

Also at play here is Patrick's unconscious belief in the importance of his male role. He has come from a family where the father earned the income and the mother stayed at home to take care of all the domestic matters. Whereas Rachael has come from a broken home where her father walked out and left her mother to fend for the family, becoming both the income earner and domestic carer. Her unconscious belief system is that you must be able to take care of yourself because you can't trust a man. Eventually he may leave.

While some of these scenarios may sound a little antiquated it must be remembered that we are looking at belief systems that have been absorbed from parents, and although we may pay equal rights lip service, often there is a deep unconscious belief that men should be served. We still live for the most part in a patriarchal society

LET'S TRACK YOUR RELATIONSHIP

Now spend a few minutes thinking about your own particularly knotty, uncomfortable relationship. Perhaps it would be helpful to jot down a brief outline of the problem so you are clear about the main issues, as above. If the difficult other could also be asked how they see the situation, so much the better, as the problem will become more evident. If you don't feel comfortable asking the other person for their perspective, could you imagine what they would say and write it in your workbook?

With the image of your particular issue and trying other in mind, write down all you are saying to yourself about him or her. After focusing on that relationship, it would also be useful to choose the next three most impossible people in your life, and think of what it is about them that you find so difficult to tolerate. You could discover that they share many of the same characteristics. Some of those characteristics may resemble those of a parent that we found difficult.

It may help to scan through the following list to see what adjectives or what behaviours come to mind to describe them or the relationship. As you go, think through what you find particularly difficult about each person. For instance, you may think the "difficult other" is a nice guy generally, but his tendency to brag and big-note himself really irritates you. It is also very possible that what gets under your skin and annoys you intensely is what society would normally deem a good quality, such as somebody's beauty, their attention to detail, or their punctuality.

IDENTIFYING THE UNATTRACTIVE QUALITIES OF OTHERS

Here we go with all these less than perfect qualities:

Lying	Shrewd	Negative
Stealing	Cunning	Procrastinator
Blaming	Sabotaging	Powerful
Criticising	Deceptive	Charismatic
Insincerity	Short-tempered	Unproductive
Big-noting	Distasteful	Lazy
Bullying	Unpredictable	Helpless
Aggressive	Withdrawn	Communistic
Abrasive	Too energetic	Fascist
Violent	Unintelligent	Dictatorial
Conceited	Dependent	Racist

Egocentric	Dishonest	Intolerant
Selfish	Manipulative	Careless
Thoughtless	Indifferent	Dogmatic
Domineering	Authoritarian	Pompous
Doubting	Over Advices	Calculating
Fearful	Submissive	Doesn't try
Disbelieving	Power hungry	Self-involved
Indiscriminate	Belittles others	Self-centered
Angry	Foolhardy	Extrovert
Talkative	Cowardly	Introvert
Skeptical	Boasting	Eccentric
Cynical	Too demonstrative	Shallow
Ironic	Conventional	Envious
Over-religious	Unconventional	Mean
Irreverent	Exploitative	Inconsiderate
Intense	Scrooge-like	Over thrifty
Under-confident	Over-emotional	Lifeless
Over-confident	Undemonstrative	Too demanding
Paranoid	Too controlled	Foolish
Phobic	Controlling	Vengeful
Phony	Too rational	Jealous
Too giving	Irrational	Bitter
Too taking	Too wealthy	Superficial

IDENTIFYING THE PROBLEMS IN RELATIONSHIPS

Anxious	Too poor	Judgemental
Fundamentalist	Unskilled	Insecure
Derisive	Inefficient	Misogynistic
Passive	Too efficient	Secure
Stressed	Unhappy	Vulgar
Clumsy	Depressed	Need to be right

Perhaps you can think of more.

Now rate these less than perfect qualities that you have identified using the numbers one to ten, with one being the least unpleasant and ten being the most disgusting behaviour that you can barely tolerate. Put your numbers beside each adjective. For example, you dislike Joe Blow. He is deceitful, yet lies with total conviction, which you fall for every time. You may decide to rate his deceitfulness as a 10. Your sister-in-law is the most manipulative person you have ever come across, and you can't abide that. So that might rank as a 9. She may also be controlling, so that's another 9. Her negativity also irritates you intensely, and that ranks as a 7 for you.

YOUR SECRET SELF

Now we have come to the difficult part, and this will require great courage and honesty. Know that all the qualities you find incredibly irritating in someone else probably tell you more about yourself than about the other person.

Unfortunately what you find the most irritating about others tells you more about YOURSELF than those others.

For example, you can't stand others being judgmental, but in judging their judgment, you are being judgmental. Often we do not realise, that in criticising others we are doing exactly the same thing. This is our secret self. It lurks so well hidden that often we are totally unaware of its existence: it is buried in our unconscious. It only becomes visible when it is reflected in the mirror the difficult other holds up for us. It then takes great bravery to look into that mirror because the things you dislike about others are likely to also be part of you. It is important to accept that we each have the ability to have all the qualities or attributes that we have chosen from the list, as well as many more. That is one of the reasons we are such powerful beings. We have the ability to be many things and behave in many different ways. The more self-aware you are the more you will recognise the truth of this. Far from running away from this fact, it needs to be embraced.

This may come as a shock and a challenge. This secret self is the disowned part of us. While we will cover all this in detail in the following pages, it is important to lay down the framework here so we can clearly follow how our secret self works, and understand how amazingly adaptive and complex we really are.

Our secret self comes from our childhood programming. As we have already covered, when we were vulnerable infants, we were so dependent on our caregivers for our survival that we learned that in order to be loved and cared for, we had to modify those aspects of ourselves that our parents deemed unacceptable, such as: wanting whatever we wanted, whenever we wanted. This programming or behaviour modification went down into our unconscious, to later wreak havoc in our relationships without us knowing it. It is revealed through projection. We see other people's faults very clearly, meanwhile, not acknowledging that we have the same faults. We can spot our own projections when we recognise our triggers. Triggers are our emotional reactions to a stimulus, i.e. one or many of the characteristics on the list.

We all dislike various characteristics in others, but do not realise or perhaps do not admit that we too may harbour the same characteristics, in varying degrees, within our secret self. Probably some 99.9 % of the world's population is in the same boat. In understanding how this secret part developed without our awareness, how it's camouflaged by our unconscious, and how it influences our day-to-day life, we will learn how to use it to become happier, healthier, more integrated people. In fact, the more we become aware of our secret self, the stronger we become, because most of the time it runs our lives without our knowledge. Scary stuff!

Your first response to learning about your secret may be to dismiss this as rubbish. For example, you may argue that because you recognise that your sister-in-law is manipulative, it doesn't mean that you are manipulative. You are probably right, and you aren't manipulative to the same degree.

If we look at manipulation on a continuum, we see:

Ability to be manipulative____Manipulative____Extremely manipulative

Ideally, when we are aware, we can move along that continuum as we choose. However, if we are unaware that we have a range of choices or ability, our behaviour will tend to be stuck in one place. Your sister-in-law may have no awareness that she is being manipulative because her behaviour is set in a certain position. When we can acknowledge that we are capable of being and having the attributes that we despise in others, we are aware of the scope of opportunities to choose our behaviour in a particular circumstance.

Exploring this part of ourselves brings rewards. In learning about ourselves we are also learning about others. So this work, that you have already begun, is about everyone becoming more understanding. Perhaps you do not like what you see and want to fight it. Perhaps the prospect of exploring what underlies the difficulties in your relationship daunts you. I encourage you to persevere because the rewards are rich. We will find a freedom from the perceived tyrannies of others, or more particularly, freedom from our own self-imposed inflexibilities. The effort of keeping illusions alive and maintaining these far from fulfilling associations is much harder than looking at the truth. We can also reassure ourselves that we are among a small minority that has the courage to want to look honestly at what's going on at a deeper level, below the problems that the association is throwing up. We have already discovered from the work we did in the first chapters that we are amazingly adaptive and have a lot to be proud of, and as we uncover even more we will discover that the essence of us all is beautiful.

4 THE SECRET SELF

Now its time to understand exactly how the secret self works and also to track it down in our unconscious. If we only had gut feelings and dreams to rely on to find our secret self it would be a very hit and miss affair. However, we are lucky because our secret self likes to come out to play, usually to cause a spot of havoc here and there and then it becomes easy to see. Your secret self points the way to your unconscious, which wields so much power and influence in your life. Let's recap on exactly what the secret self is.

The secret self is a concept that became widely known as part of Carl Jung's work. He is considered the father of modern day psychology. Jung talked about the shadow, which I have called the secret self as those aspects of our own being that are not in our awareness, those parts of us that we do not, cannot or dare not acknowledge. The secret self, just like the unconscious, is out of our awareness until we start to recognise it. As we recognise and accept its existence, the secret self shows itself more clearly and enables us to become our own therapist. Whilst examining the secret self we will find many more signposts pointing out how our jigsaw fits together and this is where we will start to get to know this secret part of ourselves more intimately. We may be a little fearful of it because we don't know or understand how it works. However, as we start to understand and appreciate this precious part of ourselves we can embrace it. It adds dimension, depth and richness to our lives plus creative energy.

Our secret self apparently starts to develop at about two years of age, evidenced by the onset of the tantrums thrown by the "terrible twos," as we resist the world's restrictions. As a smiley gooey baby we are very adorable but staying our own person meets a few conflicts and limitations. We soon learn that unacceptable behaviour does not produce the attention and rewards we seek, and to survive we repressed or hid away certain aspects.

Our secret self is emotional. We cannot get a precise handle on it, but we sense it. Usually it is made up of greed, laziness, envy, jealousy, desire for domination, prestige, and aggressive or sexual urges. The seven deadly sins of pride, envy, gluttony, lust, wrath (anger), greed, sloth (laziness), probably cover them all, which is a fairly scary thought. What? Us with those vices? No never. Some of these urges will be promptings from our untamed human or animal nature, which is part of the limbic system. Many will be the attitudes that society has taught us should not be revealed, yet are a fundamental part of us all.

You could think of your secret self as a separate person who has all the attributes that you would not like to be seen as having, such as meanness, dishonesty, dirtiness and aggressiveness. All those aspects that are good to criticise in others but have nothing to do with us. This is why the secret self is often called the disowned part of ourselves. When we are completely unaware that we have a secret self we compare ourselves to "those bad people" and it allows us to feel holier than thou, or better than them. A nice feeling and one that can motivate a lot of our behaviour.

MINING UNDERGROUND

Theoretically if we lived on a deserted island, totally alone and had not gone through the programming that we do as children, we would not have a secret self. We would do exactly what we wanted when we wanted, as there would be no one else to please. We would not need to modify who we are. We would have nothing to hide, so no "bad" parts. While it sounds good being able to be completely ourselves, not adapted to suit others, our chances of survival on the desert island would be very slim and it could be exceedingly lonely.

Although we have talked primarily about the negative aspects of the secret self, there is also a positive secret self. For example, while one person may not like to think that there are aspects of greed, domination, anger and lust lurking deep within them, others may not like to express their sensitivity, gentleness or compassion. Although these are qualities that society normally deems very acceptable, a child may have learned that they were unacceptable in his or her particular environment. A sensitive child may have been criticised for his gentleness and been accused of being unmanly, so that innate gentleness goes underground into the secret self. While goodness and creative potential would make up a good secret self, the typical secret self is the one that is repressed, the disowned part of ourselves that our caregivers and society deemed unacceptable or "bad."

Surprisingly, in mining or dredging our "bad" parts, we can expect to find lots of gold. In fact, our excavations could be considered all gold. Even the most negative attributes are all useful information, enabling us to turn over more of those pieces of our own jigsaw. One of the ways it becomes gold, is to bring up the dirt from deep underground into the light for examination and to turn it into valuable material. We don't need to be alchemists to do that.

In the light we can look at aspects of ourselves clearly, they come into consciousness. Light brings awareness, enabling us to act with rational intention and intelligence. Personal growth comes from awareness. On the other hand, the unconscious is usually associated with the dark side and because it is unacknowledged, hidden or unknown, we fear it. It represents the part of us that is outside our conscious knowledge and control, which is scary until we do this work. In recognising our secret self we gain confidence as it no longer has the power to cause mayhem.

FEAR IN THE SECRET SELF

Ideally we all like to think we are heroes, beyond good and evil, and consequently we have no secret self. However, rather than deny its existence, the way to psychological good health is to embrace it.

Fear holds our secret self aspects down. We fear that if people could see us in our imperfection we would be judged imperfect and probably rejected. So the fear of rejection, of loss of love, keeps our secret self in darkness.

Jung believed that we have both constructive and destructive forces within our personality. To become whole, to be a real person, it is essential to integrate the dark side of our nature, with its primitive impulses such as selfishness and greed, into the light of our consciousness. He also believed that whatever we think our characteristics are, we possess the opposite, in equal measure. He called this the law of opposites. The self unites all opposites: light and dark, good and evil, masculine and feminine, conscious and unconscious. So for example, an outward femininity implies an inward masculinity. It is highly unlikely that there is a mathematical exactness to this, but the tendency is most certainly there.

If someone is always good, always smiling, always anything you want him or her to be, be aware that the secret self is probably hiding, unless they are indeed perfect. The secret self of good will be bad, resentful and "scowling," or as in the simple tale below.

> Ms. Perfect was a pillar of society, who did lots of good works. She always portrayed a delightful, sunny disposition. However, she was becoming increasingly irritated with her neighbour Ms. Untidy. Everything Ms. Untidy discarded seemed to be thrown into her back garden rather than in the rubbish bin, so her garden looked like the local tip. Unfortunately, Ms. Perfect house overlooks Ms. Untidy's garden from her kitchen and family room, so the rubbish lying around is a continual eye sore. Ms. Perfect is frightened of Ms. Untidy's fierce temper, so doesn't dare protest too strongly. She did ring the local council to complain, but to no avail. Eventually, driven crazy, she sets fire to Ms. Untidy's house, in the hope that with everything

> destroyed, Ms. Untidy would move away. Her crime was discovered. All her charitable good works and the charming, generous, kind image she had worked so hard to acquire and maintain was shattered.
>
> Ms. Perfect had worked so hard to be beyond reproach that she didn't dare complain and make a fuss, in case her image slipped. Inevitably, when there are gaps in our conscious willingness to see and own part of ourselves, our unconscious mind will create situations, if we can be honest, so that we become aware of our secret self and deal with it. Ms. Perfect had to deal with it when her cover or social mask was completely destroyed. Often, because we have invested a great deal of energy keeping our social façade intact, we do not realise the extent of our own self deception.

The problem is that when we try to deny the secret self, it multiplies. However, when we choose to integrate it instead, we gain stability and expansion of consciousness. We loose our self-righteousness and become flexible instead of rigid and defensive. The integration of our secret self adds to our richness of character, giving us balance and opportunities for growth, experience and creativity. As Jung says, everyone has a secret self, and the more we are unaware of it, the blacker and denser it is. It often acts as a snag, thwarting our best intentions, playing a dangerous covert game.

Going back to the story about Daniel and Neil (page 66), Daniel knew that Neil wanted approval, but he found it difficult to give because he had rarely experienced it in his own upbringing. This was a disowned part of himself, and part of his secret self. There was no one to blame for this situation. Daniel's father raised him in the same way he had been raised, with scant acknowledgement or approval, and Daniel's mother was also brought up in a household where praise was sparingly given. It would have been difficult for Daniel to be any different until his awareness increased.

Although Daniel also craved approval, he found it extremely difficult to see other's actions as being worthy of his validation. If you have rarely experienced acceptance it is extremely difficult to be able to give it to others in a natural and spontaneous way, which validates who they are. This is what was happening in Neil and Daniel's relationship, but neither was aware of it.

In Sue and Barbara's case (pages 29, 66) Sue's laid back, more casual approach to life was part of Barbara's disowned self. As a child she had learned that to be messy and casual was not appropriate behaviour. It alienated her from love and attention, and was suppressed.

In explaining the secret self, it may help to look at it another way. Imagine if all was light, you would not be able to recognise it as light. The intensity of brilliant sunlight on a tree needs the shadow that it throws to highlight the brightness. To have light you must have the contrast of darkness. It is as simple as without night there could be no day. If there was no dishonesty how could there be honesty? If people weren't unkind how would we recognise kindness? The two are complementary and are, in fact, on the opposite ends of the same continuum.

MOVING BACKWARDS AND FORWARDS ALONG THE CONTINUUM

A complaint that has probably been leveled at one time or another to everybody living on the planet is, you are selfish... Let's look at the continuum below.

Abusive to others_____Selfish_____Selfless_____Abusive to self

We are covering the extremes, but we can see that we cannot have selflessness without having selfishness. The secret is to get the balance in the middle of the continuum and have the flexibility to move comfortably along the continuum to suit each situation. If we were forever selfless we would in fact be self-abusive, as we would be denying that we had any right to do what we wanted, when we wanted, which is a receipe for disastrous relationships.

Back on our desert island we would be selfish, because there would be no one to ask us to do anything, and we would continually do what we wanted. If there was chocolate, we could eat the whole bar and not feel guilty. In fact, marooned on our desert island we would have no opportunity to have a choice about how to be.

The ideal is to have a choice of which position on the continuum we want to be in. If we can learn to live there, not needing to identify with either extreme but accepting both sides at once, we start to live a transformed life. We won't get hooked in to judgement in the same way because we realise that one cannot be without the other. If we deny or fail to recognise, the existence of either end of the continuum, it becomes part of our secret self, waiting to show its face at the first opportunity, and probably in a destructive manner, such as with Ms. Perfect.

FINDING THE BALANCE

We can't get a balance unless we can acknowledge that, at times, we are selfish and that is appropriate. We would not be human otherwise. The difficult part is to throw out the childhood programming that said it is always wrong to be selfish, and to accept some healthy selfishness, and to be comfortable with that. Because we have selfish thoughts doesn't mean that we constantly act on them, but the fact that we are able to acknowledge the selfishness allows us more choice in our actions. Without awareness we have no choice about what action we will take. Making the choice is empowering, and enables us to feel more fulfilled about ourselves.

ARE WE SELFISH

Maybe these questions will give you some clues.

Your journey

- Would you leave your baby locked in the car while you go into the club and play the poker machines?

- Do you insist on having the light on at night because you are reading your book, when your partner would prefer to sleep in the dark?

- Do you expect your friend to always buy the beer when you go out drinking?

- Do you expect your friend to top up your car up with petrol if he has borrowed it?
- Do you expect to do the clearing and washing up after you have cooked the meal, for yourself and others?
- Do you expect others to clear up after themselves?
- Do you repay money that you have borrowed or hope that in time the other person will forget?
- You want to go out to the movies but you can't get a babysitter for your two small children, do you leave them tucked up in bed, but alone for a few hours?
- Do you sneakily eat the whole chocolate bar without offering anybody any, when they are around?
- Do you force your partner to have sex?
- When your boss congratulates you on a job well done do you accept the praise and pretend you were responsible for the entire job, or do you tell him it was a joint effort with your team mate?

Write down in your workbook if anything came up for you as you read those questions. Your comments or feelings may be more clues to consider. These questions can raise the issue of selfishness but, more importantly perhaps, they raise interesting questions about respect for others, rights and responsibilities. Sometimes the issues are difficult to distinguish, and seem to be often lumped together and called selfishness. What one person may consider selfish another may consider irresponsible. The point of this exercise is not so much to illustrate how selfish or selfless you are but to highlight how we might consider someone selfish, when in fact from their point of view they have merely forgotten to consider your rights.

It seems possible and highly likely that we are all inherently selfish and only become less so because we realise that if we acted on our impulses all of the time we could not live harmoniously and may ultimately not survive, in which case even unselfishness is selfishness.

Can you take a flight of fantasy and imagine a glass of water being an analogy for your energy. Before you can offer anyone a drink your glass has to be largely full. The less water you have in your glass, the less you can give out to others. To be able to give selflessly you must give to yourself first, thereby keeping your own glass topped up.

Any time we recognise that we feel very strongly about something it could be very useful to stop and ask ourselves am I being very dogmatic or judgmental. What is the opposite way of looking at this? Do I like what I am seeing here, knowing that the more one-sided my point of view, the further toward one end of the continuum I am? You may decide that you are exactly where you want to be. That's OK, because it means you have a conscious awareness of your position. Or you may choose to ask what do I need to look at, to counteract this tendency in me?

Gradually we learn to balance the different extremes between selfish and unselfish, childlike versus mature, work versus play and so on. We see that we have both aspects. The conscious and unconscious minds can meet one another in harmonious play. As we learn to balance our inner contradictions we become consciously creative and aware of the consequences of our actions. Our awareness and creativity guides us onto a steadier middle course, while allowing us to consciously choose how we want to be.

Acceptance of the dark, or secret self, does not imply being dominated by this dimension of our being. It means recognising that this is a fundamental part of our nature. Instead of not even daring to acknowledge the parts of us that were modified in childhood, we can now own these thoughts, feelings and actions that we previously tended to disown by blaming, judging criticising others. This is called projection and we'll come back to exactly how it works in the next chapter. Before we started this journey of awareness, disowning and projecting our "bad" bits out onto others was our way of keeping the secret self locked into the unconscious.

It is easier to see the "bad" in others than recognise it in ourselves

Becoming aware of the secret self is uncomfortable and so we developed defense mechanisms to push the discomfort away, by repressing, which means not thinking about it, blocking it out and projection. It is always much easier to see the "bad" in others than to even acknowledge its existence in us. While that is the case it will inevitably cause psychological and interpersonal difficulties.

When the secret self explodes into consciousness, often in times of stress, it can either manifest as physical behaviour that can be destructive, and may range from table thumping, plate throwing, bashing, hurting, killing… Like the pressure cooker has to let off steam, otherwise it explodes unless the heat is turned down, our discomfort does the same. Turning down the heat, dampening down the urges from the unconscious may take many forms including drugs, alcohol or an angry outburst. Often after we have lashed out at someone or had too much to drink or used whatever avoidance mechanism we have used to cover our discomfort, we may feel intense feelings of guilt and unworthiness and try extra hard to be pleasant again which pushes the secret self even further back down.

DISOWNING THE SECRET SELF

Disowning our secret self plays a vital covert part in our relationships, and can't be emphasised enough. Each of us has learned and consequently must acknowledge that we do have thoughts that society, our friends and loved ones would probably be shocked to know about, such as spite, theft, murder, revenge, the seven deadly sins and so on. Barbara would not be unhappy if Sue accidentally dropped under a bus. "She's an appalling daughter-in-law and she really trapped poor Mark."

However, those of us who can look at ourselves honestly will realise that our thoughts are no worse than those portrayed in novels and movies. In acknowledging that to ourselves, we can make a leap into knowing our unconscious. We are starting to own the disowned aspects of our personality. We make an even bigger leap into the unconscious when we can talk to others about these thoughts. The fear that stops us telling others is that we will be judged unacceptable. Yet we are no different from the rest of the world.

It would be more productive to be honest about our feelings, at least to ourselves. This way our unconscious would not be as full, like a computer hard drive that needs downloading from time to time before it fragments. Neither will it covertly continue to control our actions. It would be healthier, if after acknowledging such thoughts we could accept them and not judge ourselves negatively for being human. Otherwise, whatever we deem too negative to express, whatever goes against our highest ideals, will be conveniently projected out into the world.

> Let's go back to Tom and Cherie, (page 67). Tom's irritation with Cherie's happy go lucky nature and spontaneity is part of his disowned self. From a young age Tom, knowing he wanted to be a doctor, had learned to repress his spontaneity, and focus on doing what was necessary to achieve his ambition. Over the long years of training, his sense of fun and spontaneity had been so repressed that it was now deeply buried, and he resented others being happy and free. Tom's secret self was disowned and projected onto Cherie. When Cherie understood what was happening she did not feel so disheartened and put down by Tom. She realised it wasn't about her, it had a lot more to do with Tom, although her behaviour brought the problem to light. Tom now had a choice about how he was going to handle the situation. Would he be able to take responsibility for the dynamic that had occurred?

Most of us are constantly checking our social mask to ensure that no one finds out who we really are, and that takes a lot of energy. Energy we often don't realise that we are expending but we are certainly aware we feel tired, and all because of our largely unconscious fear that if others saw our faults they could reject us.

RECOGNISING OUR SECRET SELF AT PLAY

If we meet someone socially and decide after a few minutes that they are inflexible and pompous, we are now aware that there will be a part of us that can be inflexible and pompous. What is difficult, is judging exactly where on the continuum of each characteristic do we stand? Are we just a modicum inflexible, or are we really quite rigid? Naturally, we want to have only the teeniest smidge of rigidity or pomposity,

We cannot become Mother Theresa unless we can look at our Hitler.

but how do we determine if that is the truth or only what we hope? There is no easy answer. As a rule of thumb the more we recognise this trait in our other relationships, the more it is a trigger, and as such part of us. The only sure fire way of knowing, is to check it out with our friends and relations. Have you noticed this tendency of mine to be rigid? Most people will give you genuine feedback if that is what you want. Perhaps the most important point is that whatever happened in the past is the past, when you did not have this awareness, so you do not need to judge yourself harshly.

From now on by recognising the trigger, you know you have choice about how flexible or inflexible you choose to be, at any given moment. Naming a feeling or thought means you are no longer so tied up in it. You have immediately achieved some measure of distance and a degree of choice over the mastery it can have over you. You are then able to influence the degree and the expression you give it.

The more we recognise the secret self and bring it into the light, the more objective and honest we can be in our relationships. *Whenever there is great energy in denying something, know that we are seeing part of our own secret self that is alive and flourishing.* Once you are aware of your personal triggers they become easier to spot. "You can't become Mother Theresa if you do not have the courage to look at your Hitler and get rid of him," wrote Elizabeth Kubler-Ross. Exercises further on in the book will help you identify your secret self very clearly.

SIGNPOSTING THE PATTERNS

The patterns that repeat themselves in our lives are another signpost. They are clues to what is underground, how the unconscious is working, and which parts of us are in our secret self, and disowned. Jung explains it by saying "the psychological rule states that when an inner situation is not made conscious, it happens outside as fate."

> Doreen and Ian have been married 28 years. Their three children have grown and left home. Doreen has always been a housewife and mother. Ian is a high powered business man engrossed in his work, which involves very long hours and much overseas travel. Doreen feels increasingly isolated and her life seems to lack meaning. She thinks, I've lost my purpose, what am I achieving? Ian

is totally tied up in the business, and all the committees he's on. I have social activities, yoga and art class, but it all seems a bit pointless. I can't ever see him really retiring. Without his job he'd be lost. He's a workaholic. Even the kids are too far away to pop in on easily. They all have jobs and are busy. Perhaps it will be different when I have some grandchildren. The only time we really seem to have a marriage is on holiday a couple of times a year. It's like a four week a year marriage when Ian and I are really together.

Ian can't understand why Doreen is not happy. "After all she has everything she could possibly want, there is no shortage of money, a beautiful home, her time is her own, what more could she want. I think she's being selfish. She can't expect me to provide absolutely everything. She has to make an effort. I'm very busy working and can't be at her beck and call. I think she is just bored and wants me to entertain her. She says things like I've always been there for you all these years and now it's time you are here for me, as if it is some sort of payback time. Furthermore, I am worried that she is starting to drink too much."

In this marriage the increasing arguments over the years was always the same, Doreen complained about Ian's unavailability. Surprising though it may seem, this was really all about Doreen. All her life she had been taught to give to others, she had little sense of self unless she was caring for others. Now she has no one to lavish her care on, and felt increasingly isolated and useless. However, much she nagged Ian, nothing changed, the pattern of arguments continued at regular intervals. Eventually Ian, totally exasperated, told her to get some professional help, he couldn't stand it any longer.

With help Doreen realised she had a life script of "you must take care of others," and why she felt unfulfilled, unloved and rejected. She took responsibility for the problem. Part of the solution was accepting the status quo, and the rest was immersing herself in the things she had always wanted to do, but told herself she couldn't because they were too time consuming and selfish. In Doreen's adherence to a life script, she had not realised that part of her disowned self wanted to do more things for herself, in fact desperately needed to do things. She hadn't acknowledged that to herself and had thought it was about Ian, hence the arguments. When she went back to full time study, she found great satisfaction. Part of her secret self was emerging into the light. The end result was that Ian found her more interesting and started to want to be around her more. A further pay off for both was, they realised how similar they both were. Both validated themselves by working hard.

To start with, their unsolved arguments were the result of the energy they were generating that had no place to go, a bit like the pressure cooker building steam. It continued to be repressed because after an outburst, Doreen would feel guilty and settle down again, but because nothing had fundamentally changed, the situation continued to "cook" building energy, causing tension and stress, even physical disease. Fortunately in this case the pressure was finally safely released.

- In your workbook, can you identify any repeating patterns in your life that may conceal your secret self?
- What patterns are there when you think of your relationships with difficult others? Perhaps the following questions will help identify some of them.
- Do your close relationships usually end in the same way?
- Is there a similar pattern in what goes wrong?
- Do you find you need to change jobs for similar reasons perhaps because you don't get recognition?
- When you look at what you are saying to yourself about that difficult other, is it similar to what you have said about other difficult others?
- Do you feel you are often ripped off or have become a victim of a situation?
- Do people tell you the same thing about yourself again and again? Is there some truth in it?
- Are you aware of often having the same argument?

The patterns you identify are useful as they may point to linkages in your jigsaw.

THE COLLECTIVE SECRET SELF

Secret self energies can be much bigger than just the disowned parts of us. Up to now we have only been concerned with our personal secret self, but Jung believed there is also the collective secret self, which is mankind's secret self. It is our human history, an aspect of which is universal and belongs to each of us. For example, people may carry in their secret self the energy of the country they are living in.

Take the Irish, living in an environment where there has been fighting for over 400 years. Many, particularly those who are politically aware, will, by having been indoctrinated, carry the unconscious and collective anger and grief of generations. The same could be said of the Jews and countless other persecuted people. If people are still being persecuted they will naturally need to do everything in their power to demand respect. However, the difficulty comes when people are either unaware that they may be carrying the anger of their forebears, or feel responsible for continuing the fight that their ancestors fought.

We can see with the continuous political situation in Israel that Jews will not allow themselves to be pushed around or controlled in any way, despite mounting negative international opinion. Their long history of persecution has forged a very strong collective energy of determination. (Energy used in this sense means the determination and pain carried by their parents and their grandparents is passed on down the generations, i.e. as a child you are taught never to forget what happened to your grandparents and how they suffered and were killed.) So understandably the people of Israel are doing their utmost to preserve what they have. It is almost as if they cannot afford to back down because to do so would betray their history and culture.

The secret self side of true strength is to be aware of rigidity as well as weakness. The risk is of going too far to the other end of the continuum thus losing flexibility.

Australian Aboriginals were dispossessed of their land as a result of European colonisation, and that anger is still present in today's political scene. It was, and still is a great motivating factor in their fight for land rights and native title. The Stolen Generation, (when paler skinned Aboriginal children were taken from their families and put into homes in order to integrate them into white society) is seeking to heal, by finding their roots and identity, which they were deprived of as children. Often it seems that the energy of the past is carried on through generations in search of final resolution. This can be such a valuable healing tool if it can be obtained by respectful means. If the final resolution comes through violence, the secret self aspects are merely perpetuated.

Perhaps the recent Croatian and Serbian war was expressing a rage, which could not be expressed 400 years ago when the Muslims invaded, in which case, the events of the past have transmitted an energy from generation to generation. This can change when the unconscious part is exposed, examined and expressed as it comes to light in our personal lives. Then we can make decisions. Often the underlying conflict is between rigidity and flexibility, the longer we hold onto the past the more rigid we become.

Extremism, fanaticism, one-sided bigotry and dogmatic conviction are evidence of a repressed secret self. The part being suppressed is the more moderate balanced point of view. In the West, Osama Bin Laden is generally classified as an extreme fanatic. Suicide bombers are another example, We believe that to go to such extremes, an important part of these people is being starved, so they create a compulsion. In the case of the suicide bombers they probably feel that at some deep level that they are valueless so, by committing their life to their political ideal, it becomes a way of being noticed, of being valued. Instead of being an unimportant cog in the wheel, perhaps they will have fame and maybe immortality.

Mankind's collective secret self may never be totally integrated into the individual, it will always be bigger than we are. However, our own personal light will grow stronger while we carry awareness of our personal secret self, and as others do their work the collective secret self will diminish. Our secret self is our teacher and when we ignore what it wants to teach we will again be thrown an opportunity, because "when an inner situation is not made conscious, it happens outside as fate."

According to Jung, the psyche is always striving for wholeness. He also says: "That part of human nature is to be constantly developing, growing and moving toward a balance and complete level of development." He believed that humans naturally tend to move toward the fulfillment or realisation of all their capabilities. He regarded the integration of the conscious and unconscious aspects of our personality as "being an innate and primary goal."

The secret self is a vital, living part of us all. To get to know ourselves, to achieve a greater degree of self awareness, it is absolutely vital that we meet it, embrace it and learn from it.

Although it has fundamentally come about by hiding our "bad" parts from ourselves, it can be gold if we embrace it and learn what it can teach us. Not all secret selves reflect the negative aspects of a personality, there is also the positive secret self. When we meet someone we truly admire, we are seeing part of ourselves in those qualities. We have similar qualities to a greater or lesser degree. The stronger the energy around the person, both positive and negative, the more we are looking at our secret self. To contain the secret self we disown, suppress or project it, but that does not resolve the underlying issues or problems. To use our secret self, we need to recognise both positive and negative aspects and then find the balance to suit each situation. It is a reconciliation and acceptance of the opposites within us that leads to healing and a minimisation of conflict.

We know that what we don't own or recognise we will often see in others, and it is highly likely that we will have the same characteristics in some measure.

Your journey

So to end this chapter, let's pick up the work book again and write down some of the positive qualities you admire in others because they are also within you in some measure. Facing our secret self expands our capacity for love, so that eventually we can love everything inside and outside of us.

5 PROJECTION

THE OLDEST TRICK IN THE BOOK

Projection is one of the key underpinnings to psychology. Projection is one of the mechanisms we use to deceive ourselves and to blame others, without even being aware of what we are doing. We project when we don't know we have a secret self, or disowned aspects of ourselves. It allows us to avoid the pain of recognising or embracing our secret self. We see other people's faults very clearly while not acknowledging that we have the same faults, or if we do, they are only miniscule in comparison. It obscures the picture of our personal jigsaw. It stirs up the mud in our pool, so we lose most of the clarity. To restore clarity and understanding, we need to know exactly how projection works.

It is the oldest trick in the book and has been part of mankind's armoury since we first walked on the earth. Jesus made one of the most famous comments about projection when he said, "Cast out the log in your own eye, so that you can see the mote in your brother's eye."

PROJECTION AS A MECHANISM TO DECEIVE OURSELVES AND BLAME OTHERS

Awareness of our projections, like the secret self, is a portal into part of our unconscious. The following example illustrates how important it is to understand it well, because it plays a huge role in all our relationships.

> Craig was feeling depressed and inadequate. A few months earlier, he had started a new job, working as a sales manager for Martin. To start with, their relationship went well, but gradually Craig felt Martin was putting him under enormous pressure to get the sales up and he was feeling anxious about being able to deliver. The products were not as good as he had been led to believe, but he didn't want to complain in case Martin thought he was making excuses, and was a lousy salesman. Then he realised that Martin himself was under substantial pressure from the chairman, to produce good sales figures and that Martin's own job was on the line. Craig realised that Martin was relying on him to deliver those results to protect his job.

What is going on here is that, Martin is projecting his anxiety about his own job prospects onto Craig. Meanwhile, Craig is feeling unhappy and uncertain under the huge pressure, he doesn't want to tell the truth about the product line, in case he is thought inadequate in his role as a salesman. He no longer has confidence in his boss, nor does he have confidence in the product he is trying to sell. This has a negative impact on potential clients, who are not motivated to buy. A negative spiral has been set up, largely based on projection.

Martin unconsciously wants to blame Craig for poor sales, but that's not where the problem lies. It is compounded because Martin, although the managing director, is not a good communicator and so out of touch with his people, that although he's aware of problems with the product, he doesn't want to address them because his performance is being judged by the chairman. Without consciously realising it he is hoping that Craig can produce magic, and prevent the whole situation unravelling. He blames others for being inadequate in their jobs when he himself is not performing adequately.

How could this have been handled differently? If, as soon as the relationship started to sour there had been honest communication about the situation and the root causes of everyone's anxiety, it could have been different. This lack of openness is going on to some extent in all organisations, from the simplest two man bands to the boards of every major corporation. If people could be more self-confident they would be able to talk about what was going on for them rather than protect an image. Imagine how much more effective we'd all be if we could talk openly about our fears without fear of being judged inadequate.

Your journey

- Using your workbook think of social, work and personal situations
- Can you be comfortable enough about yourself to tell people how you are feeling?
- Can you think of any examples where you have felt safe enough to be totally honest?

Your journey

- Write down the situations where you know you modify your behaviour in order to be seen as "better." Can you see a pattern?

- If so what is it about?

- What is the underlying fear beneath the need to be seen differently by others?

Do you blame others to protect yourself? It is a useful tool. We all learned it well as children. Terrified of being caught for our latest prank, we quickly pass the buck and blame Joey, Johnny, Kathy, or the dog. It's not our fault, we are not responsible. This blaming others is such an ingrained part of our survival mechanism that we often don't know we are using it. That is when it comes back to bite us, and creates general mayhem in our relationships.

SEEING FAULTS IN ANOTHER

Sometimes the secret self is so repressed that people are firmly barricaded behind their social mask or persona. They avoid any kind of negative reaction or emotion. They are too good to be true or too frightened to be themselves, like Ms Perfect, (page 81). We sense that these people are somehow false and generally don't feel comfortable around them, perhaps because no judgemental comments pass their lips, yet we instinctively feel they must think it, after all we do. Gossip can bring a wonderful sense of connection with others, although a far from respectful pastime. We criticise others or comment in a derogatory manner on their behaviour and can feel quite superior, totally unaware that we are projecting our secret self. Projecting our baggage onto others is the repressed energy of the secret self coming to the surface.

If you spot it you've got it.

Generally the person being criticised or being projected upon, will be a "good hook," i.e. they will be manifesting that characteristic or quality clearly, so it is easy to see. They may be mean or critical, or people that have any number of the huge list of characteristics that we looked at in the second chapter, (page 71).

Coming back to you:

Your journey

- Are you generally very critical of others or only occasionally?

- Can you see their faults clearly?

- Are your thoughts often critical but kept well guarded?

- Can you still keep them guarded when you are provoked in an argument, or do they burst forth?

'If you spot it, you've got it' is a good rule of thumb. We have all got it, we know it is part of being human. The only question is to what degree do you have it? The more you recognise it within yourself, the lower the chance that you will project. Although you may not be able to see the characteristic that is driving you crazy in yourself, it may help to cast your

mind back to when you were a child and see if you recognise the behaviour from much earlier in your life.

Does it help to think of the irritating other as being somewhat child-like when they are being exasperating? Remember how as a child you could get fixated on some idea or thing, that same tenacity that we had as children may be reflected in the other person, in their need for you to be different. The aspect of their character that is triggering you may be them behaving in that childlike manner.

PROJECTION AS A COPING MECHANISM

It is important to realise that projection can also serve a valuable purpose and could be considered a protective, defensive coping mechanism. It takes the aspects of our secret self that we cannot accept and sees them in others. The more we lack insight and awareness into our own behavioural characteristics the more we will project. It is a method that allows us to cope while we are not ready to confront our own traits, perhaps as a first step to embracing them. Even though we may be devoted to the ideal of self-knowledge, we are unlikely to have the resources, time, and courage to deal completely with every situation. So projection lets us set aside certain issues for the time being.

> Chris and Jane had a mutual friend Anne. Anne, somewhat drunk, had been very hurtful to Chris who then decided that he didn't like Anne. After the party, the friendship lapsed. About 18 months later Anne and Jane got together and Anne was going to come and visit, Chris was furious, "I

> don't know how you could have anything to do with that terrible woman. I don't want her in my house." His dogmatic attitude made Jane angry, she defended Anne and attacked Chris's critical judgement.

Later it emerged that Jane felt that Chris's rejection of Anne was also in some way a rejection of her. This incident shows Jane's secret self at work. She was critical of Chris's harsh judgemental attitude, yet was unaware that she was being equally judgemental. So effectively, each was holding a mirror to the other's behaviour. Jane was criticising Chris's behaviour, while at the same time doing exactly the same thing. Unfortunately when we are judgemental of others we are playing the same game. While it is unconscious it stays hidden in the secret self and exerts its energy, generally as criticism and conflict.

PROJECTION OF OUR OWN UNACCEPTABLE DESIRES AND ANXIETY

How often would we see ourselves as being lustful, aggressive or dishonest? Yet we can see those same impulses out there. When an aggressive man accuses others of being angry, projection is at play. Maybe the cheat is convinced everyone else is dishonest, which helps him normalise his behaviour. The would-be adulteress accuses her husband of having an affair, when in fact she is seriously contemplating a liaison. Unfortunately, we will all have been guilty of using projection as a way of avoiding our own issues at some time or another.

Another useful tactic is to "displace" our anxiety. Neil is having a hard time at work, as Daniel is threatening to sack him, (pages 66, 82). He feels intimidated by his work situation and unable to deal with it, as that might precipitate his sacking. In coming home he unloads completely unnecessary hostility onto his young son who left his bike in the driveway. He did not do this consciously, but he has chosen a safer target on which to dump his own anger and fear, thus avoiding for the short term, the danger and the real issue of conflict.

> Neil's wife Jill notices Neil's tension and dumps her own anxiety and fear onto their daughter with an angry outburst about a school bag left in the middle of the kitchen floor. She then notices that her daughter proceeds to pick on her brother, or the cat comes in for a mauling. We choose more vulnerable targets than ourselves to be our victims. The sad and difficult thing about this is that we are often unaware of what we are doing.

POSITIVE PROJECTION

However, projection is not always negative behaviour. For example, someone who never lies assumes that no one else lies. He projects his truthfulness onto others. Projection can also be about identification and is a useful social tool as it connects us with others. Our national flag symbolises our country and many of us feel a national pride as we look at it, particularly if there is a moving ceremony taking place. As a society we share communality when we project our emotions onto our flag. When watching a football game, virtually every person is pulled in to supporting one side or the other. The players carry our projections and hopes of success.

PROJECTION AS THE OPPOSITE TO INTROSPECTION

Projection is really the opposite of introspection. When we are not introspective we may rarely think about our own behaviour and our motivations, but we probably recognise others' motivations. In understanding others, we can become aware of what motivates us. If projections were not first projected onto the world we would not be aware of them. We can learn even more when we become aware of the projections that other people place on us. They may complain about our moodiness and although we don't feel we are moody, we recognise that they are. A teacher projects failure onto a student, who accepts the image and gives up trying. The recovering drug-addict, drawn back into an addictive life style by people who are incapable of kicking their own habit, is the subject of their projection as well as his or her own lack of will power. Pop stars and movie stars often feel stressed by the expectations and projections of their thousands of fans. Princess Diana undoubtedly was the focus of other people's projections. When she was married she epitomised the fairy story of the princess who married Prince Charming and lived happily ever after then, as the fairy story became a tragedy, she was portrayed as the victim at the mercy of the wicked family-in-law. Projections have the power to distort the truth and unless we spend the time to reflect on the facts, we can easily become caught up in a projected illusion.

DISTORTED PROJECTIONS

Projections are always charged energy. They distort our thinking, which affects our actions. Our impression of a person is mixed with our own projections. We may vote for a politician who seems strong and powerful because that is what we want to see. He absorbs the projection of leadership qualities and plays along with what the public want to see, yet in reality, he could be quite an ineffectual leader. Over time even great leaders lose their magnetic appeal as voters grow tired of the same face and withdraw their projections, they then have to rely on history to restore their "greatness."

Sexuality is often projected onto pop stars or film stars, either male or female. Usually this energy is well carried by the stars be they Marilyn Monroe or Madonna, Gary Grant or Hugh Grant, the Beatles or Kylie Minogue, and they act out this projected energy. It feeds their image, which may have little to do with reality and much more to do with projection. However, when the stars become older and lose that sexual quality, it can have damaging psychological effects if they haven't realised that what their fans wanted is an image of perfection, and not the reality of being human. Exactly the same situation applies to successful sportsmen, they carry our hopes and dreams for success.

Young girls reading fairy tales can absorb a belief that when their Prince Charming comes along he will be completely devoted to her, always putting her needs and wants ahead of his own so they will live happily ever after. This belief, which is a myth, can then be projected onto boyfriends, partners, husbands, and cause considerable grief. The same can be true of boys, they like to see themselves as the heroes and yet when they have been in a relationship for some time they realise their partners do not see them as heroes, but more often as the cause of their suffering. Each has been under the spell of projection.

Have you experienced a relationship where you felt you never got it right? Whatever you do, you feel it is never quite good enough; it always seemed to be criticised? What happened?

Your journey

- Were you able to come to a resolution and if so what led you there?

- If you didn't come to a resolution what action did you take?

- What did you say about it to yourself, what was your self talk?

- Reflect on the pattern if there have been a number of relationships where you never felt you got it right.

- How much could the difficulty have come from the other person's different upbringing, unconscious programming and life "rules"?

It is possible that if you have been in a situation where you have felt criticised that you decided that others thought you were inadequate. Perhaps what is happening is that deep down, you feel you are inadequate, and their criticism triggers that aspect of you. You project criticism onto them and are constantly on the defensive around them. It is possible that if you checked it out with them, that they would be astonished to learn that you think like that, in which case, your feelings were about you and your projection and not about them at all.

Ask for feedback

One of the best ways of finding out if what we are thinking is true is to ask the other party. So often, our actions are responses to what we perceive, and if the perceptions are incorrect our actions may be inappropriate. This can be difficult to accept but it is important because it can so easily colour all our relationships. It can cause conflict, which detracts from the original problem and stops us looking at ourselves. The sad part about projection is that unless it is recognised and acknowledged, our relationships cannot be intimate or effective.

Often we are interacting more with our own projection about a person, than with the person himself. Similarly, the person is interacting more with his or her projection of us, than with who we really are. Relations then become strained and each feels misunderstood. Projections result in what Jung called "imaginary relationships." In effect, each person is playing out a relationship with himself or herself, which is not really an effective way of communicating. Many young people are desperate to fall in love for the first time and in doing so may project a very unrealistic expectation onto their new partner. Often unconsciously, they expect their lover to be able to set their world at rights and that they won't have any more problems, they will live happily ever after, just like the princess, and the hero in the fairy stories talked of earlier. The expectations placed on such a relationship soon become overwhelming and the cracks appear.

Miriam had felt rejected by her mother's coldness. At an unconscious level, she decided that her mother was not safe and she would not let her heart be broken again, so she emotionally distanced herself. This went on for some 36 or 37 years, and most of the time she felt deeply resentful of her mother. At times, she would feel guilty about this and try to be the "good" daughter. Her mother then took advantage of this "goodness" and would demand more emotional energy than Miriam was prepared to give. This would start yet another cycle of resentment for Miriam, she read her mother's actions as manipulation and would withdraw and close off emotional contact. Although Miriam had been consciously aware of this cycle for about 25 years, she had no idea of the unconscious motivation. Suddenly one day, after considerable therapy, she understood that she played a major part in keeping this dynamic going, resentment, then feeling guilty, coming closer, then distancing again, and decided it was time to stop.

Miriam's mother had been born into an emotionally closed family and Miriam suddenly realised that her mother did not intentionally distance herself. Distancing was what she had learned to do, to keep safe as a result of her conditioning. After many hours of reflection, Miriam was able to see the pattern. She talked to her mother and explained how she felt and what she was doing. This in itself was a huge step forward, and testimony to how hard Miriam had worked to understand the dynamic, and to honestly examine the part she had played rather than continue the projection. Both dissolved into tears, hugging each other. Finally, they understood what had been happening and the love that had always been there was

> able to flow more freely. Miriam realised that all these years she had been projecting onto her mother her own fear, that if she got close she would have her heart broken. Her mother realised the impact of her own behaviour, which she had not been aware of. She was aware that every time Miriam had opened up by being the good daughter, she was desperate to hold onto that love and attention, and forced herself upon her daughter. The relationship does not always run smoothly now, but they are both quicker to identify the dynamic and sort it out.

This is a classic example of how projection had completely distorted reality. Miriam was interacting with the projection she had of her mother, rather than who her mother was. It had become so bad, that neither she nor her mother could really discern the other's actual words, actions or other communications, such as body language. Both were trying to cope with the situation in the best way they knew how, until Miriam became aware.

The irony is that Miriam was unaware that in her distancing she was copying the very behaviour that she despised in her mother. It was Miriam's secret self at play, and demonstrates the subtlety of unconscious behaviour. It is a fair assumption that if Miriam had not recognised her behaviour this pattern would have continued down to yet another generation. It is likely that Miriam's grandmother and maybe even great grandmother had learned as small children that it was not safe to trust, and consequently become emotionally closed.

Ideally, the way out of this type of bind is self-reflection and honest communication, to clarify exactly what is going on.

LOSS OF PERSONAL POWER AS A RESULT OF PROJECTION

Projection can bring about loss of control over our lives. We unconsciously select certain people to be our friends or enemies simply because they are suitable recipients for our projections. For example, a man might choose as a friend a guy who is a successful businessman as well as an excellent sportsman. When seen with him he hopes others may think he is like him, also a successful businessman and good sportsman, however, for all this man's outward attributes he may not be a good friend.

People can manipulate us all if we project our power onto them, such as the politician at the rally, or the leader of a cult. It is possible, even easy, to miss the reality beneath the projected image. A boss seems to wield considerable power. We do not see the weak ineffectual man beneath his authority. When he fails to live up to our expectation of powerfulness, we realise our expectations were inappropriate and maybe our projection all along.

A disturbing thought is, that if we deny a quality in ourselves and project it onto others, we give away this aspect of ourselves. It is no longer available for our own use; i.e. my boss is all powerful and compared to him I am weak. By thinking that, you do indeed become weak in comparison to your boss. Projections take energy.

> Amanda is very insecure in her relationship with her boyfriend, when he comments admiringly about another women Amanda immediately feels threatened, she compares herself with the women and invariably feels she's lacking. This not only takes physical and emotional energy but also serves to diminish her already fragile self esteem. It is triggering into her deep sense of vulnerability from childhood, in this case her mother constantly told her that she did not look good, she had brains but no looks. Even knowing how destructive this programming is, Amanda still continues to compare herself to most women she sees walking down the street. She says to herself, Brian would like her she has nice legs, or nice hair etc. This behaviour diminishes Amanda more and more, she only sees what she lacks, rather than what she has, a nice figure, beautiful eyes and so on. Her reality becomes totally distorted. If Brian is unscrupulous he can use Amanda's insecurities to make himself feel more powerful. Unfortunately, this type of power play is quite common.

Anorexia and Bulimia are good examples of how distorted reality can become. People suffering from these disorders cannot see how thin they may look, they only see how fat they are and that they still need to lose weight. They lose more and more energy as they chase an unrealistic projection. (Eating disorders or food issues are much more to do with perfectionism, power and control, as well as intense pain rather than just physical appearance.)

Often undue or exaggerated reactions such as fascination or obsession will indicate projections, as will intense infatuation, irritation, hatred or praise. If we see the world as being full of violence and evil, is it really like that, or are you concentrating on the small percentage of the population that may well be violent and evil? Is your own world looking scary and unpredictable? Are you seeing reality or projections?

What we see in others we also need to be able to see in ourselves, the good and the bad. The degree to which we see it or choose to exercise it will be our choice.

> **Your journey**
>
> - In that difficult relationship are you projecting your own image of that person? For instance, are they always spiteful or is it only you that sees them that way? You could check it out with others.

A fraught area in relationships is that others hold views that we are powerless to change. If they are adamant despite what we do or say, then the more we try to force them to change their mind the more likely we are to be disrespectful and possibly abusive. Indeed, if we do try and force them to change we are perpetuating exactly the same behaviour and the same inflexibility. We are looking at the same rigidity, thus our own secret self. Difficult though it may be we need to be respectful and allow the differences.

We can't force another to change. The only behaviour we can change is our own. The interesting thing is that as we change, others change around us. If you change one part of any system the rest automatically have to shift. Often this shift is uncomfortable, and the other party tries to make you revert to your normal behaviour because, to coin an old expression, the devil we know is better than the devil we don't. When we are aware that others feel more comfortable with our old behaviour, even though they may not like it, we do not have to take their reactions so personally, when they try to make us change back. We can understand that they are feeling uncomfortable with our new way of being.

SPLITTING

Going back to our development as children, we initially learned to deal with difficult situations and conflicts by using a mechanism called splitting. In play we used different characters to represent different feelings. For example, there is the good fairy or the good Queen, and we will also have the wicked witch, and the evil Queen. In *Star Wars* we have Luke Skywalker and Darth Vader. Then there is Robin Hood and the evil Sheriff of Nottingham. In *The Lord of the Rings* we have the hobbits pitted against the evil wizard and his cronies, the same story applies in the *Harry Potter* series. Recently we had the good guys in the US and the bad guys in Iraq, (the simplistic way governments would have us look at it.)

By splitting we get some relief from the conflict of thinking about the issue. It becomes so much easier to deal with when we can just polarise it in very simple thinking, it makes it bearable to look at difficult situations. In the West, shortly after 9/11 and contemplating the US/Middle East situation, there seemed to have been a ground swell of opinion that wanted to cast all Muslims as villains. Rationally that is a ridiculous assumption, but it reduced a hugely complex situation into a simple matter of good versus evil. Furthermore, the more people share the same projection the better we feel, security in numbers, perhaps. We must be right because we are not alone. It saves us looking at the issue in its entirety and complexity. For children splitting and projection are the predominant defenses for avoiding pain and criticism, it helps them to make sense of complexity.

OWNING OUR PROJECTIONS

As we become more aware, we can learn to hold previously separated feelings, such as good and bad and allow both aspects to be part of the whole. We are no longer denying the existence of our secret side or secret self, but embracing it and bringing it into view.

Once we realise what we have been doing it, it can be painful for us to take back and own our projections. However, until we reclaim and acknowledge those elements, they will continue to be projected onto one person and then another. We repeatedly encounter the same difficulties in relationships with lovers, family, employers, co-workers, friends and others. We could think of ourselves as victims and think we are really unlucky to be coming up against the same situation time and again.

- Look back at the work you did in the last chapter identifying your own patterns in relationships. Can you see projection?

The secret self does not always get projected but in most cases it does. Unless the energy from a situation is expressed or released somehow, it is repressed and slowly builds. The ideal way to avoid repression is to talk about the situation with the other person in a respectful way. When this is not possible or feels too difficult, you could pretend they are sitting in a chair opposite you and imagine telling them all the things you dislike and would like them to change. This exercise can allow you to let off steam without it doing any harm and can be a precursor to an actual discussion in due course, when the anger or strong feelings have largely dissipated. Writing down all the things that really irritate you can do the same thing. Usually we feel a lot calmer and more in control when we have acknowledged to ourselves just what is eating at us.

When we get the courage to look at our projections and own them, splitting becomes much less frequent. The great benefit of this is that polarisation is reduced, as is antagonism and conflict between people, which promotes integration and co-operation. Stress starts to dissolve as the need for the social mask slips, tension lessens and people have a much higher chance of happiness. To do this we must be able to hold onto the conflicting projected elements, so that we can discuss issues and think them through before reacting and acting them out in destructive ways within the relationship. Assimilation of projections requires self-acceptance and humility as we acknowledge the unpleasant aspects that we have thrown onto others. The great redeeming feature of this work is that we realise we do not deliberately set out to project our own baggage onto others, it comes from the child in us who could not carry the pain and shame of feeling unacceptable.

ACCEPTANCE OF OUR CHARACTERISTICS

Acceptance of our characteristics is an enormous step forward. We know we cannot move forward until we recognise and acknowledge our undesirable traits. We accept this but it does not mean that we have to like these parts. Once aware we can choose how to deal with them. It is important to keep remembering that these characteristics are merely the symptoms of our defence strategies to cope and survive as healthily as possible.

> Samantha is very dissatisfied with her defacto relationship with Will. She complains that when they go and do the household groceries she always pays the bill. Will conveniently forgets his credit card, or doesn't have any money, but says he will pay next time. Samantha is very careful with her money and does not like spending it. To her, money represents security and when she supports Will her nest egg is depleted. She feels resentful particularly as in her mind the relationship goes all Will's way. When Samantha challenges Will he says, "It doesn't really matter because we are a couple. Everything I have I want to share with you anyway." This keeps Samantha hooked into the partnership. Eventually when she tires of empty promises, she decides to leave Will.
>
> In the past, Samantha had been stung by criticisms of being mean and stinginess from her family and some friends which had hurt, and rather than focus on whether she was being mean, she could avoid her discomfort by focusing on Will's lack of financial contribution. Projecting meanness onto Will, allowed her to feel better about herself. Like Samantha, unconsciously we tend to pass that hurt on by concentrating on someone else's mistakes and undoubtedly Samantha had a valid point, Will was avoiding his responsibilities.

This story has a happy ending, when Samantha understood what was really going on, she was able to talk about it with Will. They laughed about their similarities, and the relationship strengthened. The money issue had to be identified and separated for Samantha to appreciate how it had contaminated her whole perspective of the relationship. When she could identify why and how her mean trait had developed she was able to accept this trait within herself, it was no longer disowned. At that point she also realised she had choice. By talking about it, Will could see the part he had unwittingly played and realised if he wanted the relationship he had choices to make around responsibility.

HOW TO DEAL WITH OUR PROJECTIONS

In your workbook write down as many examples as you can think of where you project onto others. It might be helpful to go back to the list you made after reading pages 71–73, these are some of the characteristics that you could possibly be projecting. The ones which really provoke emotional "heat" (i.e. get you mad) are the ones to particularly watch. The next step is to learn to manage those particular characteristics, if anger is a problem, learn some anger management techniques. If arrogance sticks in your craw, check out how arrogant you think you are, perhaps ask others if they perceive you as arrogant. We have to learn to manage the emotions that lie beneath the projection, we can't just pin it onto others and blame them for something that is all about us, and which has come from our need to protect ourselves at some time.

Many clinical disorders are about projection. Paranoia is a projection of fears onto innocent strangers. Many Schizotypal symptoms, where suffers believe that aliens or beings from other worlds want us to "do" things, are projections. Perhaps most commonly the person with a Borderline Personality Disorder will often project onto others their fears that they are going to be abandoned, that others do not care or do not love them.

We can now begin to appreciate that our projections come from a need to get away from pain and shame, largely laid down in childhood. Focusing on the other's faults makes us feel better about ourselves. We develop compassion for ourselves, which brings about an automatic flow-on response to others and we no longer judge them harshly. We recognise that we are also capable of similar traits and by accepting this, we may even come to like the people upon whom we previously projected the then despised trait.

Projections are charged with energy. We expect the person who we are projecting onto to live up to our expectations. This takes our energy and when our expectations are dashed brings anger and disappointment. When we learn to manage our projections we recognise their golden quality. We also regain the energy that has been trapped in them. We now know that whatever generates a lot of emotional energy within us gives us some vital clues as to what is being projected from the unconscious, and in becoming conscious it releases its energy. We no longer have to work so hard to keep our façade intact. Our secret self is no longer so secret and we can play more freely, with greater creativity. We release power and potential. Our secret self emerges like a butterfly from its cocoon, and gives us choice. Our personal growth is about embracing the disowned projected parts of us.

As the last part of this chapter pick up your workbook:

- Reflect on whether that impossible other you are trying to live with may have characteristics that perhaps you can start to identify with.

- Thinking back to those people that you identified early on in the book (pages 71–73) can you think a little differently about them. If you can't, don't worry about it.

6 TRIGGERS

We know that our secret self and our ability to project it is an integral part of us and up to now has played a valuable part in our growth and socialisation, even though we never realised it. Now let us understand how we can learn to use the secret self if we choose, so we can harness its power and empower ourselves.

Imagine if Hitler had been aware of the play of his secret self and projection. If he had realised how he was ruled by his unconscious the world may have been different. He symbolises for us one the worst monsters of the last century, yet he was far from being all bad. He played the mouth organ, was a pretty good landscape artist, and had a vision to improve the world. Perhaps it would have all been different if his upbringing had been different. His psychopathology has been attributed to many different theories. These include "paternal violence, maternal over-protectiveness, childhood trauma due to an over-eager goat's successful attempt at biting off one of young Hitler's testicles, sexual inadequacy resulting from an organically derived testicular defect, a Narcissistic Borderline Personality Disorder," ... to name but the few quoted by Ernesto Spinelli, in his book *The Mirror and The Hammer*.

It is interesting to speculate that maybe he wasn't truly loved and accepted by someone who appreciated his talents and understood the context of his insecurity. Perhaps then he wouldn't have felt compelled to impose his violent, megalomaniac vision on the world, or maybe he epitomised the power we all have, but hopefully eschew. The world could have seen its own ability to be evil, its secret self in Hitler's actions, but this is too terrifying to contemplate so we comfort ourselves by casting him as inhuman, a monstrosity. This reasoning, conveniently, stops us from thinking that we possibly have a similar ability, if circumstances presented themselves. It is in the very denial of this secret self that we can more easily be sucked into its power. Is it so impossible to contemplate being a prison guard in Nazi Germany, or a soldier in the army? Isn't the only difference the scale of the abuse of human rights? Although we talk of Nazi Germany here, there are scores of examples throughout the world right now. The only thing different about Nazi Germany was the scale of destruction. Perhaps we need to face the fact that regardless of social class or profession, ordinary citizens get caught up in committing atrocities. It seems that "evil can be enacted with surprising ease by even the most normal and sanest of men and women", as Spinelli points out.

Coming back to the secret self aspect of ourselves, we have the ability to be brutal and cruel as well as divinely beautiful. When we can embrace that, we are far less likely to enact the brutal cruel aspects of ourselves. We may not have any conscious recollection of being brutal and cruel, but to deny that possibility within ourselves is lacking insight, and deprives us of the ability to deal with evil.

HARNESSING THE SECRET SELF

We harness the power of the secret self by examining our personal triggers. (In this case a trigger is the emotional reaction we have to a stimulus, a reaction often greater than the stimulus warrants.) Our principal triggers are the list of characteristics that we noted in the first chapter, (pages 71–73.) Face the discomfort and spend a few minutes to revisit, yet again, the list of characteristics we hate in others. The higher the number you attributed to these characteristics the higher the likelihood that they reflect your secret self, and the more control they are likely to have over your life. The greater the intensity of emotion they evoke in you, the greater the power they have over you.

The person you find so difficult can tell you a lot about yourself.

Now we also know that although we may clearly see the despised trait in someone else, we do not necessarily possess it to the same degree. You may say this has very little to do with me, I'm not like that and you may well be right. The person carrying those projections will be a good hook, i.e. it will be easy to see the particular characteristic you hate in them. That said, your challenge will still be to accept everything you wrote down after reading the list and think to yourself, umm – maybe I could have that tendency, but now I am aware of it and have a choice of how I think about someone. The gift is that the person you find so difficult to live with can, if you look long and hard, tell you a lot about yourself. Information that you never even realised, perhaps never even knew about.

SELF TALK AND BELIEVING OUR OWN STORY

If you are having trouble accepting this, become aware of what you are thinking, or listen to your internal dialogue.

Your journey

- What are you saying about that difficult other?
- Are you replaying in your mind all the many niggling incidents that have happened in an effort to reaffirm that this is not really about you at all?
- You may notice that your self talk has nothing to do with you, it is all about them. If you are replaying scenarios from the past you may be saying things like:

It's got absolutely nothing to do with me, it's his or her fault.

He just won't see or hear what I'm saying.

He hurt me.

I did so much for him and still he's so ungrateful, never lifts a finger to help me. Doesn't matter what I say, I just can't get through to him.

She's such a bitch, always bringing up every little thing I've ever done wrong.

She can never let go, got a memory like an elephant.

She blames me for everything that goes wrong in her life.

She never thinks about all the good things I do for her all the time.

He deliberately makes spiteful comments to hurt me.

The more upset I become the more he ignores me.

No doubt you could add to this list, by referring back to what you wrote earlier.

The same repetitive thought whirs on and on, like sandpaper. As it grinds, we are slowly smoothing away doubts, increasingly believing our own story. In a perverse way it is quite a comfortable process. We are the innocent victims, unfairly treated by whoever it is. It certainly isn't our fault... Listening to the self-talk is quite comfortable, we are like a dog with a bone, and don't want to let our hurt and pain go.

> Karen has a love/hate relationship with Jessica. They have known each other 25 years and when they are relaxed in each other's company and there is a degree of trust, the friendship works beautifully. Each feels heard, respected, and a deep connection is forged. Both are insecure around each other. Karen's insecurity comes out when she makes patronising derogatory comments at times. Jessica's insecurity is revealed when she is unable to ask what Karen means or to retaliate when she feels the poisonous dart of a comment. Her lack of voice to express either hurt or anger signals her fear. She fears that if she retaliates she will lose the precious times when they are really able to connect. Consequently, she puts up with the barbs for the sake of peace, but spends hours having imaginary conversations with Karen telling her exactly how she feels and how hurt she is. She does not have the courage to do this face to face.

One day when she finally tires of the putdowns, she may take her courage in her hands and take responsibility for the part she plays in this dynamic, and express her feelings instead of allowing the barbs, moaning and playing the poor victim. The victim role allows us to justify, rationalise and comfort ourselves. It is so easy to blame others for our discomfort, and it lets us off the hook beautifully for a time, but unfortunately keeps us helpless. We don't have to take any responsibility for what has happened and consequently we don't need to take any responsibility for solving the problem. We can go on being the hapless innocent. We avoid the pain that arises if we looked candidly at ourselves and the work that could entail.

There is a cost in smoothing away our conscious awareness. We become less in control of ourselves as human beings. When we take a good hard long look we will find that the problem has a great deal more to do with our thoughts and our actions than we would care to admit.

As we all know, when a relationship goes bad it generally becomes a downhill spiral until the only way out is to break off the relationship and write it off as bad luck. The internal dialogue could be, I picked the wrong guy, girl, friend, boss etc. At least when we say we picked, or were attracted to the wrong person we are taking some responsibility for what went wrong. However, it is a different matter with our family, mother, father, brother, sister, son, daughter, uncle, aunt, cousin and so on. That is certainly not our fault, we never chose our family. Most of the time

> *The more responsibility we take for our feelings the more empowered we become.*

we rationalise our failed relationships by saying it's their fault. "If my relationship with my mother had been different my whole life wouldn't be in this mess" or, "Because my father walked out when I was a small boy I've been in trouble with the law."

The more characteristics we marked in that first exercise, the more aware we are and the less projecting we'll do. This allows us to take responsibility, which in turn is very empowering, as the more we take responsibility the less our unconscious is running our lives. The greater the awareness of our secret self, the more control we have over our life.

Awareness brings knowledge, which brings choice. Choice is empowering.

CHOICE AND EMPOWERMENT

Unless a person is mentally ill, not even your worst nightmare of a person continually deliberately sets out to be mean, vindictive or destructive, although it may appear that way to you, hurting as you may be, due to the other person's barbs or actions. People resort to vindictive behaviour when they are scared or threatened. They may not consciously realise what they are doing and will probably deny it vehemently, because they are genuinely unaware. Their behaviour triggers us because, at some level, it resonates with our own secret self.

> *Empowered people do not resort to manipulative, intimidating behaviour because they can ask for what they want.*

Empowered people do not need to resort to manipulative, intimidating, vindictive behaviour because they have worked out what they want and are able to ask.

This exercise of identifying our secret self characteristics can be pretty terrifying the first time you look at it, but consider its implications. When we are aware we can become far less reactive to other's comments or actions. We can pause and think how much of this is about my secret self and how much is it about the other person's secret self. We can make a conscious choice and thus protect ourselves from feeling unnecessary pain.

Let's look at this process with Melinda. Melinda ranked meanness as a 9. It is likely that as a child she suffered someone being mean to her, quite possibly on numerous occasions and as a child she was unable to defend or protect herself. If she had been strong enough she would probably have retaliated with violence to avenge the mean action or actions, or at least complained about it. As she had been "socialised" and because she was a child, the pain and the powerlessness she undoubtedly felt went into the secret self, perhaps to come out at a later time. When Melinda became an adult she could not tolerate meanness. At some deep level out of her consciousness, when she encountered this characteristic it brought up uncomfortable feelings, which if analysed, would probably reveal powerlessness and pain. It wasn't so much meanness that Melinda reacted to, the trigger was the bullying that had accompanied the meanness in her childhood. When Melinda next encounters a mean spirit, instead of feeling hurt or angry she can say to herself, this is a trigger to feeling powerless but I can choose to react or not.

> Later, Melinda is quietly sitting in the lunch room at work eating a bar of what she considered well needed chocolate when some of her work mates came in and eye her chocolate, someone even asked for a bit. She was desperate to finish the bar but could not tolerate being judged as mean, and made a conscious choice to share. She also made a mental note of her desire not to share, thereby acknowledging her secret self, and determining that if she saw others eating chocolate she would not judge them harshly if they did not share it. She would totally understand the feeling.

When we recognise one of our triggers, we know that a red flag is being waved, pay attention! We may have a choice about how we act.

Like the archetypal figures Adam and Eve, we have eaten the apple from the tree of knowledge and we recognise the temptation of greed, of lust, of revenge etc, the seven deadly sins. This knowledge of good and evil was implanted, in childhood, by our caregivers and socialised into the unconscious, in the form of life scripts rules and the secret self. It is vented in projection and controlled by understanding, which brings acceptance and choices.

In due course, you may like to move along the continuum further toward the quality that inspires you, rather than its opposite, but there is no way you can do that unless you acknowledge where you stand right now.

It can be easy to deny the above, ignore it and forget about it, but you will do yourself a disservice if that is the decision you make. What takes true courage and grit is to be able to accept yourself as you currently are, otherwise you cannot move forward. You need a solid foothold in the now before being able to advance. Unfortunately most people do not have the courage to do this type of work, it is too scary. If they did, they would realise that once they accepted their own traits, their reactivity to other's comments would not have the same intensity or power to hurt. You can work out if the action or comments that irritate and hurt you are about your triggers, or if it could be the other person's secret self at play. You begin to feel more comfortable in your own skin and as a bonus your own sense of identity grows.

Like Melinda, we may despise meanness but we now recognise this propensity within us. We realise that we have the capability to be mean. It doesn't have to follow that we act on the trait: in fact usually we go in the opposite direction. Knowing that this is a trigger, we now have awareness and thus choice in how we behave. We are in the powerful position of creating who we want to be at any given moment, and our unconscious has far less of a hold.

FEELINGS ARE ANOTHER CLUE TO YOUR SECRET SELF TRIGGERS

You have identified some personal triggers, there will be others. The exciting thing is that they always give you useful clues. The clues come from your feelings. Whenever you find yourself in a situation where you feel uncomfortable, know that the discomfort is waving a red flag. It is trying to say STOP. Feel what is going on here, and think about it. What is happening is about you, no-one else. Sure, the other person or people are acting as triggers and they may exhibit behaviour that you can't stand. They are only messengers waving the red flag, it is not about them, it is about you. The fact is that you have encountered a trigger that is alerting you to anxiety or discomfort. Triggers indirectly signal that there is work to be done here, if you choose to do it. They are a gift if you take your self-development work seriously.

DUMPING OUR GARBAGE

Generally the more acute your discomfort, the more intense is the trigger. As said before, the greater your emotional pain, the more likely it is that these uncomfortable feelings will be projected away from you and onto someone else. It is possible that you feel the other person deserves it, but it's highly unlikely they'll feel they deserve your projection or your emotional garbage. Do you really want to dump your garbage when you could usefully recycle it? Imagine if we all dumped our rubbish onto our next door neighbour's lawn. We would quickly have total chaos, plus a neighbourhood war. All sense of peace and harmony would be gone, yet symbolically, that is what we all do most of the time with our emotional garbage.

Any situation that doesn't leave you feeling good about yourself is giving you clues about how you currently operate in the world. It is your choice to look at what the situation offers you, or to walk away. Without doubt, the same feeling will come up time and time again, in lots of different circumstances. Eventually you may be forced to look at it. This can be seen in many stories about second marriages. The names, faces and places are different but when people present for counselling the issues are generally very similar to the issues that arose in the first relationship. They weren't dealt with then and until they are dealt with, they will continue.

> Jake's wife had been telling him for some years that she wasn't happy but because it was uncomfortable, Jake tended to ignore what she was saying, or just gave it lip service. He wanted the issue to go away and secretly hoped that it would evaporate. Unfortunately, it doesn't work that way. One day she told him she was in love with another man and wanted out. Finally, he was forced to look at the part he played in the situation, but by that time she wasn't interested.

It is easy to slip into ignoring situations until they become desperate. It is usually better to deal with sooner rather than later. Or as the cliché goes, what goes around comes around, we reap what we sow. If you ignore the warning signs of uncomfortable, distasteful feelings, unfortunately, you will pay the price in due course.

AIDS FOR A NEW WAY OF THINKING

When we start something new we usually need aids, an instruction manual, training wheels or floaties if we are learning to swim, tools to help us learn. In this case we want tools for learning to deal with uncomfortable feelings and how to uncover the gold they hide. You have already taken a great step forward by recognising that you have been triggered. Various ways of going beyond the old fear based pattern of behaviour when we would project our discomfort, can include the following: take yourself away from the scene, have a cup of tea or coffee in a quiet place, listen to what you are saying to yourself about it or feel what your body is saying about it. Test yourself by writing down some of the self talk. When it is in black and white, it is easier to learn from and harder to run away.

Thinking things through is hard work, although it may sound easy reading it here. Every trigger is a pathway to an understanding of difference, to forgiveness, to strengthening your own self, which of course means you can feel more secure. A person who learns Kung Fu seldom has to use it. It is portable security that has come about as the result of disciplined insight.

AVOIDANCE MECHANISMS

When you recognise a trigger, you will probably find a million reasons why now is not the time to look at it, and think about what it may mean. You may find that your mind has wandered off the subject completely or you have just dismissed it. You may mentally tag it as something you will come back to, but when you have time, not now. Another great defense mechanism is to suddenly feel tired and want to go to sleep. We all have a huge variety of ways of avoiding looking at things that might prove uncomfortable, busyness, rescuing others from their own discomfort, as well as any of the addictions, work, sex, alcohol, drugs, and so on. There is more about these coping mechanisms in the next chapter. If any of these symptoms occur, know that it is a vital clue, the unconscious is at work again, hiding what it does not

Is the person you find impossible finding you impossible?

want to acknowledge. It is painful and difficult thinking about your own issues. Listen to the excuses you make to yourself for not dealing with it.

As your own therapist, know that what you find the most difficult to think about is the very area that most needs thinking about, so that you can bring it out from the secret self. If you shine light on it, you become more confident about who you are. You start to know yourself at a deep level. You know that you can meet a challenge and deal with it, rather than sidestep the situation. It is also worth considering, although uncomfortable, that the one you are finding impossible to live with is finding you equally impossible.

Your journey

- Knowing that your personal triggers were those noted on pages 71–73, go back to look at that list and note if any of the characteristics have changed? In your workbook can you identify three good reasons for why you or others, may have developed that so called negative characteristic. For example, you may have chosen meanness, yet meanness is also an ability to being careful. Could you have learnt meanness growing up in a poverty stricken family? Could the person you dislike this attribute in, have grown up in poverty? Could that same person unconsciously have a great fear of lack? Could they have been brought up with a family rule, don't throw money around you never know when you may need it.

> ■ Do you have compassion for yourself when you look at the list, knowing that these less-than-perfect qualities comes from our fear of being judged as "bad" by others?

Your journey

It is your reaction to the other that is invaluable, when you choose to look at your own self development. The stronger your secret self energy, the more control it has over your life and your actions, unless you have awareness. Effectively, you are in the back seat driving your car and the disowned, projected parts of you are in the driver's seat.

To move forward on our journey of self-development we need to accept where we are now. The acceptance brings comfort and a sense of our own identity. We consciously move into the driver's seat of our own car. We are no longer victims, we have awareness, we have choice and we can take actions that allow us to be who we want to be.

Although every situation we encounter can throw light onto how we conduct ourselves, it is important in times of danger that our unconscious, which guards our survival, is allowed to take over. For example, in times of severe physical risk our flight or fight mechanism will be triggered. There is little sense in overriding it and making a choice to be peaceful when you are about to be assaulted. In such times there is no time to make choices. Instinct takes over on behalf of reason and thank goodness it does. Later, when you are feeling physically safe it will be useful to explore how you came to be in such a situation and what it can tell you that will be useful on your journey of self-discovery.

Your journey

- Can you think of any examples of this type of situation? Write them in your workbook.

- What aspects of you do they highlight, maybe your bravery or perhaps the pleasure of risk taking.

7 TAKING RESPONSIBILITY

You will now be aware that the feelings you have about the person who sets your teeth on edge the most are largely of your own making, but that there are lots of reasons for why you act as you act. We know those reasons largely relate back to childhood. As you gain this understanding about yourself there comes a time when you need to make some decisions. In order to give yourself choice there is both good and bad news. The bad news is that you need to acknowledge the past knowing that it is gone and can never be recreated but the good is that it is up to you to create who you wish to be now. Right now you can empower yourself and take responsibility for your feelings and actions.

You and only you are responsible for your own feelings

Responsibility is not demanding others change so we can feel less anxious, frustrated, upset, depressed, angry, or victimised. Responsibility is recognising what we are feeling and taking control of our own emotions. Your thoughts and feelings are yours, wholly and solely yours. Although they may be motivated by external factors, they have nothing to do with anyone else. You run your own control center. You may be ordered to do something, but you are the one who actually does the action. Ultimately you have to accept culpability for your action and the effects it may have. No one else can get into your head and physically manipulate or control your feelings, thoughts, and actions. Responsibility for our relationship begins and ends with us, no one else, just us. We choose how we relate to everyone and everything else in our life. This is difficult to come to grips with because it kicks away our old behaviour patterns.

NO ONE TO BLAME

Taking responsibility takes guts. After all, it is convenient to blame. You drop a cup, and your first thought is the cup slipped. (A useful cop-out the cup is responsible for its own demise.) Perhaps the reason the cup dropped was because we simply were not paying attention to the task. Why is it so hard to take responsibility for even simple failings? Why do we try to avoid this responsibility? In most cases we are probably not even aware of what we are doing. We find it so difficult to acknowledge our mistakes.

Avoiding responsibility has a long history. It goes back to Adam and Eve in the Garden of Eden. When God asked Adam if he had tasted the apple, Adam promptly blamed Eve for giving it to him, Eve in turn blamed the snake. Perhaps if the snake had been asked, the blame might have been passed again. He might have blamed God for creating the forbidden fruit in the first place. If it wasn't meant to be eaten, why create it in the first place? All that aside, we have eaten the apple from the tree of knowledge. We know what's right and wrong. Symbolically, we have been thrown out of the Garden of Eden, out of the safe place where all our needs were met. Now we are adults on the journey of life and because we have eaten the apple of knowledge and know the difference between good and bad, we have choice. The Garden of Eden could be compared to childhood, or innocence when we were largely told how to be. Now we can choose to do the right thing for ourselves. For instance, do we choose to look at our relationships as a vehicle for self development and personal growth, or are we quite content to continue to blame the system and irritating others?

> *Successful people are those that grow from their mistakes.*

What if Adam had taken responsibility for eating of the apple? Maybe our story of creation would have been different. How many deceptions, secrets and betrayals could have been averted? Even political promises are notorious for being misleading and misguiding. The US/Iraq war may have been averted if the story of weapons of mass destruction had been accurately portrayed. Imagine the guy on death row who is convicted of a crime he didn't do. Many stories of betrayal started as small lies to avoid detection, and then built up to much greater proportions. People become defensive and in an attempt to cover their tracks, they sink deeper and deeper into the mire. In the corporate world many major companies would still be here today, providing livelihoods if this could have been avoided.

Employees that take responsibility and learn from their mistakes are usually highly valued by their employers.

Successful people are not necessarily any better than others, they are just more willing to see their mistakes as opportunities to grow. Jeff Keller in *Attitude is Everything*, says, "There is no such thing as failure, only results, with some more successful than others."

Perhaps it is worth speculating on how different our own story may have been if we had always faced the consequences of our actions. Can you think of incidents in your life when you didn't take responsibility? Imagine how the scenario would have been different if you had.

Your journey

- In your workbook write down some of those occurrences.

- After each incident write down how you would deal with the situation today with the knowledge you now have.

Imagine how different our lives will be when we start owning our actions, or inactions. We will certainly kickstart our personal growth.

If Adam had been responsible and God forgiving we may still be in Eden not needing to do anything for ourselves, forever looked after. That maybe a nice thought, if a touch boring, we would not need to grow. Personal growth and evolvement only seems comes from struggle and effort.

YOU CAN CHANGE WHAT YOU ARE RESPONSIBLE FOR

Whether or not you like it, you are responsible for the choices and actions that have put you in your present circumstances. The good news is,

You can change what you are responsible for

If you are not responsible you have no control or influence. Someone else is in the driver's seat of your car.

Often one of the most common reasons for being a victim and avoiding responsibility, is because at some level we feel helpless and powerless. Fear and the inner constriction of being unable to cope and to change things can be almost overwhelming. Your childhood patterning may have eroded your sense of being valued and heard. Perhaps for you it wasn't safe to feel, maybe your sense of self-determination was largely taken out of your hands, others knew better, when you tried to have your say, you were immediately repressed. If this is how you feel, acknowledge that, knowing that things have already started to change, you are increasing your awareness. However, there is work ahead.

You can now begin to rebuild yourself and to allow who you really are to emerge. The result of this work will be like a butterfly emerging from a constricted cocoon. You will need to learn to identify your feelings and needs, just as the butterfly needs to spread its wings and allow them to harden and strengthen before flying. (Needs are discussed in the next chapter.) Although you may have come from a difficult place you still have choices. Am I going to spend the rest of my life in this situation or am I going to do something about it?

There are many magnificent examples, in books, in all libraries, of people who have overcome horrendous personal experiences to come out on top. They turn their personal nightmares to their own advantage, to become inspirational to others. They could not stay defeated, they helped themselves, and made the best of difficult circumstances. Equally there are millions of stories not reported in books and newspapers of unsung heroes who have overcome enormous obstacles. There is no reason why we cannot do the same.

HOW WE AVOID FACING WHAT WE DON'T WANT TO FACE

How do you escape the feelings of discomfort or anxiety, which are probably masking feelings of sadness, loneliness, anger, or self-destructiveness? Your clues lie in your body and observing your physical feelings. Sometimes you may be so used to a level of discomfort or anxiety that you feel quite normal. Let's check that out.

- Conjure up a situation that would definitely feel uncomfortable, like being caught lying or saying something incredibly tactless.
- Stay with the discomfort for a moment and observe your bodily sensations. Is the physical feeling a heaviness in the pit of your stomach, do you turn on TV, pick up the paper, watch sports, eat or go and do some exercise? Do you immerse yourself in a book or go and do some work? Switch on the computer, surf the net, or go to the chat room?

> Whatever you do, recognise that it is, in all probability, an avoidance mechanism to help you disconnect from those feelings of discomfort or anxiety.
>
> - In your workbook write down the clever ways you've invented to avoid feeling what you don't want to feel.

Your journey

In more extreme cases some people genuinely can't feel what is going on. Although they are obviously physically present, they are emotionally distant or absent. Do you feel emotionally detached or dissociated much of the time? If you do, know that for you it has been safer to blank out your feelings, but now to be fully aware you will have to start the journey of reconnecting emotionally. To do that try to become aware of how your body reacts to the day to day ups and downs. In time as you keep trying to connect with feelings they will eventually emerge. Your unconscious will be delighted that finally it has one of its greatest danger signals on hand to use. Admittedly it was your unconscious that said it was safer to close down your emotional center, but now with growing self-awareness you have the ability to look after yourself better and you are no longer a child.

It may be helpful after identifying your avoidant behaviour to tie it to a particular trigger. For example, when I feel anger____ I eat, or when I feel powerless____ I rescue, when I feel fear____I need to sleep and so on. When the trigger is not immediately clear you can use your personal reaction to help identify the emotion or the issue. This can be useful if the emotion is too strong or frightening to deal with, i.e. terror, abandonment or annihilation.

John (page 23) hates being largely dependent on his folks, and can't abide the critical nagging voice of his father, telling him how inadequate he is, so he uses drugs to get rid of that horrid feeling. It numbs the anxiety. Sue (page 83) either walks the dog or picks up the phone to talk to a friend when she's feeling uncomfortable. Immersing herself in their life enables her to switch off from her own discomfort or anxiety, when she can give others solutions and advise it enables her to feel good about herself. This is only a different more subtle form of addiction. She solves their problems and that enables her to ignore her own. Tom (page 90) goes into his study and puts on the classical music when he feels he can't cope with the chaos and noise of home, so his tactic is withdrawal.

If you have worked out how you physically avoid feeling those unpleasant feelings, you are a long way down the track. In becoming aware we give ourselves choice about how we should behave and it becomes more difficult to slip back into those old avoidance mechanisms. You start to intuitively observe and monitor yourself. You build up a data base of your own methods of coping, and avoiding.

DIFFERENT STRATEGIES FOR DIFFERENT FEELINGS

In order to take responsibility for our feelings and actions we need to be aware of all our different strategies, most of them will be largely unconscious, until we stop and think about what is motivating our behaviour. We have looked at avoidance mechanisms and below we may cover more but some will also be coping mechanisms. When we become angry that our favourite team has lost the match, we may decide to walk the dog as a way of coping with our disappointment. After a big argument with a partner we may slam the door, walk out and go to the pub to drown our sorrows. We may, if we feel let down and betrayed by a situation, find ourselves in the midst of either a verbal or physical fight, or we may just take ourselves to bed to shut out the world. We can clearly see different coping mechanisms in the behaviour of a child during a parental fight, when he either retreats to the back of the garden or creeps into bed, or goes to see a mate, or even caused some sort of fracas himself to divert the parent's attention away from their fight. If the child felt the situation was desperate enough, he would do almost anything to get the furthest away from the parental home and the tension and stress there. The only difference between a child and an adult is the number of choices or strategies available.

As we become aware we give ourselves choice.

One very common way of dealing with a stressful situation is to deny it is happening. We deny the reality of it and hope it will go away. Alternatively we may acknowledge the situation but deny the impact it is having on us. Most of us will typically spend a lot of time and energy avoiding the thoughts, feelings and activities that provoke, irritate or cause us discomfort. This is a very normal and natural thing to do, the problem is that it is not helpful, because a large part of those feelings go underground into our unconscious. This makes us feel better temporarily but ultimately erodes our self-awareness and self-control.

At times, after a particularly stressful event some avoidance may be important, as it allows us some ability to cope, and continue functioning to the best of our ability. However, prolonged emotional avoidance or suppression will result in numbness, or dissociation. This is what has happened to people who say, "I don't really feel anything, or who say, "I don't know what I feel." Over time as children they gradually taught themselves to go numb, (i.e. not to feel). They weren't aware this was happening but often if they expressed feelings, parents, caregivers and even peers probably said, "No, no you don't, don't think about it, it's OK." The underlying message is don't feel like that. Slowly but surely, children learn to discount their feelings, after all, we only learn to identity our feelings through adults naming the feeling in the first place. How do you name hunger if you have never heard the word hunger? A child may hear the word sad in a story however, when he tries to use it an adult may discount it saying, no you don't feel sad. He then absorbs a very confusing message about sadness and can't connect fully with the feeling.

> *Denying and hoping a difficult feeling will go away erodes our self awareness, self-control and ultimately self-confidence.*

Many drug addicts and alcoholics use chemical substances to suppress their feelings, to blank them out. They didn't necessarily use drugs or alcohol with the intention of blanking out feelings, but addicts quickly realise that the effects of the substance make them feel better, at least temporarily. This begins the cycle of using. Some of us may use food to push down the feelings. Workaholics operate on the same principle but it is just socially more acceptable. Any addictive behaviour is a mechanism to avoid the fear, frustration, anxiety, sadness, or whatever the feeling is, of a particular situation, that we don't want to know about. Not feeling is dangerous because it effectively erodes and blocks our self preservation or defense mechanisms. If we have the courage to face the feelings, we don't waste precious energy trying to anaesthetise ourselves and much less is hidden in the unconscious.

RECONNECTING WITH FEELINGS

For many people their feelings have been driven so deeply underground that to even start acknowledging them is a big step, but it is a step closer to reconnecting with themselves. When we reconnect with our feelings we feel safer. In recognising our emotions we gain awareness of what is going on, and that knowledge enables us to make choices and take measures to protect and care for ourselves. For example, our programming may have been, "don't feel, just get on and cope, don't think about yourself, thinking and feeling just makes things worse. Get on and eventually you will feel better." There is a measure of truth in that solution, but it is a short term way of dealing with issues and they don't go away. They go into our unconscious, which will call the shots at a later date.

> Not judging our feelings but allowing them to be felt enables us to reconnect with the deepest parts of ourselves. We can then make choices that are in our best interest.

Gallina came to therapy with her husband Zoran because their marriage was on the rocks, she could not control her temper and the slightest provocation would unleash a torrent of abuse as well as physical assault. Gallina had met Zoran and left her native Russia to come to Australia, where she felt totally alienated. Everything was different, the language, the culture, the climate and furthermore, Zoran, born in Australia, had his network of family and friends around him, while Gallina only had him. Back in Russia her family and particularly her large circle of friends had been very important to her. They had given her a sense of belonging, of acceptance and love. Deprived of that support network she really struggled and her anger escalated, what she had not acknowledged were her deep feelings of grief and isolation. As therapy progressed, it became clear that Gallina had not learned to identify and feel her feelings. They had been buried in the unconscious but were still making themselves felt through her outbursts of anger. Her anger was masking all the pain and grief of not only leaving everything that was familiar to her, but also the trauma of her childhood that she had covered with an active social life. Without the cover of friendship these disowned feelings were like an active volcano spewing molten lava.

When feelings go into the unconscious they build up another layer of what is already there. Most of the time, we will never know exactly what happened to drive our feelings into the unconscious in the first place, but as long as we recognise the trigger, we can always assess the current situation and react appropriately.

JUDGING OUR FEELINGS

Another way to avoid feeling is to pass judgement. We criticise ourselves, telling ourselves that it is not OK to feel selfishness, guilt, sadness or any other emotion, usually judged as negative.

> Angela is 60 years old, and is dealing with a husband who has bipolar disorder. He is heavily medicated to avoid the highs followed by the deep troughs, so it seems to Angela that he is completely disconnected from his feelings. He spends his day reading the paper or working on his computer. Meanwhile her mother, nearly 90, is also depressed and self absorbed about her own health. Angela spends a lot of her time looking after both her mother and husband and feeling that she is not getting any recognition or appreciation. After sacrificing too much and at the end of her tether, Angela lashed out at her mother, feeling guilty immediately afterward, and beats herself up about her dreadful behaviour. She finds it almost impossible to have any compassion for herself, as she was taught to think of others first. Even though she has put her life on hold for years, to look after these two most important people, the strain and anger is now percolating to the surface, to vent itself as vitriol.

This is a denial of the secret self. In this case, Angela is not recognising and giving herself credit for all the good things she has been doing. Whenever she starts to feel resentment she immediately squashes it, and says, "the least I can do is be kind." A very important point to remember is that actively avoiding or suppressing unwanted negative emotions, thoughts and memories, actually intensifies the negative emotional response.

If you are aware that you are being judgmental or critical of yourself and are reluctant to talk to a friend, consider finding a good therapist to get a reality check and help to master some skills for insight. Writing in a journal, or using a tape recorder to record how you feel can be helpful. Some people will embark on a creative enterprise in the wake of pain. They may stitch a quilt, build a garden, write their own story, a piece of music or sculpt.

Through creativity we can often work through pain in a safe way. Sometimes we deny or are not aware of what is going on, but perhaps encoded in the selection of a piece of wood for a carving, or the shape of a pottery piece, or in the pattern of a quilt or a piece of weaving, we are telling a story and releasing our emotions. We may not even be aware on a conscious level that we are expressing our feelings.

> Cherie (page 67) depicted the story of a close friend who died of cancer by making a beautiful quilt out of pieces of her friend's clothing. In this way she achieved some sense of closure around her loss and was able to give the quilt to her friend's husband. He felt wrapped up in his wife's love, when he was snuggled under it.

If, at this stage it is too scary to talk to someone, tell yourself out loud when you are alone how you feel, this is very therapeutic and really helps. Another good mechanism is to acknowledge exactly how you feel. It may be, "I feel really down and depressed," and then allow yourself to sit with that and feel the depression. In giving yourself permission to stay with the feeling, it is often much easier to deal with and tends to dissipate quite quickly. As we have just read, when we try to push things away or hide them from ourselves the feelings become more intense.

WHAT YOU RESIST PERSISTS

You've probably all heard that expression, what you resist persists. This works, because everything in our world is built around a dynamic tension between opposing forces. There is a balance between rest and activity, between expansion and contraction like the ocean tides, a pendulum, summer and winter, night and day and so on. When you think of your uncomfortable feelings, or your difficult relationships, you create a dynamic tension in wanting what you do not have. These polarities are the driving force of all action, they are neither good nor bad, they just are. However, by creating the polarity, in this case wanting the uncomfortable feelings to go away, you are actually creating a tension that enables you to feel them more strongly, hence they become more intense. If you can allow the discomfort to be there, to sit in it, it will subside. For most of us the need to avoid unpleasant feelings is so strong that to stay within the discomfort may seem a very strange idea. In today's world we want and expect instant gratification and resolution. However, if we stay with the tension and tolerate those moments of chaos and confusion, we can generally find a more profound and lasting solution. The ambiguity opens up different perspectives.

Unlike what you have probably been taught, instead of avoiding thinking these thoughts, as many of us have been taught to do, it is healthier to allow the thought to be there and think about it, accept that this is how you feel at this moment and then allow it to pass. Where it becomes unhealthy, is when we can't stop ourselves thinking about a particular negative emotion and it becomes obsessive.

WHAT WE DON'T CONFRONT

What we face dissipates, our fears arise from what we do not confront, not from what we do confront. When we look fully and deeply at the source of the discomfort and the fear driving it, the fear loses some of its intensity and power. The truth is that there is nothing within us that can hurt us, after all, whatever is inside us is what we have already felt and judged. It is only our fear of re-experiencing our own feelings that keeps us trapped. Sometimes, when we face what we do not like we don't find immediate resolution, instead we realise just how complex a situation can be. If we can be courageous enough to sit within the tension at this moment in time, something will inevitably shift.

SOCIETAL PRESSURES

Going back to Angela, (page 152) the imposition of the traditional selfless female role of caring, distorted her natural humanity and brought out bitterness, manipulation and guilt inducing behaviour. If you are taught to be "good" and to sacrifice your needs for the sake of conforming and making others happy, you end up feeling guilty when you give to yourself. Deep down and often at an unconscious level, our true motivation for giving is because we want approval and to be liked. Before we can give from the heart, it is important to learn that it's acceptable healthy behaviour to say no. This can be difficult, as our natural desire for autonomy and independence can often feel selfish and wrong. A major disadvantage of teaching children to give unselfishly is that it can undermine their ability to act assertively and develop spunk and competence. Without these qualities, they can be manipulated by others to martyr themselves and give away their lives, putting the needs of others before their own.

Often, societal pressures demand us to conform to the stereotypical image of masculinity and femininity, and behave appropriately for your gender and your role. Men should act tough otherwise they are not men, they can be shamed if they are vulnerable, they should be the providers. Women must act caring otherwise they are not deemed feminine, they should not be angry or have a desire to win. They are supposed to care more for others' feelings than their own.

When people are somehow coerced to do the "right thing" inevitably at some time or another, resentment forms. Some typical scenarios are the resentful wife, parents who lay guilt trips on their children, and men who are unhappy at work and come home and order the family around like a sergeant major.

- Does your own gender role and societal expectations impact on your difficult relationship?

- Write down the impact of your gender conditioning in your life.

- Is it keeping you stuck, preventing you from pursuing your own development and growth?

We each have a responsibility to find out who we really are, what our original blueprint looked like before the influence of our programming. If for example, you have been taught to put others first, you may never have developed initiative and the courage to follow your passion, yet they may be integral aspects of you and pieces of your personal jigsaw.

THE VICTIM MENTALITY

There are lots of ways to avoid examining what is painful and we have looked at the strategy of denial and blaming. Being a victim for a prolonged period of time, also allows us to avoid pain. When we are long term victims we don't have control and are usually quite negative people. We see life as giving us a raw deal, and negativity gets free rein. It is much easier to be negative than positive in a difficult situation. Negativity often allows us to rationalise and justify our behaviour, so we don't have to take responsibility.

> Blake is a student enrolled in a course beyond his capability. Struggling, he complains the teaching is poor. It was easier to find fault and blame the teaching rather than take responsibility for his part in choosing a course that was beyond his capability and seek help.

There may well be people in our lives that simply are not able to understand the part they play in the relationship and will choose to blame or find fault rather than take responsibility. When we recognise this we can choose to walk away or choose to help, either way we do not need to get hooked in emotionally. Admittedly, this is easier said than done.

However, that said, each of us has an aspect of victim in our make-up, we wouldn't be human if we didn't. That part of us all is alive and well in some form or another, which is as it should be. If we denied the victim, it would be sitting firmly in our secret self, playing its role covertly and destructively. Acknowledging the negativity and victim part of us openly, means we have choice about how long we choose to sit feeling victimised. We will all have had some bad experiences and been victims at some time or another. It becomes unhealthy when we decide that life is so unfair that it's not worth trying, we effectively give away our own strength and power, and ultimately become disempowered. It is helpful when we find we are a victim to ask yourself, "what can I learn from this situation? How can I recognise a positive potential in a negative experience?" Before we get there, we need to acknowledge and feel our own sense of powerlessness and frustration. That's the first part of the process of moving through the difficulty.

Victim behaviour means that we don't confront our situation and decide what we can do about it. We blame the circumstances, the person, people, the system, and we feel vindicated. The vindication feels quite safe, but probably somewhat stuck. While we blame our self development grinds to a halt. To avoid "stuckness" we have to take responsibility.

Every step of the way we have choice. Every minute of every day we are making choices. They may be tiny: shall I have a cup of tea, or a glass of water? But the choices, regardless of size, make up the fabric of who you are.

A good question to ask is, "have I got a vested interest in being a victim? What does it give me?" We know we don't have to take action. Furthermore, the endless cycle of mind chatter, "it's not fair, if ____ hadn't happened it wouldn't be like this…" is quite comfortable. However, as we already know, the reality is that we are disempowered and because we have given away our power, we are less safe.

Here are a few reasons for being a victim:
- We don't have to try.
- We don't have to work at making it better, or changing it.
- It gets us sympathy and attention – for a while. (Eventually people get sick of victims. They are negative, and negativity saps our energy.)
- It saves us from failing.
- It allows us to keep face.
- It's better to be a victim than a failure, may be a preferred way of thinking
- It absolves us of responsibility.

Do any of these strike a cord for you?

> Write those down, because they are signposts to uncovering more of your secret self. The same applies to any situations where you are not proud of your motives, it is all valuable information.

REASONS AND MOTIVES FOR OUR BEHAVIOUR

Shocking though it may be, there is a vested interest, albeit unconscious in all our behaviour. We may be totally unaware that we have a motive for behaving as we do and are consciously unaware of possible reasons, however much we try to fathom it out. At the deepest level our answer will lie in the unconscious and will be to keep us feeling safe and OK. (As we already know our survival mechanism is incredibly strong.) The motive may be to always do the right thing, because that is how we choose to be. An act of kindness and love may be just that, a wonderful act of love, or the motive behind it may be like Ms. Perfect (page 81), motivated by wanting others to think she's wonderful.

When we are aware of the motives behind our actions, or our true intent in most situations, we are living consciously with choice. Our unconscious is not pulling the strings and our secret self is becoming more transparent. It is good practice to check in with ourselves and ask, what is my motive? With practice and honesty the answer will come. Remember with every choice you are determining who you are right now. Not yesterday or last week, but who you are right now. Who you are right now will influence who you are tomorrow.

JUSTIFICATION

The other very common tactic for avoiding responsibility is justification. We justify and explain why we can't take responsibility. "It's not my fault, my mother made me like this... I get mad because he treats me so badly... It's the taxman's fault... If the system was fairer I wouldn't need to break the law... It's only fair that I should be able to earn a decent crust... Big business does it all the time... and they are talking mega bucks, not just a few paltry dollars... ". If you fall into the category described above, you probably have every excuse for doing what you have been doing. No doubt your justification was a valuable survival mechanism for you, and may still be for the time being. It probably allowed you a sense of being an OK person. To a greater or lesser degree, we can all justify why we are the way we are and why we do what we do, but that is past. The question is who do we want to be now?

The same reasoning applies to denial. It can protect us until we gain the skills to face our pain, and see what has been going on. We cannot confront all our problems at once and little by little as we learn we may choose to make changes. When we accept and suffer the pain, not reject it through denial, we can move through it to embrace new challenges and try new behaviours.

Sometimes, if we decide we can no longer blame nor deny, nor continue to justify, we will decide to hold onto our weakness and fears. For example, we now acknowledge that we are afraid of the dark. Previously we always tried to keep it a secret and perhaps even projected it by making fun of others who are afraid of the dark. We are now courageous enough to accept, that for the time being, that is where we are at. Although ideally it would be more comfortable not to be afraid of the dark, by openly expressing that it is our fear we have taken a big step forward.

> **Your journey**
>
> ▪ Are there areas in your life that you could bring out into the open, fears that you have held or weaknesses that you have always tried to hide? Write them down. After quiet contemplation you may decide that you do not need to justify what you feel you can accept that for the time being that is how it is for you.

Personal responsibility for our feelings is a lifetime discipline and no easy path. As we have discovered sometimes we don't understand why we have the feelings we do. So many different factors, including our perceptions, our understanding and our intentions all come into play. Nevertheless, we choose to feel whatever it is we feel, regardless of how miserable it makes us. Difficult as it may be we have to own this. We know no one can make us feel any particular way. We decide how we want to feel.

Victor Frankel, a Jew in a prison of war camp illustrated this most poignantly. The prisoners were forced to watch executions of fellow prisoners. After the executions this particular man fell to his knees thanking God. When questioned what he had to thank God for, when their fellows were being killed, he said, because I know that I could not kill others like that. So even in the most dire circumstances this man was choosing what to feel.

INTERPRETATIONS AND DECISIONS

A useful exercise is to recognise how many decisions we make in the process of becoming judgmental, aggressive, emotional or upset. Firstly, we must perceive what is going on; then we interpret the situation, whether it is right or wrong and what motivates another's actions. We then use our view of the situation, our interpretation of why the other person did whatever they did to decide, exactly what we ourselves are feeling or thinking. Our feelings and thoughts then prompt us into action. Our intentions or motivations determine how our feelings and thoughts actually get expressed, and finally we decide what to do with these feelings. We have a huge range of options open to us. We may blame, deny, justify, we may repress, or we may convert them into physical symptoms. We may demand that others change or we may express inappropriate anger, judgement, sarcasm or disapproval. We may threaten, moralise, argue, or accuse to name but a few of our options. Alternatively, we may choose to respond to the situation appropriately by checking out what the other person meant, or by expressing how we feel using "I" statements. I feel____when____. Finally, we could choose to change our feelings. There are choices to be made every step of the way, ideally we have a responsibility to be aware of what we are feeling and thinking and how we express ourselves.

Imagine how quickly we would change if each thought cost us a dollar, or better still gained us a dollar. John Kehoe uses this idea in his book *Mind Power*. He goes on to say that your thoughts cost you energy rather than dollars. No thought is produced without it having an effect.

RESPONSIBILITY

To be responsible is to be "response-able," "able" to make a response. "Able" to do something. Responsibility leads to action. When we accept responsibility we are in charge, we can change our thinking and attitude and plan a course of action: we can change our behaviour. We can accept and deal with our emotions. We can claim our power and make changes by saying, "I am responsible." We empower ourselves when we claim and exercise our responsibility, and our lives inevitably improve when we do so.

Then there are some people who are over responsible for others, rushing in to help or meeting most of their needs for them. We have all heard of the over-responsible mother always there doing everything she can for her child. This is taking inappropriate responsibility.

> Jaques is a habitual drug user and he expects his mother to always bail him out when he gets into trouble. To fund his habit he started dealing drugs. When the law caught up with him his mother got him out of police custody, and paid for his court defense. Each time Jaques promised it would not happen again, but unfortunately it became an ongoing cycle. When his mother, almost at her wit's end, decided enough was enough, she was not going to give him any more money, he threatened suicide. This threat was enough to get Mum back where he wanted her. After seeking professional advice about how to deal with the situation, she was told that she should not give in, that Jacques was an adult and it was ultimately his choice to live or die. When he realised that his mother was finally serious and that she had come to the end of her tolerance, he decided to go into a drug rehabilitation center and, unlike previous times, he stayed the course.

Perhaps things would have been different if Jacques had been left to face the consequences of his actions earlier. If you take responsibility for what others do or are feeling, you are disempowering them. (More about this in Chapter 11.)

(Addicts often tend to be perfectionists, and because they can be so critical of themselves, they use substances to try to deaden their dissatisfaction. Paradoxically, the harder they are on themselves, the more likely they are to use substance abuse. This is what had happened to Jacques, when he realised how unrealistic his expectations had been he stopped being so self-destructive and started to take responsibility for his actions.)

> This example of over-responsibility would be hard to beat: a grandmother of 80 years old, who did not drive, would walk two suburbs to her son's house, to cut his lawn. Meanwhile he, perfectly able-bodied, would sit inside watching the sport on television. When she had finished she would walk home, even though her son had a car and could have driven her.

It is interesting to speculate why she was doing what she was. Perhaps it was the only way she could see him, maybe she thought he was incapable of cutting his own grass, or he only loved her if she gave to him. Was her gift taken for granted and thus devalued? It is possible that she lived in a retirement village and wanted the exercise, but this seems somewhat extreme. The possible explanations for her behaviour are endless.

EMPOWERMENT

It is much easier to want others to change, so we do not have to suffer and as such, don't have to take responsibility for our suffering.

"If she wasn't like that it would all be so different...." Meanwhile she is thinking the same thing, "If he wasn't like that it would all be so different.

Examining these statements we can see how each person is giving the other so much power in the relationship. In his mind she is the one totally responsible for how things are, the implication being that if she changed the relationship could work. Meanwhile the woman, in blaming the man, is giving him all the responsibility for being able to make things better. By not taking any responsibility for the way things are between them she is effectively saying I'm powerless to change anything. As we know relationships don't work that way, it takes two to set a dynamic in action, and although we may not be able to change the other person we can change ourselves, our perception, our attitude and ultimately choose if we want to be part of this dynamic.

What we focus on is what we will see.

Taking charge of our personal choices is empowering. What we choose to think about our relationship is how it will eventuate. If we think it is going to be bad, it can't fail but be bad, that is the energy we are feeding it. If we continually think critically, we will always see the other person in a critical way. What we focus on is what occurs and is how we set up self-fulfilling prophesies.

Albert Einstein once did an experiment to illustrate this point. He held a big round sieve into which he put a green marble and a red marble. He then asked two small boys to choose a marble to watch, he set the marbles spinning around the sieve in opposite directions, and after a while asked each boy what he had seen. The first boy said he only saw the red marble, and the second boy had only seen the green marble going around. Yet both marbles had been going around, but because each boy had been concentrating on his own marble, both had failed to see the whole picture. This is precisely what happens to us most of the time. We get an idea into our heads and it takes an enormous amount of energy to shift or enlarge our way of looking at things. Our brains have a natural bias towards judging others, whilst not looking at the part we may play. This then remains firmly in our blind spot.

We know that we are largely a product of our programming, and that once our unconscious mind has accepted a belief or idea, whether true or not, that belief remains there until it is actively and continually challenged by our conscious mind. So taking responsibility means continually monitoring our thoughts and the impact they have on our relationships. This takes guts as it is much easier to blame, than face what is really going on. Furthermore, our unconscious wants us to be safe, and not rock the boat causing relationship disturbances. We may be operating under societal role expectations, which leave us feeling powerless and frustrated and not knowing who we really are. You can choose to ignore and not confront a situation because you are afraid that feelings you have already experienced may hurt you again. The fear of re-experiencing pain then keeps you trapped.

Your journey

- In your workbook write down the times you have avoided conflict, or avoided confronting a situation in case you get hurt. As you contemplate that what is it exactly that you are avoiding? Is it what someone could say? Write down what you think they could say and see if you can see the underlying message that is triggering your unconscious. Is what they are saying appropriate for you now, as an adult?

- Are you avoiding a possible conflict situation now? Is it because you don't feel you have the skills to handle it appropriately? How could you go about gaining those skills? Who could you ask?

If you feel life circumstances have conspired to "make" you a victim, it means your personal power is in your secret self and not available to you, until you decide to reclaim it. To take control and responsibility means confronting those difficult situations, which leads to action, and is empowering. We sit in the front seat of our own car doing the driving, deciding how we look at events and people.

When you take responsibility for what is happening in your life you are on a journey toward wholeness and healing. It will change your life irrevocably for the better. In your case, because you are reading this, it has already begun to do so.

8 LIVING WITH THE MOST IMPORTANT PERSON IN YOUR LIFE, YOU

We have absorbed a huge amount about how our relationships are impacted by our unconscious, our programming and the development of our secret self, all of which has given us a great deal more understanding and hopefully compassion for ourselves as we struggle with our arduous, sometimes impossible relationships. We are starting to see the part we've played and can focus more clearly and hopefully, less reactively on the troublesome dynamic we have contributed to setting up.

It is now time to look at the most important relationship of all in your life, the relationship you have with yourself. As said earlier it sets the tone for every other relationship you have.

We have all heard the saying, that as people near the end of their lives, they never say they regret not spending more time in the office. Nor do they regret that they didn't make more money or become famous. The regrets always seem to centre on relationships: I wish I had been a better father, mother, husband, wife or friend.

Your journey

- Was I kind and gentle to them?
- Did I do enough for those I love?
- Did I help them to be happy?
- Did I think about them enough?
- Do people love me?
- Do my children really care?
- Will they miss me when I'm gone?

In your workbook jot down your responses. Perhaps the least considered but probably the most important questions of all are:

- Do I love or even like myself?
- Am I gentle and forgiving to myself?
- Have you come to an immediate answer?
- Are you able to stay with the question or is your body wanting to do something else?
- Does it want you to put the book down, and go and do something different? If so, ponder on why you think it feels a bit uncomfortable.
- Your responses are valuable clues: an insight into yourself. For instance, if you are pushing the question

away and feeling vaguely irritated, then introspection is probably new to you and may feel somewhat scary.
- Do you feel discouraged when you think objectively about yourself?
- Do you think you are not really worth thinking about?
- Have you been taught to think of others before yourself?
- Is low self-esteem a problem for you?
- Are you becoming aware that you are starting to switch off, drifting away when you hear these questions, wanting to think of something else?

If that is the case, you are not alone, it seems that along with so many others, it is uncomfortable to contemplate the answers. Although we occupy centre stage in our own lives, when it comes to questions of liking ourselves or self-love we will usually mumble something like, "I suppose so," and try to change the subject.

Why are these questions difficult to contemplate? Is it because we are terrified that we'll be considered too self-absorbed and narcissistic if we admit we like ourselves? Yet these questions are crucial because they underpin the fabric of who we are and the success and happiness our relationships give us.

It is probably easier to consider what sort of behaviour we would exhibit if we didn't like ourselves. Our insecurity and lack of self-confidence and self-belief would probably be identified as depression. This is not a book about how to love yourself, but the ironic thing is, if you read the book to the end I can almost guarantee that you will feel better about yourself without doing anything. Hopefully you are already feeling very differently about yourself, the object of this exercise is not self-judgment but self-knowledge. Don't judge the answer, just become aware of it. There is no right or wrong. However, your answer indicates where you are, right now.

> **Your journey**
> - In your workbook contemplate whether you criticise yourself perhaps unnecessarily harshly. You may even think: Am I so awful that no one can live happily with me? If you do, why do you think you do that?
> - What do you say when you have made a mistake? Are you harsh and critical of yourself, saying, "What an idiot I am, I should know better." Is that helpful to you?

If your answer was more gentle and your self talk went something like this, "That was awkward, but I didn't deliberately set out to make a mistake, so I will just have be more careful the next time," you will also be much more accepting and understanding not only of yourself but of other's mistakes.

The other most important part of all the awareness that we have gained is to have compassion. If we are really smart we will become more compassionate with our selves. In understanding how our personality has been constructed we become less critical of ourselves, and inevitably less critical of others. Once we see the secret self side of ourselves, we are no longer so quick to judge others and as our empathy, compassion and forgiveness grows, we become much nicer to be around.

LIKING YOURSELF

If you are having difficulty thinking about liking yourself then it might be helpful to think:

Your journey

- If I wasn't myself, would I like myself?
- Would I like to have myself as my friend?
- If I were my friend, could I trust myself?
- What wouldn't I like about having myself as my friend?
- For many of us it is much easier to like and love others. In fact, the idea of loving ourselves sounds quite sickly and self-obsessed.
- What does loving ourself mean?
- How do we do it? Isn't it self-centered and selfish to love ourself, and if we do, shouldn't we keep that fact well disguised?
- Do you even want to like or love yourself?

Perhaps the language is a problem here. We talk of loving ice cream, a movie, a car, clothes or our children, our friends and our partners, but we don't love them all in the same way. When we think of loving others it often seems to imply unending sacrifice, being available, or else romantic love, red roses and sweet verse. One of the commandments in *The Bible* is to love our neighbour as ourself. What does that mean? Surely not endless sacrifice or soft words? Maybe it is helpful and more useful to think of love as taking people seriously, of being respectful of others' needs. This is an easier concept to define, understand, and embrace.

RESPECT

Respect is a fundamental human need, which we learn primarily through example. When it is actively modeled to us as children, it becomes a deep-seated attitude.

The Oxford dictionary defines the verb to respect as "regard with deference, esteem or honor: avoid degrading or insulting… to treat with consideration…" It may be easier to understand respect by what it is not. Disrespect being the opposite of respect usually holds an underlying threatening tone and covers a broad encompassing range of behaviours. For example, disrespect can include being ignored, sidelined, passed over, forgotten or mistaken for another. Behaviours we do without thinking can be disrespectful, such as interrupting when others are talking, talking over the top of them or calling them names. In doing these things, not only do we degrade ourselves but we degrade others, our family and those closest to us, often without even realising we are being disrespectful.

A comment like, ""You are so stupid", is disrespectful. Yet how often do we say to ourselves: "What a stupid thing to do" or, "What an idiot" or, "I'm so dumb."

> **Your journey**
>
> ■ It would be revealing to count up how many times a day you make a negative disrespectful comment about yourself. Jot down some of the common ones you use about yourself in your workbook and see if you can start to break this destructive, self-abusive habit.

Many, if not all relationship breakdowns, start with disrespect. (More of this later.) If you can think of loving yourself as taking yourself seriously and respectfully, perhaps the earlier questions about whether you can love or like yourself will become easier to reflect on and answer. Substituting respect for love would certainly make more sense of the biblical commandment.

When we have a firmly embedded sense of respect, unhealthy relationships, which lack mutual respect, wither before they can begin to flower. Respect is the root of all interactions, and without strong root growth there are no flowers, or the flowering is feeble and shortlived. When others disrespect us and we let it pass without remonstrating, perhaps without even noticing, we are not showing love to ourselves. Nonverbally we are giving others the message that we don't respect ourselves, when we don't respect ourselves it becomes easier for others not to respect us. It enables people to take us for granted, to walk over our wants and needs, and relationships that form without strong roots invariably produce stunted, unhappy liaisons.

SELF-ESTEEM

Let's look at this question of self-esteem. What is self-esteem? It is accurately, or honestly and realistically appreciating who we are. It is not thinking that we are less than others or more than others, we are all fallible and will all make mistakes at times. It is appreciating that we are as special and as unique as everyone else.

The cornerstone of all relationships is your own sense of self.

As Glen Schiraldi says in his book *The Self-Esteem Workbook*, "Each person is of infinite, unchanging, and equal worth, which comes with birth." He goes on to say we all express our worth in unique ways and patterns, but each person, at the core, is whole, possessing all necessary attributes in embryo. (I have used the words self-esteem, self-confidence, self-liking, self-love and self-worth interchangeably. Although they all have slightly different connotations, the idea I want to convey is the importance of having a strong sense of self.) That strong sense of self, or self-esteem is the cornerstone to all relationships and is important in the development of self-awareness. Why is it, that low self-esteem seems to be an endemic problem for the western world? Perhaps our societal norms have played a large part.

Generally, we are encouraged to be modest, not to blow our own trumpet, and to hide our light under a bushel, all those old expressions. A major disincentive to telling others how wonderful you are is that they will find you extremely irritating and unrealistic, and eventually drop you from their social circle, unless of course you are exceptionally successful and influential. Who wants to see continual perfection in anybody? Of course, there is a balance in all of this and that balance is the key.

It's important to talk about the extreme of self-love, which is narcissism. Truly narcissistic people display grandiosity, a need for admiration that is well over and above what we all desire as a basic human need, and a lack of empathy and understanding for others. They believe they are superior, special or unique, and expect others to recognise them as such. Usually they only want to associate with others who are also exceptional. They tend to feel that the normal rules of society don't apply to them, as they consider themselves superior. Pop stars who take advantage of the groupies who follow them, often become more and more narcissistic the more famous they become. They may take sexual advantage of the young people who follow them, totally disregarding their own relationships, becoming insensitive and exploitative. They think they are entitled to take without consideration. If you try living or associating closely with this type of person, it will inevitably cause problems in the long-term. If you know someone who is like this, the relationship will be very one-sided, in fact, a Narcissistic Disorder such as the one above, is a very sad condition and masks a profoundly deep insecurity that the narcissist is generally totally unaware of.

> *Low self-esteem holds us back.*

Apart from narcissism, some people with low self-esteem may display overtly aggressive, bombastic and maybe overbearing behaviour as a cover for what they are really feeling, while others may seem very vulnerable and retreat. This will then play out in the dynamics they create with others. It seems almost paradoxical that people with low self-esteem can become overbearing, but the arrogance and pompousness is usually a sign of deep insecurity. However, the person themselves may be totally unaware of this, such as somebody with a personality disorder (see appendix).

Perhaps religious teachings in the west have played an important role in people's low self-esteem. Religion has emphasised that we are sinners and that we are unworthy, consequently, it's hardly surprising that many of us in western society labour under the delusion that to like ourselves is bad. This thinking is so ingrained that although we may recognise it as outdated, many of us find it extremely difficult to throw off. As we learn more about our psyches, we start to understand how this thinking holds us back, how it weakens our self-confidence and has a negative impact on our efforts in life.

In an ideal world, self-esteem is cemented into our psyche by our caregivers, but in reality, that ideal becomes mixed up with the message that we are not OK unless we modify our behaviour and that our needs don't necessarily matter. Of course, this is not deliberate, but our generally well-meaning parents pass along their own fears, unconsciously absorbed in childhood, that it is not acceptable to like ourselves. We could therefore blame them if we have poor self-confidence and certainly they are responsible to a certain extent, but that would be far from the whole truth. For instance, how can they teach what they have never learned? Consequently, if the mother has a very poor sense of self-esteem, unconsciously she is going to pass that on to her infant. It is a frightening thought that the child probably grows up feeling under-confident before he or she even starts dealing with the knocks of life. Of course the average parent doesn't deliberately set out to imbue their child with a lack of self-confidence, but if they aren't fundamentally confident themselves it is more difficult for the child to have a deep sense of self-esteem. The sad thing is, that at some level all of us feel this way. This lack of self-confidence can be rectified and later in life, when the need to change arises, the difficult job falls fairly and squarely on our own shoulders.

Here we are, trying to live with others and wondering why our relationships don't go well, when maybe, impacting on all our interactions is someone else's belief system that we have unconsciously absorbed as our own.

It certainly makes achieving a high level of self-esteem important for us all, and as a natural consequence the long-term health of our planet would improve dramatically. Imagine if we were all respectful to each other. The good news is, that it doesn't matter how little you like yourself at this minute because you can reverse this programming, if you choose. No one else can do this for you, it has to come from within, using your own determination and compassion.

How do you begin this task? Jot down some of your ideas as you consider these pointers:

- Believe in your own abilities. (If you don't, why should anyone else?) When we trust and believe in ourselves, it automatically translates into more self-confidence. Almost the same but with a subtle difference,

- Value yourself and consider your opinion valuable. It may not be the same as others', but it is just as important.

- Believe in what you think and do so you can approve of yourself and enjoy your own company.

- Work towards meeting your own needs, without unduly impacting on others. Showing consideration for yourself is respecting yourself. (There is much more about self-respect in the next chapter.)

The great importance of gaining self-esteem is that it enables you to become clear and real about what you are feeling and thinking. This allows you to be authentic, not only with yourself but also with others. You no longer need to hide behind social masks and play roles to get approval. You say what you feel while being considerate and respectful of others' feelings, therein lies the skill and balance. By saying how you feel you avoid abandoning yourself emotionally. This is not easy, especially if we want a particular outcome, like getting our own way. It's sometimes easier if we don't want to come out and say what we want directly, to just gently and unobtrusively manipulate matters to achieve our objective and hope no one notices. However, we usually sense when we are being manipulated by others, so conversely others will generally sense when we are trying to manipulate them, particularly if it happens more than once. In the long term being authentic is the best solution. Not speaking your truth, saying what you think others want to hear is emotional abandonment of yourself. You set yourself up for disappointment and instead of gaining self-confidence, you allow it to erode.

This all sounds very straightforward, but it takes consistent practice to incorporate it into the fabric of who you are. While self-liking is clearly one key to happiness, it has to be accompanied by a healthy dose of self-knowledge.

As we know, we are all insecure in one way or another at some time in our lives. That may take the form of aggressive or boastful behaviour and at other times we may be meek and mild and may not have the confidence to tackle new ventures. Self-confidence doesn't necessarily mean we can do everything. Self-confidence means that we don't mind admitting that we are not that capable in particular areas.

BALANCE OF POSITIVE THOUGHTS AND REALISM

Clearly, self-esteem needs to be a balance of positive thoughts and feelings tempered with reality. Perhaps an ideal way of looking at being positive is to ensure that at least 80% of our thoughts fall into that category and that there is room for a 20% growth as we try and be different as we grow. It seems that we will always be growing as we develop our potential to be who we choose to be, while being respectful and caring of ourselves and our needs. We talk more about our needs in the next chapter.

When we have low self-esteem we are like a ship with a broken rudder, tossed about on the sea of everyone else's opinions and demands. When others disagree with what we are thinking and doing we tend to vacillate, we don't feel secure enough having set our course to stick to it. A person with a high sense of self-esteem will be able to listen and evaluate others' opinions, but feel confident enough to persevere in the face of opposition. Obviously if we can be thrown off course easily, it becomes more difficult to have a sense of what it is we want to achieve in our lives and make headway. With self-liking we can work toward achieving interesting and meaningful goals. We self-actualise, that is, shape our lives to aspire to our highest values and goals. (More about this in Chapter 14.)

Having a balance between thinking that we can do anything and recognising the truth, is important. If we set unrealistic goals, our self-confidence and self-acceptance erodes when we fail. Yet our society often says you can do anything you choose, for example: "just do this course and you'll be a millionaire in a week." Nice advertising, but the reality for 99.9 % of us is usually very different. Judging ourselves by comparing ourselves to others who are better at something than we are is a guaranteed way of decreasing self-esteem and self-liking. It seems to be human nature that we do not compare ourselves to the masses, or to the average person, which would be much healthier, but to those who excel in their fields and then wonder why we don't measure up. Our expectations need to be realistic. Many of us berate ourselves up for not making the grade, which was unrealistically high in the first place. There is no point wanting to be a brain surgeon when you don't like studying and school was really difficult for you, or wanting to look like a model when your genes didn't provide the necessary prerequisites. We won't all be able to be Olympic athletes however much we practice. Our biology has built-in intellectual and physical limitations and although practice and training will enhance these abilities, there is a point beyond which we can't proceed. This doesn't mean you won't discover your niche in a different area. It's good to set goals and have aspirations, but keep them within realisable parameters. Once reached, we reset them with small steps, which are more easily achievable, rather than big ones which are immediately unattainable.

Set goals within realisable parameters.

Most of us are much more demanding of ourselves than of others. We can be compassionate of others who tried and failed, yet we often don't have the same degree of kindness for ourselves. What stops us being kind to ourselves? Are you kind to yourself, or are you worried that if you are not seen as capable and successful that others may not like or approve of you? Our insecurities are based largely on our self-critical opinions of ourselves, and whether or not we will be accepted and valued by our peers and other significant people in our lives. Most of us will focus longer on our failures and rejections than on our successes, and unfortunately these critical thoughts seem to come almost automatically, and they certainly don't serve us well. Self-criticism comes from fear that we are inadequate and will not meet others' expectations. It seems that we are usually/regularly comparing ourselves with others and come out of the comparison badly.

WHAT YOU DO WELL

Rather than dwell on what we don't do well, let's look at what we are successful at.

- In your workbook make a list of everything that you feel you do well, remembering not to compare yourself to others. You may be good at grooming the cat, fixing the car, making a cake, gardening, working on the computer, keeping a tidy home, or being a good friend.
- The following columns of attributes may help:

Responsible	Patient	Affectionate
Loving	Rational	Tactful
Sharing	Leads	Talented
Trustworthy	Follows	Spontaneous
Determined	Principled	Persuasive
Creative	Fun	Compassionate
Imaginative	Perceptive	Empathetic
Encouraging	Energetic	Punctual
Respectful	Helpful	Generous
Reliable	Thinking	Cheerful
Tidy	Disciplined	Organized

If you think hard enough you will be able to fill at least a couple of pages, and it doesn't matter how small or simple the things you do well are. As you start writing, remember to take yourself and your efforts seriously, don't downplay them or minimise them. Many people when asked to write this list, find it a difficult exercise because they minimise their achievements or fail to recognise what they can do. Negative comparisons are not helpful. For example, "I know I can ice a cake well, but Lucy does it much better than me."

When we were toddlers we didn't think, "I can't do this", we just went ahead and tried, and that's the thinking we can regain. It isn't even new thinking, we did it before and we can do it again. It's just turning back the clock.

WHAT YOU DON'T DO SO WELL

Your journey

Inevitably, there will be some things in life that we are not particularly good at but would like to do better.

- Write these down.

If you go down the same old ingrained path as many negative thoughts flood your mind and you feel swamped, falling back into the old programming of, I'm not good enough? Stop for a moment, ask yourself if you are deliberately trying to do badly or if you are putting in a good effort, but not getting the result you want? Is what you are trying to do within your realistic limits? Do you think that if you really focused on achieving a particular goal and tried to get help, taking lessons, or extra coaching, you could achieve it? Are you doing the best you can with the knowledge and skill that you currently have? Remember as we try to achieve what we set out to do, we will get better at it, just like the child, with practice we become more competent. When you think about the things you are not particularly good at, could you improve on them if you decided to focus on them more? Is the reason you are not so good at it because you haven't done so yet?

You may have written down that you would like not to lose your temper so often, but because you do lose your temper, does that mean that you are bad? Many of us judge ourselves harshly for not being as perfect as we would like. We think we are completely hopeless when it is only one aspect of us that isn't as good as we would like it to be. By focusing on what we don't do well, we don't recognise all we do achieve. We are complex and made up of a myriad of different parts. Because the fuel filter is dirty and the car doesn't run as it should, do we think the whole car is useless? We accept that the fuel filter needs replacing and we know the car will be functional and useful again.

WHEN YOU JUDGE YOURSELF HARSHLY IT IS LIKELY YOU'LL SECRETLY JUDGE OTHERS HARSHLY

Psychologists tell us that some 70–90% of our thoughts are critical or judgmental, which is hardly helpful, constructive thinking. What do we achieve by negative judgmental thinking? How does it serve us, other than to feel bad about ourselves and undermine our self-confidence and self-esteem? Is it a societal norm to be severe on ourselves? Are we secretly just as judgmental of others, but in order to be liked don't let on and pretend to be compassionate and gentle?

To alleviate this discomfort many of us secretly criticise others as harshly as we criticise ourselves. It would be difficult to do otherwise, however, we don't want to be judged unkind and thus words are often softer than our thoughts. It all becomes a vicious circle, the more unkind we are to ourselves the more unkind we are to others, and so the cycle perpetuates itself. Do you judge those people that you find difficult more harshly than others? Like us, they will have their faults that make them exasperating, but they will also have their admirable qualities. If we could

> *Some 70 – 90% of our thoughts are critical or negative, which is not constructive.*

remember to see our own good points it would become easier to see those of others. However, often in our frustration we choose not to think about those positive attributes, it weakens our case for why they are so difficult (if not seemingly impossible) to live with. When we see their good aspects it becomes more difficult for us to blame them for the relationship tangles, and most of us want to blame so we can preserve our own self-image of righteousness.

There is another aspect of our psychology at play here. Many of us secretly hope that we are actually better than others. This seems to be part of our genetic make-up and probably stems from the belief that the best of the species gets the top pickings. The bird with the most magnificent plumage wins the female, or the strongest lion has the biggest pride and therefore, the best opportunity of ensuring his genetic heritage. The fitter and more intelligent the man, the more money he makes the better his prospects of attracting a good mate. Likewise, the more beautiful and kind the woman, the greater her chances are of attracting a mate to support her and their offspring. So, the more "perfect" we appear to be, the greater our opportunity for accruing social advantage. However, many of us secretly fear that we are far from being at the top of the heap, and then there is a further complication. If we did think we were "special," we would need to be wary of displaying it because society does not encourage braggarts. Tall poppies are cut down, as are people who think they are better than the rest of us. It seems there is something of a conflict between in-built genetic programming and societal norms. All of this makes it difficult to have a genuine and realistically based self-esteem.

RESPECTING AND FORGIVING YOURSELF

Your journey

- Coming back to that thorny question, do you like yourself?
- Think about this question, even ask yourself out loud. "Do I like myself?" What response do you have now? Jot it down in your workbook.
- If the answer was negative when you began this chapter, are you looking at yourself differently now?
- Can you begin to respect yourself and take yourself seriously?

That is a fundamental prerequisite to this journey. If the answer is still no, you have work to do to change your mindset, perhaps to forgive yourself for whatever you have done that does not allow you to respect yourself, and to find compassion for yourself. Remember that we don't deliberately set out to do the wrong thing, often it just seems to happen and sometimes because it is the easiest option, we shy away from taking the harder road. Judging yourself harshly for your part in relationship breakdowns will not change the past, nor will it serve the future. If possible, recognise and take responsibility for your part of the dynamic that was created, admit liability and move forward. It sounds easy but if your heart is in pain, it can be difficult.

Personal emotional learning, as said before, comes from suffering, so you could choose to see a painful experience as an opportunity to grow, to release yourself from the pain of the past, and put the newly acquired knowledge to good use in your future. Forgiveness means releasing our hold of the past. Holding on to what is gone only stunts new growth, and you and those close to you deserve more than that. If you feel you have a tendency to hold on to the pain of the past it would be worth asking yourself:

- What investment is there for you in that behaviour?
- How does it help you?

Remember that we are made up of lots of different parts. For example, we may be responsible parents but may not take care of our own health when we are sick, which could be considered irresponsible. Because a mistake is made by an aspect of us that we may not be proud of, it doesn't mean that all of us is contaminated, only parts need to be worked on, not the whole.

The beauty of self-esteem is that we have innate self-confidence which decreases our reactivity. We can hear what people say, take it away and think about it before becoming defensive, upset and retaliating, meanwhile criticising them as the worst person in the world. We all tend to think we should be better than we are or somehow different from how we actually are, and this leads to a continual self-doubting, which ultimately is very destructive. Sometimes with the resentment and frustration of not getting it right we end up discouraged.

Self-confidence increases our ability to get on well with others.

Instead of fighting we could see conflict as an opportunity for growth. The challenges it brings enable us to become more empowered and more evolved human beings.

9 IDENTIFYING OUR NEEDS

The next part of having a good relationship with ourselves is to take ourselves seriously and be considerate of our needs. This is important, but many of us emotionally abandon ourselves by not considering our needs and not telling others what we really feel and think. If we emotionally abandon ourselves, how can we truly be there to help others be true to themselves and their needs? When we take ourselves seriously our confidence and self-esteem grows stronger, which enables us to be more empowered.

Ascertaining our real needs can be difficult once we dive beneath those wonderful surface wishes of fairy tale partner, lots of money, new car, bigger house, great figure and brain, clever children and the wish list is never ending. However, for those type of needs to be easily satisfied, we need a fairy godmother with a powerful wand and unfortunately this book doesn't cover that.

As adults living our own lives we, and only we, are responsible for getting our needs met. It would be wonderful to have someone supply us with whatever we want, when we want it, like living back in the Garden of Eden, but unfortunately that is not the real world, though many of us tend to think it should be. The expectation often is that our partners should meet our emotional, sexual, and even financial needs. Our employers should supply a happy, well paying working environment, and our friends should provide us with additional entertainment and stimulation as well as make things better if life goes wrong. Our families should be behind us supporting our journey every step of the way. We usually expect this as our right without having to work to reciprocate and maintain these relationships. This is almost inevitably a recipe for disappointment and conflict when our expectations fall short.

Good psychological health means recognising our needs and working toward getting them met. When we are happy being who we are, everything else including physical health, tends to follow. The problem is many of us assume that others know what we want, we expect them to be mind readers, when we may not really know ourselves.

Tom (page 147) arrives home tired and irritable. The kids are playing tag and as he gets out of his car a couple of them call, "Hi Dad," and continue their noisy game, followed by the dog, barking madly in excitement. He nearly falls over the bike and in the hall are a mass of building blocks. The place is a shambles and Cherie greets him up to her elbows in flour and says, "Hi darling, afraid dinner will be late tonight, I have to make a cake for Jo to take to school tomorrow. It's a good thing she remembered as I had completely forgotten." Tom has had enough of the disorganisation and explodes. Cherie also loses her temper

> and suddenly the house goes quiet except for the parents' shouting.

Like all such situations this could have been handled differently but so often we let things slide until one day it all gets too much and there is an explosion. If, instead of waiting, both had sat down and talked through their needs and concerns, this wouldn't have happened.

> Instead Tom shouts, "I am tired and uptight after the day at the hospital and I need a calm and organised house, not the kids running wild and everything in a mess."
>
> She says, "But you are only thinking of your own needs. What about the kids? They've been doing what they are told in school all day and when they come home they just want let off steam. They follow rules and regulations all day. I don't want home to be more of the same, which is what it seems you'd like. You're not thinking of me, I feel happy when the children are happy and I hate the idea of a household being run like a hospital. There's no joy in that."
>
> After the yelling subsided and the anger dissipated somewhat, they resolved to sit down over a glass of wine and work out how the situation could be improved. Both recognised that changes were needed.
>
> After a huge fight Sara and Jason went for marriage counselling, which gave them both insights. Sara learned that she automatically assumed that Jason should always be able to sense what was going on for her. As she said, "I never for one minute thought that it may have been helpful to tell him how I was feeling, and what I would like. If I had been more in touch with what was going on for me, I could

have handled it all in a completely different way, which would not have resulted in a fight. If I could have calmly stated what I need I'm sure most of the time I would get it." Sara goes on to realise that the problem is that it's really quite difficult for her to work out what exactly she wants, and that she had just assumed that, "We've been together long enough, and he should know what I need when I'm feeling tense or anxious, and act accordingly." She goes on, "I know what he wants when he's having a hard time. When he doesn't respond as I want him to or seems uninterested in my problems, I lose my temper thinking that he doesn't love me." Sara had not realised that her anger concealed the fact that it was easier to get mad and feel sorry for herself, rather than talk about what was really going on for her.

Your journey

- Do you know what it is that you want from other people?

PROJECTION OF UNCONSCIOUS NEEDS

Jill battled for 25 years of marriage to try and get her mother-in-law to validate her. She thought when she became engaged to be married that perhaps she could have a deep, honest, and loving relationship with her mum-in-law, something she had not been able to achieve with her own mother. Her own mother was fairly critical and it had been safer not to tell her things than risk being criticised. As a result, Jill worked extremely hard to be the perfect daughter-in-law, even though a lot of the time the relationship bored her, she felt drained by all the effort she had put in. However, very occasionally she would receive a positive comment, but most of the time the comments were directed at how Jill could make a better wife and mother. Eventually Jill was so tired by her efforts, and becoming increasingly resentful and bitter toward her mother-in-law that she sought some counselling.

Jill was surprised to learn that unwittingly she had engaged in a power struggle, she was struggling to receive validation for all the work she had put in. She wanted love and approval from her mother-in-law, and in trying desperately to obtain that, she was slowly killing herself with effort. Jill had not recognised the depth of her own need. She had wanted to replace her own mother with someone who could give her the love and approval she had missed out on as a child.

Jill was projecting her unconscious need for mothering onto her mother-in-law, who had no idea what was motivating her daughter-in-law's behaviour, nor did she have any understanding around the simmering resentment and bitterness that she was sensing. How could she have understood what was going on?

Furthermore, Jill's mother-in-law had come from a family where showing emotional closeness and intimacy was frowned upon. Jill suddenly saw her mother-in-law for who she really was, and not for the fantasy that she wanted. She realised that it was all about her need, and really had nothing to do with her mother-in-law. It was only then could Jill accept her for who she was, and not try and change her. After that, the whole relationship shifted dramatically. It became much more natural and comfortable. Jill was finally able to detach from her need for validation from her mother-in-law because she could understand that she was looking to fulfill a need from an inappropriate source.

WANTING OTHERS TO BE DIFFERENT

The basis for most conflict in relationships is that we do not accept people for who and what they are. We want them to be different. Recognising why we want them to be different, what need in us we are seeking to fulfill, is an enormous step forward. Perhaps in recognising those needs and taking responsibility for meeting them ourselves, we would find it easier to live with others.

YOUR NEEDS

We know that to be responsible we need to connect with feelings, but we also need to know what our needs are so we can take action and be responsible for getting them met.

What do you need? You may think it sounds like a really simple task. You may say I know exactly what I need: a new car; bigger house; better job; more money; trimmer figure; a partner that really cares for me; kids that listen to me and do what I want; happiness; more fun; and, so the wish list goes on. Unfortunately this book cannot

> *Knowing what we need enables us to take responsibility for meeting those needs.*

guarantee those, but with better relationships they may become more likely. Some of us may simply say we want happiness. That is a good start, but what constitutes happiness for you? According to a recent survey done by the American Psychological Association, (APA) popularity, influence, money and luxury are not what make people the happiest. What makes us happiest according to the survey, are autonomy (feeling that our activities are self-chosen and self-endorsed), competence (feeling that we are effective in our activities), relatedness (feeling a sense of closeness with others) and self-esteem.

In working out what we need let's first consider our emotional needs. When we can't or don't get them met, it often makes us angry, resentful and revengeful. At a conscious level, we don't always realise what's motivating our behaviour, but hiding in the unconscious are the emotional needs that we didn't get met by parents, friends, peers and teachers when we were children. They are still there, making themselves felt covertly, waiting to be fulfilled. So without being consciously aware of it, we are trying to correct our childhood experiences, and in doing so, heal ourselves. We are looking at others to fill these needs, and if we look very carefully at our most conflictual relationships we will usually see the same issues that haunted us as children. Consequently, in our interactions with other people those needs will unconsciously direct our behaviour. The problem for the most part is, that we are not exactly sure what we need in order to rectify the childhood pain and suffering.

Do some of the words in this list strike a cord? Phil McGraw uses some of them in his book *Relationship Rescue*. They probably cover most of the key issues in our lives;

Relationship	Criticisms
Intimacy	Being used
Truth	Addictions: work, drug, alcohol, sex, sport
Trust	
Family	Being a victim, Being persecuted
Lack of passion	Children
Boredom	Money
Jealousy	Lack of time
Fear	Rage
Underachievement	Communications
Harshness	Overachievement

Your journey

In your workbook jot down those that resonate with some of your deep needs. They may not necessarily be just about your childhood. What are you not getting now? Alternatively, what are you getting now that you find so difficult and are there similarities to childhood situations? Spend time reflecting on these questions and journal your answers.

> Rebecca was desperate for a relationship. She had been sick for many years and although not cured, was improving. She felt that if she could find the right man her health and her life might get back on track. She found a man, however, her health deteriorated instead of improving and she started having anxiety attacks. When she sought help and started therapy she realised that she wanted to find security, someone who would look after her, even if she was in ill health. The partner she had found was not willing to make the necessary changes in his life to accommodate her needs, and this was prompting the anxiety attacks. As a child Rebecca had never felt really loved and unbeknown to her consciously, she wanted a partner who could give her what she felt her adopted parents didn't.

HUMAN NEEDS

Let's look briefly at what constitutes the most common human needs. Survival is at the top of the list. As each need is satisfied, the next becomes important. Following survival is the need for safety, which is closely followed by the need for love. Love includes security, protection, warmth and shelter, as well as the physical needs of touching and caressing. Then there is the need to belong and to achieve this we know that generally we learned to please our caregivers, often irrespective of ourselves. We didn't demand justification and clarification as to why things were a particular way, we accepted. That acceptance becomes, for many of us, the basis on which we live our lives today. As we grow older many of us try and get the love and approval of our peer group, or organisations to which we belong. We may become a couple, believing unconsciously that our partner will provide us what we need, a sense of acceptance and belonging gives us emotional security and satisfaction. When we feel as if we are accepted and belong, we can then move to a place where it is acceptable to be different, where we do not always have the same views or do things in the same way as our group. This is called differentiation. We are confident enough in ourselves to allow ourselves to be different when it is appropriate. It is from this platform that true self-esteem and self-worth can grow.

BEING TRUE TO OURSELVES

This is an important key. When we can allow ourselves to experience our feelings, be it anger, sadness, despair or helplessness and so on, we are much closer to owning and taking responsibility for our needs. In taking responsibility for our own needs we don't threaten others, unless of course we threaten them to fix it for us. It is when we don't take responsibility that others will often pick up our covert demands, which can arouse many different emotions including; aggressiveness, vulnerability, fearfulness and distancing. Sensing their reaction, we will often backtrack and deny what we want, emotionally abandoning ourselves. The needs then go underground, often to be covered by inappropriate behaviour, but eventually they surface again later, often to cause a greater level of resentment, pain and

> *When we don't express our needs they often emerge covertly causing tensions in our relationships.*

angst for more people. It is important to note, each of us has a legitimate need to be noticed, taken seriously and respected.

According to the APA survey, (page 198) a lack of security and a lack of predictability are the most difficult for us to handle. Both of which, we often take for granted. If one single need is picked as being the most important to satisfy, it was self-esteem.

True self-esteem is a lot more than just recognising one's attributes and special qualities, talents, beauty and so on. Inner strength is derived from coping with problems, owning and taking responsibility for the authenticity of one's feelings, and dealing with issues that arise from them. It is much more about being comfortable with being true to yourself. "To thy own self by true, And it must follow as the night the day Thou canst not then be false to any man," says Shakespeare in *Hamlet*. From this solid platform, happiness and satisfaction are much closer and more easily attainable.

LOOKING TO OTHERS FOR VALIDATION AND TO MEET OUR NEEDS

Many of us look to others for our self validation and the sole source of our emotional satisfaction. We become reliant on their approval for our sense of self, which often compromises our own truth. With maturity, hopefully, comes a more grounded sense of who we are and what we stand for. This then decreases the need for external approval, which can be a precarious position, as it is reliant on other's constancy, if they happen to change their mind about us for some reason, that can severely damage our self-esteem. Consequently, it is important that our self-esteem is based on our own internal validation.

At a deep instinctive level we know that the single aspect of our life that contributes most to our satisfaction and to our sense of psychological well-being, are our intimate relationships. Most of us, if asked what we want from those we spend most time with, would say trust, respect, friendship, companionship, honesty, good company, understanding, and where appropriate love, good sex, similar interests and the list goes on. It all sounds ideal, but to have all those things 24 hours a day, 7 days a week is unrealistic. For many of us our relationships are a bit of a disappointment, sometimes everything is fine, then something happens and we start to feel angry, frustrated, let down or sad. Generally, we believe it has nothing to do with us or our unrealistic expectations, it is just the way the other person is treating us. We are victims.

When we feel angry or threatened we know we are not living exactly the way we wish to. If we take the risk of stepping off the edge of our own conventionality, to live the life of our choosing, we need to accept the consequences of that choice. When we feel maimed by giving too much or inappropriately, or feel put upon by other's demands, it is time to explore what we really want to give.

- What do you want to give and what is just placating others?

We understand that knowing what we need and having the courage to ask, is a big step forward in avoiding the victim role. We also realise that once we let go of the expectation that others will meet our needs without our direct intervention, it changes the need. Instead of an unexpressed unfulfilled expectation with a covert agenda, it becomes a clear statement of what you need and what you are prepared to do to have that need met. In most cases this can be as simple as asking. Often you'll have changed the need from being external and risky, in that it relies on others to read your mind, into a solvable or "meet-able" internal need. Sometimes just the identification and conscious realisation enables us to take responsibility and shifts the energy, instead of an unconscious gnawing, it becomes an opportunity to act.

DIFFERENT CATEGORIES OF NEEDS

For many of us there is a need to give, to support, to encourage, to connect, and share. In the giving, we can get immense satisfaction and feel that we are fulfilling an important part of our life, but maybe you feel there is a lack of opportunity to do this. If this is the case, maybe there are other outlets you haven't considered, perhaps to a larger community, maybe doing some type of charity work. Most people involved in a charity have a higher sense of self-worth because they know they are giving of themselves in a useful way.

In your workbook:

- Where do you feel there is a lack in your life? (It is often easier to focus on what you feel you are lacking.)

- How am I going to work toward fulfilling those needs?
- What do you need to do?

If this feels overwhelming know that, by the mere identification of your ideal requirements, you have already shifted the energy by throwing light on them. Although you are unlikely to instantly change your circumstances, you may have a much clearer path ahead of you. These are easy questions to ask, but often the responses can take a lot of soul searching. (Your answers may overlap to some extent with some of the previous or following exercises.)

THE ISSUE UNDERLYING THE NEED

Like all this work, there are layers underlying yet more layers. Recapping the list from page 199: relationships; intimacy; truth, trust; family; lack of passion; boredom; jealousy; fear; harshness; criticisms; underachievement; being used; and, addictions: work; drugs; alcohol; sex; sport; being a victim; being persecuted; children; money; lack of time; rage; communicating; overachievement and, adding the basic needs of feeling safe; supported; encouraged; respected; connected to others; sharing and acceptance.

- What underlies the issues that you have marked as resonating with you?

If we take an example, such as the need to be supported, you may read this as a financial need and it may be helpful to determine what underlies your need for money. Is it about money? It's an outward commodity, but is it really about what money buys for us? Is it the security to know that we have enough to be safe? Or, is it about having the new dress to make us feel attractive, because we have a belief that we are not attractive enough, or the new car to make us feel important? Ask yourself the question, what is the need? Below each of the things you've listed in your workbook, be it the need for respect, the need to belong, the need for more time, the need to overcome the addiction etc. Is it a longing wanting to be fulfilled? What is it you really want? Make yourself a flow chart such as on page 207, after reading the following example.

> Patrick (page 68), heading up his department at the bank feels under continual pressure to increase profitability and to be seen as excelling. There are numbers of younger, highly qualified people just below him on the corporate ladder and he is not feeling confident that he can exponentially "grow the profits" fast enough to preserve his position. Consequently, Patrick works extremely hard and both his parents and Rachael see his ambition as more than just keeping abreast of competition, he was driven and as a young child, and always wanted to be at the top. What Patrick unraveled when he looked beneath his need to achieve, he saw:

> Overachievement is the surface issue or the need,
> ↓
> Working so hard makes me so tired.
> ↓
> Under the tiredness is a certain sadness and questioning: when will it be enough?
> ↓
> Under that uncertainty, fear emerged.
> ↓
> The thought was: will it be good enough?
> ↓
> And if it is not good enough, is it because I am not good enough?
> ↓
> If I am not good enough, will others want to be with me?
> ↓
> If I am not enough, no one will love me.
> ↓
> If no one loves me, I will be rejected and left all alone.

So the bottom line of this exercise is that Patrick's deep unconscious fear is that if he doesn't work really hard to achieve he may be abandoned. Perhaps a childhood message was in order to get approval and love you have to achieve. When Patrick could see it clearly he was able to make some conscious decisions about how much he was willing to sacrifice to climb to the top of his corporate tree.

Your journey

- As you are doing these exercises be aware of what comes up for you.
- What physical symptoms is your body manifesting right now?
- What is it doing to try and divert your focus from these difficult questions?

FEAR

If you are finding it hard to determine your reactions, consider the possibility that your unconscious isn't even allowing you to consider these questions. What is that about? It is possibly avoiding triggering fear. The main areas of fear are rejection, abandonment, annihilation and the fear of being inadequate. You may feel inadequate in any number of ways, physically, mentally, socially, culturally, sexually, and spiritually. Any one of these can usher in a fear of disappointing yourself and others. We can go to great lengths to avoid these uncomfortable feelings, so un-tackled, they go underground into the unconscious and the secret self, possibly to be projected out at others and to become more intense. It is much easier to criticise others who do not wish to look at their problems, than to look at ourselves. Back to that adage: "if you spot it, to some degree you've got it."

BACK TO RESPECT

Relationships that become teeth grinding contacts that have gone sour will be most unlikely to have the vital ingredient, respect. The resultant resentment builds as toxic waste. To help alleviate discomfort it is easy to project and find fault with others, sometimes blaming and criticising them. This can have a ripple effect sucking many people into a cycle of annoyance and reactivity.

When we don't feel respected it will be highly unlikely that we are treating the difficult other person with respect. If it was interwoven into all our relationships, beginning as children, we probably would not be reading this. Respect is again another vital key. Although we have already talked about this and continue to talk about it in Chapter 10, it is important to deepen our understanding at this point. We all know the following but it may be helpful to refresh our memories.

Respect is:

Treating others as I want to be treated

Being considerate

Treating people with civility, courtesy and dignity

Accepting personal differences i.e. different racial or cultural backgrounds, sexual orientation etc.

Working to solve problems without violence

Not intentionally ridiculing, embarrassing or hurting others

Ideally when we first meet people we have a respect for them, this will deepen as the relationship grows or it diminishes if we find we don't particularly like the person. We may find we respect certain aspects of a person, perhaps their drive and determination, but don't respect their business ethics. Does that taint your whole relationship?

Your journey

- As you think about that impossible other can you think of occasions when you have been disrespectful? Use your workbook to journal these.
- What did you learn?
- How has the difficult other in your life been disrespectful to you? (You could probably write a book about this but keep it very short and try not to go into feeling persecuted. Try to see both points of view.)
- Is there any truth in what they have said that could be useful to you?
- Are there any aspects of that trying other that you can respect?

Daniel's treatment of Neil (pages 82, 106) is overlaid with disrespect. He feels Neil is somewhat pathetic and acts like a victim. He complains bitterly about his work and threatens to leave but never follows through with his resignation. He doesn't walk the talk, to coin the jargon. Neil feels that Daniel is disrespectful of the fact that he never acknowledges the overtime that he puts in. Financial reasons are dictating the behaviour of both, so on another level both are selling themselves out by being disrespectful of their own needs. Neither is happy and both would like to be shot of the other. In fact both men are holding up a mirror to the other as both are feeling a victim of

> circumstances and stuck, which only exacerbates the situation.

Unfortunately this tends to be a fact of life. Sometimes we can't just leave our jobs because we don't feel respected, but we can acknowledge the fact and work with it by finding ways of dealing with it so it is not a continual thorn in our side.

If we have not been treated with much respect in our lives it is possible we will project disrespect. Worse still we will not have respect for ourselves, and find that self regard difficult. Projected disrespect does not have to be in anything said or not said. It is an energy that we automatically, at a subconscious level, read, absorb, and then react to. If we are the victim of this we may be unaware consciously of what is going on, but we know that we don't feel comfortable and relaxed. We are automatically on guard, at some deeper level we feel unsafe. Neil feels this around Daniel. Sometimes another will project disrespect, but we may not have the confidence or discernment to recognise it, and then take it as a personal insult.

RESENTMENT

When we are not treated with respect we often feel resentment. One of the most common reasons why relationships become difficult, and then seemingly impossible, is that people don't feel appreciated for what they do or for who they are. When they don't see things coming back to them in the way they expect, or don't feel respected, they get resentful. Resentment is really unexpressed anger, as is revenge. We will all have experienced this at some time and quite possibly recognise the feeling well. It underlies so many relationship knots. When we are not getting what we want it raises its head.

Your journey

- Spend a few minutes with your workbook and write down the biggest resentments that come to mind. Now praise yourself for your courage and honesty because this is not easy work.
- What was the need that was not getting met that caused the resentment in the first place?
- How can you go about fixing that?
- What do you need to do?
- What are you saying to yourself about the incidents?
- Does the self-talk go something like this, "I do all this stuff, and there is no recognition or appreciation, they just expect me to do it, even worse they don't even realise I'm doing it. It's all bad."
- How can you change your thinking and modify your self talk?

Like many of us you may have a ton of toxic waste buried as resentment. In all probability the offenses may stem from similar issues, clamouring for a voice, and using different scenarios to be heard. Little by little as you become aware and deal with the needs, by talking about them as they arise, this dump of toxicity will reduce of its own accord. It is only building up because it has not been dealt with earlier. Sometimes our resentment builds to such an extent there is an almighty row, and it all gets aired. This, while unpleasant, may be a healthier option than letting it fester, although it is not an ideal solution. If the other person doesn't want to talk we have to work out a satisfactory solution for ourselves. This can be difficult; journaling may help in seeking resolution, or asking a friend to talk it through with you or seek some counselling. What can happen when it is not safe to get angry with the person involved be it our mother-in-law or our boss we may project all our anger and resentment at a safer target, someone who will not bite back hard, or fire us.

PROJECTION OF RESENTMENT

Choosing these softer targets is done at an unconscious level. As a general rule we don't go around thinking, I'm really mad, who can I pick a fight with? We are not even consciously aware that we need to dump our anger or frustration on someone else, and most of us would be horrified to realise that is what we are doing.

> Sue (page 147) complained that she didn't know why, but she was going around acting like a policewoman. She had been lying on the beach and saw someone with a dog. Dogs were prohibited on the beach, so she promptly reached for her mobile phone, walked up to the sign saying dogs were not allowed on the beach and phoned the number given.

> Normally it would not have bothered her. Later that day in the library she watched someone use a computer that they had not paid for and went and reported them. The next day she experienced so much anger on the road that she gave another driver a mouthful.

This was uncharacteristic behaviour for her. It transpired that she was feeling angry at Barbara the mother-in-law from hell, but it was not safe to explode at her, so instead she was going around projecting her irritation at others. If we are not able to direct the anger at the appropriate place, it inevitably escapes in some way. It seeps out and will find any target it can. No doubt the person walking their dog on the beach, or the person using the computer in the library were not doing the socially accepted thing, but they do not deserve to be a target for our misplaced feelings.

The flow-on effect of that behaviour, is the person on the beach, in the library, or in the car feels picked upon, and in turn that anger, frustration or irritation will in all probability find a target. In not being aware of our needs or taking responsibility we can perpetuate an ongoing ripple effect of bad feelings. Imagine those three people then finding another three people to vent their frustration on, and so on. It is interesting to speculate what a different place the world would be if we all took responsibility for our own needs. Maybe we could all live in peace and harmony. What we can do is stop and think, what is going on here if the man or woman next door to you in the train or the shops is rude and unpleasant. You could ask yourself is this really about me, do I deserve this? How am going to choose to react in this situation?

WE EACH HAVE DIFFERENT NEEDS

How do we discern if we have been fulfilling other's needs at the expense of our own?

If our programming has been to be obliging and helpful we may need to look very carefully and logically at what it is we do and what others in our life do. It is possible that the person you find impossible to live with is asking too much of you, or to feel loved and secure you have been doing too much, and are now full of resentment and can't abide him or her.

Your journey

- Are there any people that spring to mind?

IS IT SELFISH TO MEET MY OWN NEEDS FIRST?

In thinking about fulfilling our needs many people ask, "Aren't I being very selfish if I take care of my own needs first?" Chances are if you are asking the question the answer will be, "No." If you were always out to have your own needs met, the question would not cross your mind. It would be out of your consciousness because you would automatically think of yourself first.

We touched on this briefly when talking about the secret self, but it is an important point and one of the reasons many relationships finally collapse under the pressure caused by too much giving. Imagine you are a golden goose and lay golden eggs that are very valuable. You can give those golden eggs to whomever you choose. However, if as the golden goose you are forever laying eggs there will come a time when you are not able to lay the same quantity and your supply will dry up. If, on the other hand, you nurture yourself and don't overlay, the supply of eggs will be stable. Work the golden goose to death and there will be no more eggs. When we can give ourselves what we need we can give to others more fully. If you are running yourself ragged looking after everyone else's needs and trying to please them, doing what you think they want, it will be useful to stop and think about your motives. Are you fearful that if you don't they won't like you and could reject you?

If our actions are motivated at a very deep level by fear, fear of being rejected or abandoned, our needs will often come second to everyone else's. Going back to our analogy of a glass of water, if we don't refill the glass we have less and less to give, like the golden goose. The more our old childhood patterning says, "Give," the drier and drier we become. Eventually, fulfilling everyone else's needs depletes us completely. Generally, before we get to that point our bodies get physically sick and this then gives an opportunity to look at our lives and make different decisions. That point comes at different times for different people, but it always comes when we are forced by some sort of a crisis, be it physical illness, loss of a job or loss of someone or something dear to us, or when we decide that life is not working as we had planned, and we need to reassess. Often it occurs around mid 30's to mid 50's. Something will happen to precipitate a rethink; it's like a wake up call.

Have you had a wake-up call? Perhaps this book will act as one.

Your journey

- Write down in your workbook what happened and its impact on you.

- Or if you think you are on the edge of one now, what is it trying to tell you?

SELF-CENTERED PEOPLE

There can be many reasons for this character trait, it could come back to childhood programming and conditioning. If caregivers were unbalanced or had a personality disorder, perhaps people learn very early to grab what they can to survive, possibly, because they have a deep fear that they cannot trust or rely on anyone to be there for them, to love them. A general rule of thumb, one that can be helpful when we see others being selfish, is to understand that the greater the degree of selfishness, the greater the lack of love in their early years. In an ideal world, if we were always surrounded by love and kindness we give out love and kindness.

ASKING FOR WHAT YOU WANT

If we could wave the magic wand and have others tell us what we would most like to hear, what would you learn about your most powerful emotional needs? How can you work toward meeting those needs yourself?

> **Your journey**
>
> - Make a list of the people you care about the most, and write down what you would really like them to say to you.
>
> This example maybe a projection, but what most parents would want their children to say is, how much they appreciated all the work that had gone into their upbringing, what a great parenting job they had done, and how much they love them. No doubt many of us want to hear how much we are appreciated and loved by the people most precious in our lives. One of the most universal and primary needs is to be appreciated.
>
> Does this ring true for you? OK, so now you know one of your most important needs.
>
> - How do you take responsibility for getting it met?

The interesting thing is that often when we work out what we want we can start to detach from the need. It comes back to the fact that what we face and look at generally dissipates to a large extent. We have seen the need, acknowledged it and in the acceptance, can take concrete steps to meeting it ourselves. The paradox is that when we meet it ourselves, it often starts to come from many unexpected and different sources. In the need for appreciation, when we start to appreciate and value ourselves, others seem to naturally follow suit.

In appreciating ourselves, we know we are not perfect but we are growing and need to resolutely acknowledge all the things we do well and all the positive attributes we have.

> - Make a list of the things you routinely do for others. Start to appreciate yourself, and the choices you make about doing whatever it is that you do for others. Without realising it you build self-esteem and self-acceptance.

This means that you become less dependent on external approval and more self reliant and motivated. The other thing that can happen is that at times you can ask others if they appreciated a particular thing, and get their feedback. The flow-on effect of this, is that others in your circle will do the same thing.

Once a need is recognised and you start working toward fulfilling it yourself, it is no longer covert. Your awareness frees up all the energy that has been invested in trying to have them met by others.

The answers that you most want to hear will tell you that those are the things you heard least about yourself when growing up, and wanted to hear the most.

> - After doing that exercise, write down the names of the most difficult people in your life and what you would most like them to say to you. You may need to imagine you are able to wave a magic wand and all the difficulties and conflicts of the past are over, and this was the start of a new stage in your relationships with them. What could they say that would make you feel differently about them? Just let your imagination take over, so don't censor what they would say.

Many of us dance to the perceived needs of others, then wonder why we get frustrated, irritated and downright angry when we are not getting what we want. We want them to be mind readers and give us exactly what we want and need, even when we ourselves are only vaguely aware of what these needs actually are. In taking responsibility for our desires, we have to be aware of whether our expectations of others are realistic. Do we expect perfection, or near perfection from them? Can we be perfect companions all the time? Are our expectations sensible? In those teeth grinding relationships, the pitfall usually comes because neither party has clarified what it is they are expecting from the other. In all probability each party has just assumed that the other is a brilliant mind reader, and knows what is necessary. That is an over-estimation. When each person doesn't get what they were expecting, each turns into a victim, and a vicious cycle starts.

> *Many relationships go off track when we assume others can read our mind.*

Once we establish this level of need and look beneath it, we can often see exactly what is being triggered and how that impacts on our relationships. Usually they will be core issues from our childhood programming which we want others to fulfill and resolve for us. The surface need may only act as a trigger. Our bodily reactions may try and stop us looking at these deep core issues, as invariably they will touch various forms of fear; that is, until we do the excavation work and bring those fears up to the surface to be examined.

Assessing our needs and gauging when enough is enough, is challenging. Some of us will give and give until one day it all gets too much and the relationship suffers major damage as it breaks down. It is sensible, before that happens, to ascertain if we have been fulfilling others needs at the expense of our own in order to avoid the fear of rejection and all that it entails. Others may be very self-centered and as a result find their lives are not working well, but the behaviour was learned in childhood as a protective mechanism. It undoubtedly needs to be rethought.

10 POWER AND CONTROL

Some of us will have heard of the stereotypical scenario of power and abuse, when the drunken man beats up his partner after he comes back from the pub. Most of us pretend that we don't use the mechanisms of power and control in our relationships, and heaven forbid we never manipulate. The sad truth is that we've all used various ways of controlling at sometime or another. To deny that is to undo the good work you've done up to now, because you would be denying the existence of your secret self.

Let's take a look at the most common power bases that operate in society. Some of these power bases will relate more to one gender than another. For example, men will have a power base of physical strength because generally, men are stronger than women. Also, be aware of a conflictual situation in your life, where someone may be operating very much from one or two areas of power and see if you can identify which particular power tools they use.

Your journey ▪ As you read become conscious of which you may use, it can give you valuable clues as to how you think and are in the world. Jot them down in your workbook.

POWER BASES

Imagine you are at a social function where you don't know many people. Usually after exchanging your names, the question of "what do you do?" arises. He says, "I'm a brain surgeon." You say, "I'm a street cleaner." What do you think happens? Generally, unless you have some staggering quality, like two heads, or his hobby is writing stories and you may be a good character, he finds a reason to drift away. He may stay a few minutes longer if you say you are a sanitary engineer as he explores what that is. If you said you are a nuclear physicist he would probably stick around to talk for quite a while longer. Most people quickly want to place you on the socio-economic ladder. What is really going on here, largely at an unconscious level, is that he is trying to determine if you could be useful to him, in some way that might strengthen his power base. Remember how our brain likes to catagorise people.

Let's look at the different power bases. Many of these come from Sally and Rudi Dallos in their book *Couples, Sex and Power, The Politics of Desire*.

Ideological Power In our society, men's beliefs, opinions, attitudes, discourses, narratives, and explanations have been predominant for centuries, resulting in men largely holding power, and up to quite recently, dictating women's roles. Since the suffragette movement in the early part of last century, this is slowly starting to change, although the glass ceiling still restricts the number of women in senior positions within organisations.

- Do you have some set ideas of the roles men and women should play?
- Do they contribute to conflict within your life?

Economic Power This is often a man's power base. Many women, particularly with children, are unable to support themselves financially, and often feel guilty, resentful or angry about being largely or completely dependent.

- Do you hold that power card or does a difficult other, your partner, your boss or your father-in-law and his estate?

Ascribed Power This is the power that stems from the mutual acceptance of a given role, for example, a man is in charge of providing financially and the woman is responsible for home and children. There maybe an assumption that the man has sexual rights. Is the man automatically the head of the household?

- Does this apply to you?

Informational Power What is each person's expert power base, i.e. domestic tasks or technical ability? Research has found that unless the other recognised the expertise, this power edge was not seen as positive. Having some degree of power could give a controlling edge, i.e. how the house should be decorated, or how the finances were invested, however, it could mean that the task fell exclusively to one partner, (i.e. childrearing, food, lawn mowing and so on.)

- What relevance does this have for you?
- Are you always the one responsible for the finances or buying the food?

Candy is a black American. Intellectually she knows she is just as good as anyone else, white or ethnic. Nevertheless, deep down she feels that she is somewhat of a second-class citizen and it doesn't matter how often she tells herself she is not, she continues to hold that belief. Her partner, Benny, is also black. He is university educated, rising up the corporate ladder and is the breadwinner, as she stays at home with their young children. Candy has not acknowledged to herself that she is feeling increasingly resentful toward Benny, and one day he asked her to wash a particular shirt and socks for a work function that night.

Candy lost her temper, "Is that all I'm good for, washing your bloody socks and shirt so you can go out and play the cool guy?"

Benny retorted, "It's your job, I earn the money to support us."

> The argument precipitated a crisis; and, in exploration of the issue, Candy discovered just how much she always felt like a second-class citizen, and the higher Benny moved up the professional ladder, the more pronounced her own feelings of inadequacy became. She felt she lacked power.

Language Power Which party communicates more effectively than the other? Men are generally considered more rational and less emotive, which makes it easier for them to win arguments.

Your journey
- In your association with the person you wish would disappear down the plug hole, does he or she hold the power of being able to articulate exactly what they feel while you fumble around with your words feeling increasingly foolish and frustrated?

Invalidational Power This links to language power. It includes the ability to influence the other by dismissing their opinions, invalidating, or belittling; generally showing a lack of respect. There are obviously powerful links here to emotional abuse, which we'll come to shortly as we talk about how these power bases are implemented.

Your journey
- If a difficult other is using emotional abuse, do you feel they are more proficient than you in their use of words, or do you have the upper hand?

Physical Power Men have greater physical power and tend to do the bulk of heavy work. Their greater strength can be used against women in a violent way, such as in physical abuse.

- How much physical abuse are you suffering, or are you the one doing the pushing and shoving?

Contractual Power This power tool gives an ability to opt out, contract out, refuse to talk, and withdraw emotionally. Theoretically men have greater opportunity here, because women may not be able to support themselves financially. Women have the greater power of contracting out sexually.

- How much of this resonates with you?

Relational Power This is the ability to connect with significant others. This seems to be generally a woman's power base. Men have alcohol, the pub and sport, but generally little intimate communication, while women have friends, women's groups and usually a much higher level of in-depth sharing.

- In a conflictual situation, do you have more friends that you can share with and unload to or does the ghastly other?

Affective or Emotional Power There are three strands to this particular power tool.

This may not relate directly to the person you find difficult, but could give you an insight into yourself and is certainly relevant in other relationships.

- Who loves who the most? (This is relatively gender free)
- Who needs the other the most emotionally?
- Who is more capable of meeting the others' emotional needs?

Sexual Power This is predominately a woman's power base because she is usually the one that controls whether sex can take place, when, and how often it can happen. Although, in an unhealthy relationship a woman can be physically forced to give sexual favours. However, men can withhold physical intimacy, which often leads a woman to doubting her femininity and desirability, and then this power tool is totally reversed. This may not directly relate to difficult situations, but the quality of sex or lack thereof, can tell you a lot about your intimate relationship.

- How do you feel about your own sexual situation?
- Is it an indicator of more turbulent waters?

Reproductive Power This is another important power card. Birth control and abortion are choices now available to most women. Like sexual power, it can be reversed if the woman wants a baby but the man doesn't.

Social Power This is the confidence to be with others. It is a combination of a number of different power bases and its power comes from who is most able to find other people to replace difficult relationships. This is determined by who has the most friends, or is the most attractive and therefore more able to attract another partner, or fill the void caused by conflict in life.

- Do you have this social confidence or are you very unsure of yourself?

Coping Power Who is better able to cope alone emotionally? Like above, it is a combination of different power bases.

- Can you cope easily, or do you worry about how well you will cope?
- Does the difficult other appear to cope more easily than you?
- Do you think an element of jealousy comes in here?

You now have a fair idea of which are your strong power bases and may have an idea about the difficult other in a situation of turmoil.

- Which power bases do they use in their relationship with you?

Identifying this can defuse a sense of powerlessness that you may have and can build self-confidence when you realise how your abilities are spread across a number of these power bases.

Let's look at the perceived influence and importance of the power bases. Although these relate mainly to a partnership relationship, they also apply to many other different types of relationships.

POWER BASE RANKED IN ORDER OF IMPORTANCE

1. Financial: able to support self financially
2. Sexual: needing sex less often than partner
3. Social: getting on with others, social confidence
4. Emotional dependence: being less dependent on partner and vice versa
5. Child rearing experience
6. Technical expertise
7. Domestic expertise
8. Invalidation: high self esteem, less easily upset than partner
9. Communication, logical
10. Communication, emotional
11. Coercive: able to punish, threaten, physical coercion
12. Coping: able to cope better than partner when alone

(Fromm 1996 quoted by Sally & Rudi Dallos in their book *Couples, Sex and Power, The Politics of Desire*)

If we think of a couple's power tools, usually the man's are material such as money, physical strength and logic, while the woman's is sex, relationship and the non-rational. Interestingly, research by Sally and Rudi Dallos has shown that women who are financially independent are often more sexually motivated and active than their financially dependent peers.

POWER STRUGGLES

Power imbalances in relationships often present a paradoxical and confusing picture of love and hate, remorse and cynicism, blame and over responsibility, and many other contradictory messages. Abuse and coercion are at one end of the spectrum but can co-exist with intense love and friendship in a unique and painful way. Finding the way out of such dilemmas is not easy, but once the dynamic is identified, it becomes easier.

It wasn't long ago that women talking of power were seen as feminist and a challenge to men's power. It seemed to be an accepted norm that the older generations felt that women were not supposed to think or talk about their relationships in terms of power and control, but more in terms of love and affection. One reason for this was that most women were not highly educated and so their "job" was to be a housewife and mother. Against that background, if they didn't do their job properly, they risked having their livelihood cut, and talk of power would be threatening.

Men did, and many still do not like to be challenged about their privileged positions of power, so discussions are often avoided as being potentially unpleasant. Unpalatable ideas are often silenced, so for a long time power and control issues were, and often still are, pushed under the carpet not to be discussed. The problem with that strategy is that if the balance of power is not talked about and one party is getting more than the other, often a symptom may emerge to redress the balance in a more covert way. For example, covert resistance may result as a sexual symptom, the women is not interested in sex, she may have a headache or is too tired.

- Are you identifying with any of this?

The dominant partner usually attempts to coerce the other into fulfilling his or her needs, so the struggle is how the relationship will be defined and by whom. We come back to the submit/dominate pattern talked of earlier.

- Do you do the dominating or the submitting?
- If you dominate, what impact do you think that has on the knotty relationship? Conversely, if you submit, what message do you think that conveys to the dominant other?

Let's look at how men and women generally use their differences in trying to get what they want and how you identify with these strategies.

Gender differences in use of influence strategies

Women	Men
Involving other people	Withholding – going silent
Verbal persuasion – saying it is not fair	Using work as an excuse
Helpless	Blocking or avoiding issues
Supplication, crying, acting	
Bullying, nagging	

(Based on Foreman 1996, taken from Dallos and Dallos's book, *Couples, Sex and Power*)

Taking your workbook:

Your journey

- Which of these behaviours do you use?
- Which does that trying other, in the difficult situation, use with you?
- Concentrating on your part in the dynamic, how does that serve you?
- How can you break the circuit?

Let's look at how Brent and Janice use their respective power bases. We know that Janice is not happy and the marriage is coming under increasing strain (pages 53, 64). She is feeling unappreciated and unheard. Without consciously realising it, Brent is operating from both an ideological and a financial power base. He feels that she should be grateful that her living is provided for her and she doesn't have to cope with a difficult boss. He also feels, although does not articulate, that her job is to look after the family and make sure every thing runs smoothly for them all. This division of labour has never been discussed, it is merely assumed, and therein lies a major issue.

Both have informational power. Janice's is primarily in mothering and caring for the children as well as domestically, while Brent has technical expertise in his job. However, from Janice's point of view, this is not a positive, rather it means that the bulk of the caring and household organisation falls to her. Brent has invalidational power in that he dismisses her objections and calls it whining. Janice holds a trump card, in her sexual power base. The unhappier she becomes, the less emotionally available she is to Brent and she becomes totally uninterested in any sexual intimacy. She also has the emotional power because she has a strong network of friends, where Brent is emotionally much more isolated. He is very reluctant to discuss his marital situation with his mates, as he feels he would lose credibility and status if they knew his wife was not treating him "properly."

> *Power struggles usually mean that one party is feeling disempowered, unheard or not understood.*

When Brent understood that his choosing not to hear what Janice was saying was coming at a high emotional cost, he started to look at the relationship differently. Although he has the economic or financial power base, if he leaves the relationship, he would stand to lose considerably because he would still have to support his family. While his first impulse was to let Janice suffer, he soon saw that he had a lot to lose. Looking at it rationally and using his language power base, he decided to put more effort into making the relationship work better. He could see that he was using his influence to withhold, block and use work as an excuse, while Janice was using nagging and supplication, with some persuasion, as her tools of influence. The marital situation started to shift and become more positive.

Power struggles usually mean that one party is feeling disempowered, unheard or not understood.

- Does that strike a cord with you?

Neither party is respectful of the other. One may be patronising, or coming from a feeling of superiority. However, point scoring or preaching may also be trying to get a point across in a genuine attempt to be heard and understood.

When the dynamics are revealed you can discuss them. That often allows the resentment to dissipate, as well as any underlying need for revenge. Revenge may not be overt and may indeed be quite unconscious, but the balance gets redressed in one form or another, perhaps sexually or withholding affection and so on.

- Do you have fantasies of revenge?
- What would you like to do? Remember this is your secret self talking and the more open you are with yourself, the easier it will be to come to some sort of resolution.

When nothing is discussed because it is too awkward and would cause eruptions, it all goes underground and the balance is redressed covertly, which becomes much more difficult to recognise or resolve. It may even appear as something entirely different, such as ill health or tiredness that limits your ability or desire to have fun.

- Do you have any physical symptoms that may stem from an imbalance in your relationship? Try not to judge your response, let it just be there.

We all operate from a number of different power bases, be it economic, sexual, social, and so on. Identifying which of our power bases is strong and which are not so strong is useful information, and helpful in dealing with the difficult other. Naming a power struggle allows you to take responsibility for your own situation and enables choices to be made.

Generally only you and the other person in the relationship can challenge the dynamic. We all engage in power struggles at some time or another and if we are flexible enough to admit to them, the situation becomes healthier and they become easier to deal with. It is worth noting that point scoring or preaching may also be trying to get a point across in a genuine attempt to be heard and understood, rather than a power struggle.

WHO IS THE MORE CONTROLLING IN THE RELATIONSHIP?

Your journey

a) Is he/she jealous or possessive toward you?
b) Are you jealous or possessive toward another?
a) Does he/she try to control you by being bossy or demanding?
b) Are you trying to control by being bossy or demanding?
a) Does he/she try to isolate you, by demanding you cut off social contacts and friendships?
b) Do you try to isolate others, by demanding that they cut off social contacts and friendships?
a) Is he or she violent and/or loses his/her temper quickly?
b) Do you get violent and lose your temper quickly?
a) Are you pressured sexually?
b) Do you pressure sexually?
a) Does he or she abuse drugs or alcohol?
b) Do you abuse drugs or alcohol?
a) Does he or she claim you are responsible for his or her emotional state?
b) Do you claim he/she is responsible for your emotional state?
a) Does he or she have a history of bad relationships?
b) Do you have a history of bad relationships?
a) Do your family and friends warn you about the other person and tell you they are concerned for your safety or emotional well being?

- b) Do you tell your family and friends that the other person has major psychological problems, that it is all his/her fault?
- a) You frequently worry about how he or she will react to things you say or do.
- b) You don't care how your behaviour will affect him or her.
- a) The other person makes "jokes" that shame, humiliate, demean or embarrass you, whether privately or around family and friends.
- b) You make "jokes" that make fun of others, which they tell you, are cruel.
- a) The other person rages when they feel hurt, shame, fear or loss of control.
- b) You rage when you feel hurt, shamed, fearful or out of control.
- a) You leave the relationship but then continue to return, against the advice of your friends and family.
- b) He or she is always threatening to leave, but when he or she does, he or she comes back.
- a) You have trouble ending the relationship, even though you know inside it's the right thing to do.
- b) He or she is always threatening to leave the relationship.
- a) Are you the victim, do you feel a need to merge with the other to feel safe?
- b) Are you the perpetrator? Do you fear losing control over the other person?

If the answers to the a) questions were mainly yes, you are very likely to be the one being controlled in an abusive relationship. If the answers to the b) questions were mainly yes, you are the abuser in a controlling relationship. If you fall into this category, be glad that you are now in a position to honestly answer the questions. You have the tools to change your behaviour to become a much happier individual. As you read on you will understand that abusers were usually abused themselves as children, and as such need help and understanding. The core of who you really are is not abusive.

The following example shows how a small incident can escalate into abuse.

> Tim and Roxie were having a discussion. Tim's version of what happened went as follows. "I was worried that Roxie was not seeing things my way, and feeling hurt. I was trying to put things right by getting her to see things my way and stop her from arguing. But Roxie just wouldn't get it, she wouldn't stop yelling. The more she yells, the more worried and insecure I become. What if I could never get her to shut up and listen and understand? So I started shouting louder, trying to drown out her voice, so she can see it my way. Eventually when I just couldn't get her to listen, I had to hit her to finally shut her up, so I could have my say."

This is using power and control. An argument degenerates into violence, abuse, and fear. Depending on how hard Roxie was hit, she will never quite be able to trust Tim again. Her unconscious has registered that he is potentially threatening and dangerous. Wanting your partner to see things in the same way as you, may be you needing to control to feel secure. Sometimes people can rationalise that their partner phoning them umpteen times a day is showing them love, rather than needing to know exactly what they are doing, which is of course control. The shocking thing is that much of what we consider normal everyday interaction may actually be abusive.

Some forms of power and control are very subtle and often difficult to immediately identify. A whole family can be controlled by someone in authority, perhaps Mum or Dad, and it can be done with as little as a disapproving look, a tone of voice, a barely audible groan or saying, I've got a headache in an exasperated voice. Children will often immediately modify or change their behaviour when they are called by their proper name rather than their pet name.

USING EMOTIONAL ABUSE

Emotional abuse is as damaging as physical abuse, although it is often much harder to recognise, and therefore recovery is more difficult and prolonged. Emotional abuse is aimed at undermining another, it lacks all respect. It may not be done consciously but its effect is devastating. It wears down self-worth and dignity and gradually people lose self-confidence. This then erodes the ability to make choices and a sense of having options evaporates. Abuse victims often experience mental illness, clinical depression, denial, chemical dependency, extreme codependency and may

Lacking respect for another is emotionally abusive and undermining.

even contemplate or commit suicide. Many psychiatric wards are full of people who have suffered severe cases of abuse. Often the abused clings to the abuser because they believe that is all they deserve or will ever get. To make life more difficult and confusing, abusers often alternate between declarations of love, statements that they will change, or justifications that they are only acting this way for the other's good. Phrases such as, "If you loved me you would_____," are warnings of possible abuse. This is emotional blackmail. Blackmail can also take the form of having somebody tell you that, "Everyone knows you are a failure," or "You are all messed up anyway—" "You are really lucky to have me, because no one else would love you—"

Probably the most common form of emotional abuse consists of putting people down, by humiliating, degrading and calling them names.

Your journey

- Do you do that at times?
- Who annoys you enough to provoke you into calling them names?
- Ponder what triggers this behaviour in you?

Emotional abuse is also playing mind games, with the intention of getting the other person to feel bad about themselves. Interrogation is another form of abuse, as is harassment or intimidation. Checking up on others is controlling, as it implies a lack of trust and respect for what people are saying. Making others feel guilty or humiliating them by making them the butt of direct attacks or jokes is also shaming behaviour, which is abusive. This is such common behaviour when we want to modify children's behaviour.

Emotional withdrawal is a common form of abuse, when somebody withdraws emotionally, not allowing the other the opportunity to talk or discuss an issue that they feel is important. This may happen in the middle of an argument or discussion, without any prior warning. We can do this by walking away, picking up the newspaper, or turning on the TV, when the other party is attempting to discuss something. The intention is to cut off communication in a disrespectful manner. If it is not an opportune moment to discuss a situation we are all well within our rights to set boundaries by saying, "I would like to talk this over with you but at a mutually agreeable time," or simply, "Can we talk about this later?" That is a respectful acknowledgement of the need for communication.

USING INTIMIDATION

In unhealthy relationships people use intimidation deliberately, to make others fearful. They do this with looks, actions and gestures. They may make physical threats, or threaten to use weapons, including their fists, hands or belts. They may push, hit, slap, punch, kick, or bite. They may smash and break things, destroy or confiscate possessions, or threaten to destroy your personal property or sentimental items. A wife finding out that her husband is having an affair may cut off all the legs of his suits or destroy his precious CD collection saying, "Watch out, be very careful I'm dangerous and this is just the start of what I can do to you." It makes for a laugh at the movies when he comes to put on his trousers, but in real life is extremely abusive. His decision to have an affair, without telling his wife before he embarks on the new relationship, is equally abusive of her trust.

Any forcing of the sexual act, or demanding sexual acts of us that we do not feel comfortable with, is of course abusive. Young children that have been sexually abused by a beloved parent may not be aware that the sexual attention is abusive. They may not like the type of attention but can feel special to have been singled out and be sharing an important secret with an adult. Threatening to commit suicide or actually committing suicide is a terribly destructive form of controlling. However, it is worth mentioning here that many people who do actually commit suicide, rather than just threatening it, are mentally sick. Threatening to take legal action or forcing people drop charges or making others do illegal things against their will is using extreme intimidation. Obviously, in situations of domestic violence it is essential to take legal action to prevent someone from hurting you if they will not listen. It is really important to understand that it is your responsibility to take care of yourself.

Sometimes there may be silent or overt raging. Rage is, by definition, abusive. It is a shame based expression of anger. Rage can involve screaming, physical expressions of anger, violence or threats of violence, sulking, manipulation, emotional blackmail, silent smoldering, and anger used to punish. Raging actually gives the "rager" a feeling of power, even if he or she is not aware of it consciously. It allows them to cover their own feelings of shame and inadequacy.

"Ragers" were usually abused themselves as children. Abusers can also use cruelty to animals or pets as a way of displaying power and control, and frightening others into submission.

USING ISOLATION

Isolation also controls what others do, who they see and talk to, what they read and where they go. If there is an attempt to limit another's outside involvement, for example, by demanding that they stay home, cut off certain friends, activities or social interaction, the control is abusive. Denying a partner the opportunity of sharing time with a member of the opposite sex, because we feel threatened, is using isolation and justifying your demands by saying we are jealous, is also another form of abuse.

Obviously, as a parent being responsible for children, there is a need to intervene if the literature they are reading, the friends they are seeing, or the activities they are engaging in are not suitable for their age group. However, it is important to be aware that if we do not discuss with our offspring, particularly teenagers, why we feel as we do, we may just be inviting the same behaviour, but instead of being overt, it becomes covert.

USING SHAME

Shame is a not necessarily a bad thing. John Bradshaw in *Healing the Shame that Binds You* says there is healthy shame and toxic shame. Healthy shame is admitting our mistakes and in doing so, learning. We would rightly feel shame if we deliberately set out to hurt someone. It's that uncomfortable feeling when we know that we've done something wrong, that we needn't have done, or when we have been exposed, when we were not ready. We all need to experience and recognise this feeling. It is a fundamental part of being human and helps us to be caring people.

Toxic shame, however, is a totally different thing. It is a controlling tool. It occurs when others diminish us, ridiculing us for innocent mistakes, making us feel flawed, inadequate and defective. Many parents control using toxic shame and once instilled, it grows and feeds on itself, until children feel they are hopelessly defective. This gets carried through to adulthood and acts like a huge millstone around our neck, limiting in some way, everything we think and do. It only loses its hold when we do the work, like we are now, and little by little break the programming.

Your journey

- In your workbook reflect on times of shame in your life, when others have shamed you

- When have you felt a healthy shame because you could have done something differently. This helps you distinguish between healthy shame and toxic shame.

USING MINIMISATION, DENIAL, AND SHIFTING BLAME

Minimisation, denial, and shifting blame are very common weapons in the controller's armory. It stops us facing the unpleasant fact that we may be being abusive. We may make light of abusive actions and don't take any notice of other's concerns. We may say that the abuse didn't happen, it wasn't serious, or that others are making a mountain out of a molehill. Another popular mechanism is to shift responsibility for our abusive behaviour onto the other person, "You made me do it because you made me so mad—." Or, "I did it because you—."

The sad part of denial is that if we hear it often enough we take it on board as our responsibility and our truth.

> Martha's mother would tell her that she drank because she could not cope with Martha as a child. Her mother is an alcoholic and Martha feels guilty and responsible for her mother's actions. She has accepted and internalised what her mother has been saying over many years, that indeed she is responsible for her mother's drinking problem, which is patently untrue. This is destructive thinking and eroded Martha's sense of self, as she took on another's projection as her truth.

USING CHILDREN OR OTHERS

Using other people such as children or family to control behaviour is yet another form of power and control. Making people feel guilty about how they parent and threatening to tell others, including the authorities, what poor parents they are is far from helpful. Of course, if children are being constantly abused it is imperative to notify the authorities. Ideally it would be good to talk to the parents and tell them how you feel before notifying the authorities but that is not Australian law and may run the risk of increasing the abuse. Threatening to take children away and using children as messengers are all forms of emotional abuse, and are all too often used in separation and divorce situations. Withholding information about a person or disseminating private information about you to others is also abusive. Much more subtle is the use of children by their parents as surrogate spouses. When a partnership is unhappy, a parent may turn to one of their children to become their confidante, telling him or her things that are inappropriate for their age and development, effectively loading them up with the responsibility to help the parent sort out their own problems. Sometimes in a single parent family the child is made to be "grown up" to "help" the parent, which in effect robs them of their childhood.

ECONOMIC ABUSE

A very common way of keeping control is to control the purse strings. People do that by preventing others, particularly partners, from getting or keeping a job. Making our partner ask for money or giving him/her an allowance are all forms of financial control. So is taking another's money, under the guise of looking after it, if it's against their will. Another common form of abuse, particularly common in the older generations, was not letting our partner know about or have access to family income or information.

USING MALE PRIVILEGE

This may sound somewhat old fashioned, however, in a number of households men will still treat women as inferior.

They will make all the major decisions and act like the "master of the castle," they want to define men's and women's roles. If you've grown up in such a household, particularly as a boy, you may have internalised these beliefs and never really questioned them, merely expecting your partner to get your evening meal and do your laundry. In most relationships today, that will cause a great deal of conflict and would be disrespectful if it had just been assumed.

- Does this resonate with you?

YOUR ARMOURY

- How much power and control do you try to exert?
- Is this type of behaviour familiar in your life?

All of the above, using male privilege, economic abuse, using children or others, minimising, denying and shifting blame, constitute domestic violence. No doubt most of us are at some time or another culpable, and our behaviour would be termed abusive, which for many of us would be quite horrifying.

- Which behaviours do you use and with whom?
- How does that serve you, what do you gain?

Gaby is a single mum who struggled hard to bring up her daughter Louise. Money was always a major problem in their lives and Gaby is very fearful that Louise may end up like her father, irresponsible and only interested in having fun. Louise's father disappeared, deserting Gaby when she was 8 months pregnant. As a result Gaby is very mistrustful of men and now that Louise is an attractive 16-year-old who likes boys, she is feeling more and more anxious.

Louise has been brought up absorbing a suspicious negative attitude about life from her Mum, which she hates, and which causes continual friction. "You only ever say bad things about my friends. You are always criticising them and me. I am not doing anything wrong, yet you are always implying that I'm being bad, particularly when I'm out. It's not fair. Nothing I ever do is good enough for you. You'd only be happy if I was sitting at home watching TV with you. I'm sick of all your negative comments. You don't like my friends, you don't like my clothes, you're always saying I look cheap, and I'm only interested in having fun. When did you ever say anything good about me? I don't think you can see a single good thing about me, all you see is what you want to see. You are so bitter and twisted because of the mess you have made of your life and having to bring me up, that you really hate me. You always say I'm like my father a "no-gooder," worthless and useless, only out to get what I can. I am sick and tired of it, and if you continue to say those things I am going to leave."

While we can feel for Gaby as she has had a heavy load to carry, her attitude toward her daughter has been very destructive. All sense of trust between mother and daughter has been eroded, and Louise seems to have been the butt of continued emotional abuse for most of her life. Gaby has

> projected her own sense of betrayal and mistrust onto her daughter, who was an innocent party. No doubt she would be mortified to learn that her continual putdowns and criticism are in fact emotional abuse.

She justified her behaviour by saying, "I did my best. I had to make her realise how dangerous life is, you just can't trust men. I had to make her aware, so she wouldn't make the same mistakes I did." However, the result of her actions was that Louise had very little sense of self-esteem or self-worth. She had internalised the message from her Mum, that whatever she did would never be good enough. "You'll only be happy if I became a nun, or a TV addict who never went out."

In fact, unable to bear the continual criticism and her mum's efforts to control her, Louise did leave home and unable to support herself properly and wanting love and attention, eventually turned to prostitution and drugs. She had been so powerfully indoctrinated that she was bad and men were unreliable and dangerous that she acted it out. It became the reality her mother had feared would happen. Unconsciously, Louise had turned it into a self fulfilling prophesy, Gaby was devastated at what happened. She had tried to do the best she could, struggling to keep herself and her daughter afloat financially for so many years. She had little understanding her own negativity and mistrust could have contributed so strongly.

CONTROL

When relationships are going badly it seems to always come down to issues of power and control. The worse the relationship the more these factors raise their head. Control comes from fear. Fear that we will not get what we want or that we'll lose something that we already have. Fear drives us to control situations and others, so we get what we want. It all gets ugly when we cannot control those we are trying to control. They just won't listen or do what we tell them. Alternatively they listen and then completely ignore us.

Your journey

- In your conflictual situation, is control with that impossible other, an issue for you?

- Are you showing them respect?

Despite the risk of boring you, because respect is such a fundamental prerequisite to good relationships, it is worth repeating the dictionary definition again: it is, "regard with deference, esteem or honor: avoid degrading or insulting or injuring, interfering with or interrupting, or treat with consideration, spare, refrain from offending or corrupting or tempting—." It is horribly encompassing and doesn't seem to leave much room to manoeuvre, if you are trying to get another to change and they don't want to. Meanwhile you are trying to get whatever it is you think you need, prompted by your unconscious, to keep you feeling safer.

Although control often looks like being a safety mechanism, it links to fear as you can see from the diagram below.

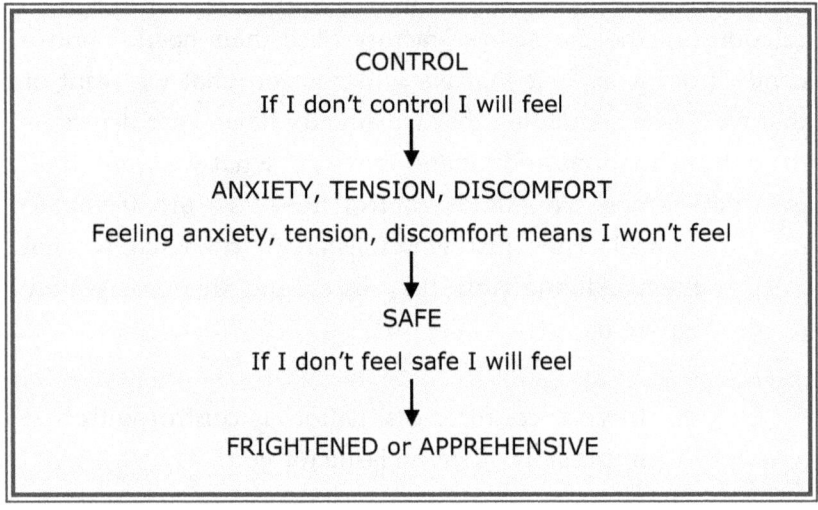

Usually controlling others is only indirectly about others. It has much more to do with our own fear. Sometimes control stems from narcissism, simply expecting to have our own way and being intolerant of anything less. Perhaps that was part of Hitler's problem, as well as many other dictators and tyrants.

- Does the fear underlying control resonate with you?

CONTROL IMBALANCE

Many difficult relationships are caused by one party being more aggressive or dominant and the other more submissive or non-assertive. Whether we are either more dominant or submissive will have stemmed to some extent from the make-up of our character at birth and also our childhood programming. Submissive behaviour usually comes from having to please others and probably, more often than not, giving away making choices to others. If we usually allow others to make the choice there will inevitably come a time when we become resentful of those people that happily make whatever choice needs to be made at the moment. This resentment is our subservient secret self side calling us to claim our dominant side, allowing us to become more balanced.

Sometimes we may think that if we can control our environment and others within our environment, that we will feel better about ourselves. The thinking may go: if you do what I want then I'll feel much better about myself. Take a moment to think of a situation where you would like someone to be doing something different from what they are doing.

Your journey

- Ask yourself, why do you need to control them?
- What is your fear if you can't control them?
- How does that fear affect you?
- What does it tell you about yourself?
- Do your answers from these questions overlap your answers about your core needs in the last chapter?

For parents, controlling allows us to cover our anxiety, and children and teenagers often cause us much angst. The following example, while simple, causes lots of conflict. Although it is about a dress code, the same dynamic occurs with messy bedrooms, or poor grades, although the stakes maybe higher. We are looking at a power struggle. Parents feel they know best and teenagers are desperate to assert their independence and move out from under parental control which they need to do to become autonomous independent adults, but it rarely happens without conflict.

> Jane's teenage daughter Anne has gone off, without parental permission, and had her eyebrow pierced, which has caused a huge family ruckus. She refuses to take out the ring out, and now she wants to wear a skin tight, very short dress that her mother thinks is totally inappropriate to a family friend's wedding. She feels that Anne will look cheap. Anne is determined and her mother resorts to all sorts of vague threats. Underlying Jane's need to control is the anxiety that everyone will take one look at Anne and say to themselves, what sort of a mother would let her daughter come to a wedding looking like that and with that pierced eyebrow? Her fear is that she will be judged as an inadequate mother, she could even be ostracised and shunned by her peers as being a bad influence on their own daughters. The bottom line is, that if she can't control Anne, she may end up rejected. Jane is not aware of this thinking at a conscious level, she hasn't reasoned out exactly what the problem is if Anne wears what she wants. Maybe, if she could stand back and think about her strong reaction, she wouldn't mind what her daughter wore, her

choice is her choice. As her daughter asserts her independence, Jane would be modelling healthier behaviour, if she was not unduly concerned. It would be a different matter if Anne was taking drugs. The more she tries to control her daughter over smaller issues the less communication they will have. If Jane thinks through her objections carefully and explains these to Anne she will have much more chance of being heard.

> ■ How often do you react at a gut level without thinking through exactly what is going on for you at the deeper levels?

Another common example of control often occurs around health issues between adults. This is an area in many relationships that causes conflict. In the guise of helping another we try and tell them what to do. However, what we are really trying to do is take responsibility for something that is not our responsibility. Our own health is our own responsibility and we have no right to expect others to care of us when we are sick, particularly if we haven't been responsible. We would hope that our nearest and dearest would help from the goodness of their heart, rather than from a sense of obligation.

> ■ What motivates your desire to control?

This is where it is so important to be aware of your thoughts, feelings, and actions. Being aware you can look at your needs. When there is conflict, sooner or later, it will boil down to a power struggle, which we usually tend to justify by thinking we are doing what we doing for the other's best interests.

Terry and his father Branson were a case in point.

> Branson was bemoaning the loss of his son. His son had not died but might as well have done from his father's point of view. Terry had cut off from his family and didn't want anything to do with them. Branson was a respected surgeon and had desperately wanted his son to go into medicine. All through Terry's early life he had been there, encouraging and pushing him to work harder in order to get the necessary grades for Med. School. However, although he achieved the necessary grades Terry refused to study medicine, he wanted to be an artist. There was no way that Branson was going to finance such a risky career, so there had been a split.
>
> Ten years down the track there was still no contact between father and son. Terry had studied art part time and had got involved in crime to help supplement his income. In his father's eyes, he was a disgrace to the family. As Branson got older he mourned the absence, but could not take responsibility for the fact that his lack of respect for his son's ambitions had effectively been the last straw for Terry. Branson justified his attitude by pointing out his son's failure to make anything of himself. It was entirely Terry's fault.

It is interesting to speculate what underlay the father's need to have his son become a doctor. That need cost the family dearly. The rigidity Branson displayed was echoed in Terry's stubbornness to renew contact with the family. So a trait Terry deplored was showing itself in his own behaviour. The secret self could be seen by others, even if Branson and Terry were blind to it.

Your journey

- Is there rigidity in any of the interactions you have with that impossible other?

CONTROL AND ALIENATION

Control almost invariably carries alienation and negativity in its wake. It creates a hierarchy with someone on top and someone underneath, so someone becomes top dog and the other is bottom dog. This hierarchy automatically assumes that people are not capable of doing the right thing by themselves, or doing the right thing to others, they have to be directed. Having said that control is a necessary part of life, however it is how we use it that is important.

> Nancy nearly 60, is divorced after 25 years of marriage, and has a son Craig. She lives alone and is lonely. She has friends, plays bridge and golf, but is a very reserved person, so finds it difficult to talk about anything of real depth to people who she feels are only fair weather friends. She feels others are probably judging her. Consequently, she feels uncomfortable about people knowing that her husband left her for his mistress of ten years, who used to be his secretary. She adores Craig, who is 23 and busy living his own life. He doesn't want to be bothered with his mother who always seems to want something. "She always

> wants me to go around there for meals and do stuff in the house like fix the fence, but when I'm there, she's so negative. She's always complaining about Dad leaving her and how unfair it is after everything she did for him for all those years while he was off having an affair. I feel exhausted and drained with so much negativity. I hear it time and time again. I wish she'd get a life instead of trying to live mine. She is trying to persuade me to live back home. Imagine what that would be like. It would kill me."
>
> Nancy says, "If only he would talk to me, young people are so closed up these days, never tell their parents anything. All I want to do is help him, and give him the benefit of my advice. After all, I know a great deal more than him. He could come back home and live in a comfortable home and have decent meals. He doesn't eat properly and all his money is just draining away in rent and drinking with his mates. He would be much better living here until he finds a nice girl to marry."

What is actually going on here is that Nancy is lonely and she would like Craig to move back home so she would have a focus in her life, and could feel useful and wanted. Ostensibly she wants the best for Craig. However, it is her judgement about what is best, and in this case that is completely different from his. She can't see her true motivation. She chooses only to see how beneficial it would be for Craig. Her need for control over Craig's life, is perhaps more about her fear of what will happen to her when she becomes old, rather than for Craig.

THE FLIP SIDE OF POWER AND CONTROL: COMPLIANCY

If we think of control on one end of a continuum and lack of control at the other end, somewhere along that line is compliancy. Most of us can be compliant. Society survives because the majority of its members are compliant and we are socially instilled to be obedient. We are taught to be submissive followers. Maybe if we weren't so submissive and we felt more confident to talk about our needs and our fears, our secret self side, needing power and control, wouldn't play such a large part in our lives.

Your journey

- How compliant are you? If ten is very compliant and one not compliant, where on the scale would you generally place yourself? (This is important and we will come back to it in the next chapter.)

Clayton Tucker in his book, *Psychological Self Help,* talks about how as a general rule, most of us are fairly compliant people. That is how we learned to survive. After all, the continuation of society largely depends on compliance. In the process of growing up we are exposed to enormous pressures to be compliant or conforming. Parents demand obedience. Peer group pressure rewards those that conform with the sense of belonging to the group. Teachers in the education system demand that you conform and comply. There is a societal expectation that we will get married and have a family. Government regulates much of our lives. It is drilled into us to follow the law. Religions tell us what to believe "with unquestioning faith" and indeed, avoid and strongly discourage doubts and questions. The military teaches, "Yours is not to wonder why, yours is to do and die." At work we are told what to do. And finally, our friends only remain our friends, in most cases, unless we agree with them on major issues. So, from the beginning of our lives we are taught well to be submissive followers.

Furthermore, our social customs and beliefs, especially in the form of social pressures, determine what we do. Christmas is a wonderful example of that. We may not have a religious belief but somehow society expects that we will participate in the celebrations and the consumerism. We are also usually "conscience directed" that is we have internalised our parents' morals and ideals so that we are controlled by our sense of guilt, not by reason. We are taught to be sensitive to how others think and feel and in most cases, we try to please or impress them.

- Would you go along with most of this, or can you and do you, stand against the crowd?

- In what ways can you be different?

The differences illustrate that you feel confident to do what you feel is right, rather than conform to social pressure.

COMPLIANCY IN THE EXTREME

The following experiment by Stanley Milgram, while very extreme, illustrates how few of us can stand up against others expectations.

In 1974 Milgram did some interesting and frightening research into how far people will go to do the "right" thing. These are well documented and famous studies. Milgram's intention was to see how much harm ordinary people would do to another person, if directed and urged to do so by an authority figure, in this case a psychologist. The psychologist asked people to give others, doing a test, an electric shock, if they got the wrong answer. The people doing the test were in the next room, and simulated receiving the shock, but the people doing the testing did not know they were acting. Each time a wrong answer was given the electric shock was increased. The range of shocks went from very mild, 15–60 volts through to death at 435–450 volts. As the shocks intensified and the person administrating the shocks wanted to stop, the psychologist would simply say, "Please go on," or "You must go on, the test is important." Meanwhile, the actors doing the test were screaming, pounding on walls and in some instances feigning death, through silence.

The results were staggering, 65% of subjects went all the way to 450 volts, theoretical death. In fact, every one of the 40 subjects administrated at least 300 volts, an extreme intensity of shock. Milgram wrote, "Many subjects will obey the experimenter no matter how vehement the pleading of the person being shocked – it is the extreme willingness of adults to go to almost any lengths, on the command of an authority, that constitutes the chief finding of this study." The subjects administering the shock were people off the street, they were not angry, nor prejudiced against the learner, nor indifferent, and neither were they sadistic monsters. They just wanted to please. The financial inducement was tiny, and they would never see the psychologist again. It is fascinating and scary the lengths people will go to, to please the powers that be.

People will generally do what they are told, when told by people in authority, particularly those higher up the pecking order than us, or in the medical, legal, and judicial professions. So our years of indoctrination, becoming "good" children, "good" church members, "good" students, may also produce the "good" torturer in Nazi Germany, the Vietnam War, the Pol Pot regime, the war in Rwanda and Bosnia, to name but a few. Recent interviews with perpetrators, or if we call a spade a spade, murderers, in both the Rwandian and Bosnian situations, said they were just following orders.

Your journey

- Can you imagine being called up to go to war, trained to kill and in a war situation then deciding you will not follow orders?

- What sort of courage would you need to draw on to disobey?

11 THE EFFECT OF OUR BACKGROUND ON HEALTHY AND UNHEALTHY RELATIONSHIPS

Sometimes it is quite difficult to ascertain what healthy and unhealthy behaviour is. Many of us will assume that we have a good idea of what constitutes unhealthy behaviour and it is certainly easy to spot if it is obviously abusive, but abusiveness can also be subtle, which is just as damaging, but much more difficult to identify.

> Sean and Belinda are passionately in love, that wonderful euphoric stage where each thinks the other is absolutely perfect. Sean cannot bear to be apart from his precious Belinda and lives for the moment he can be with her again. The feeling is mutual. Belinda has found the love of her life and can't wait to be married.

She is a make-up artist and has been offered a unique position to go on tour with a film company, who are hoping to make a blockbuster movie. Some of the stars are already becoming big names. The tour involves a 10 day stint away in central Australia. Belinda is torn, she loves her work and this is a wonderful break for her career but can she bear to be away from Sean for 10 whole days and 9 whole nights? She talks it through with Sean who feels equally devastated.

"I know this is a good career opportunity, but can't you wait until one comes along that is Sydney based?" he pleads.

"Sweetheart, this is such a unique opportunity, after all these are big stars we are talking about and, although I'm only doing the make-up for the extras, this will be a fantastic opportunity to see how the real pros work. You never know, I might get to work on one of the big names. I can't bear to leave you for so long, I'm so torn, but this is a heaven sent opportunity. What shall I do? If only I didn't love you so much. I will ring you two or three times a day, and I could email as well."

Belinda goes and Sean is heartbroken. He says, "I don't know what I am going to do with you away, I won't be able to be alone, I will have to go out every night with my mates to pass the time." When Belinda tells her friends what trouble Sean is having and how in love they are, her friends are deeply envious. "You don't know how lucky you are to have someone that loves you that much." The film shoot goes well. Belinda, although missing Sean, loves the excitement of the movie set and the gossip behind the scenes. She is good at her job and is asked to join another production. This time Sean is really difficult, and Belinda finds the decision to go even harder to make. However, once away in exotic locations, living in fancy hotels with good food, she loves the action and drama of it all. The reunions with Sean are bliss.

As time goes by Belinda is finding that she is getting more and more work away from Sydney, and away from Sean. She is now getting good money. Sean is becoming more and more demanding, and then one day when Belinda tells him she is going to Cairns for nearly a month, he just explodes. "This won't work. It is either your job or me. I can't put up with it anymore. I think you use the time to chat up guys on the set and you probably go away and have a fling with them. You're such a flirt and you probably can't wait to get away from me so you can have a fling. Is this what this is about, you get better sex from these other guys? Well, that's it. It is either your job or me. You choose. I've had it. I just sit around waiting for you to come back, and you're probably having it off with a heap of different guys. OK, if you go that's what I will do , I will go and find some chicks to screw and see how you like that."

Belinda was devastated. She had no idea that Sean could be so mean. Here she was saving all the money she was making so they could get married quicker, and he was talking like this. When she talked the situation over with her parents and friends, she realised that if Sean really loved her he wouldn't like the situation, but he would be pleased for her, if that is what she wanted and it gave her a quick way up the ladder, and he would give her his wholehearted support.

Is Sean really concerned for Belinda's well being and happiness, or is he being abusive and only thinking of himself? In the first stages of a relationship, it could be easy to mistake this intense jealousy for love and can be very flattering. However, as time goes on it can become corrosive as Belinda found when Sean became more and more controlling. Eventually she broke off the relationship because she felt totally suffocated and dominated.

Sean felt that he loved Belinda and couldn't bear the thought that she was not constantly available to him. He had no idea that his use of jealousy was a weapon to justify his demands and was abusive. As a small boy, his father had left them and his mother had gone out to work, usually leaving him with various caregivers. In the evening she often went out with other men and he was again left with others, or sometimes, as he got older, by himself. Sean had been emotionally abandoned. His mother didn't deliberately set out to harm him, but she was young and had her own life to lead as well as needing to support him. Sean had no awareness that he had been emotionally abandoned, but he had always desperately tried to hang onto his girlfriends, and each time his possessiveness had ruined the relationship. With each rejection he became more demanding and clinging. Unconsciously he wanted Belinda to be a mother figure, always there for him. With his mother constantly coming and going and different people looking after him in different places, he had been deeply affected at a critical stage of his emotional development.

CO-DEPENDENCY

Jealousy is often a primary symptom of abusive relationships and can play a large part in codependent relationships. What is a codependent relationship?

Julian and Ginelle have been together 6 years and the partnership is now turning sour. They met at an AA meeting where they were both fighting an alcohol addiction and both supported each other to overcome their addiction. Over time, their relationship had become more and more entwined. They barely let each other out of sight, except to go to work and they would ring each other at odd intervals throughout the day. When Julian became interested in model aircraft flying and wanted to spend Saturday with his mate building and flying radio controlled planes, Ginelle became very resentful. To start with, she accompanied him but she would quickly get bored and the boredom turned to anger and resentment. The weekends were their time and now Julian wanted to be away from her to pursue this new hobby. It seemed that he preferred to be with his mate than doing stuff with her like shopping, having coffee and doing the household chores. Every weekend was turning into one long argument. Ginelle felt more and more rejected and Julian very frustrated. It didn't matter how much he reassured her, unless he was physically with her, there was trouble. Her attitude was starting to eat away at him. He had found a great hobby, it had nothing to do with other women or drinking and she was always complaining that he didn't love her. It seemed that unless he gave up his hobby their relationship would continue to deteriorate.

Ginelle had no sense of self unless she was with Julian. Somehow their relationship validated who she was and when he wasn't there she felt insecure, rejected and abandoned. This is another case of emotional abandonment. Julian had also had a similar background but gradually as he progressed at work, he felt happy in his relationship, confident that he had kicked his alcohol addiction and now found a new passion he was gaining a stronger sense of self and didn't need to constantly be around Ginelle. He was become psychologically stronger and more self-confident. The stronger he became the more threatened Ginelle felt, and she was desperately trying to recreate the old patterns and control Julian to alleviate her intense anxiety. She had such low self-esteem that unless he continually told her how much he loved and needed her she felt empty and helpless.

> Ginelle's father had wanted a son when she was born and was intensely angry, convinced that somehow he had been tricked. Ginelle had tried to be the son her father had wanted, but fell far short and was not interested in sport or outdoor activities. Her father used to get angry with her and call her useless and worthless. He complained he had to feed and clothe her. Her mother was terrified of her husband and did not intervene on Ginelle's behalf.
>
> At a deep level Ginelle had absorbed this message and when Julian preferred to spend a day doing what he wanted, it somehow capitulated her back to the desperately uncomfortable situation she had felt as a child. To escape the bad feelings she started to drink secretly. When Julian found out he was furious and felt that he was being manipulated into being her permanent baby sitter.

The human race is born interdependent. We need each other to survive and thrive so in a healthy relationship naturally we want to do things together, to share and enjoy each other's company. It becomes unhealthy when we can't go off and do what we want by ourself, when we don't have the confidence

THE EFFECT OF OUR BACKGROUND ON RELATIONSHIPS

to follow our dreams and aspirations. We want to be joined at the hip with another in order to gain the necessary confidence. In codependent relationships, people have very low levels of self-esteem or self-worth. They find it very difficult to set functional boundaries and consequently, find it difficult to own and express their own reality. Ginelle could not tolerate the boundary Julian wanted to put up on Saturdays to go flying. Sean wanted Belinda to give up her career. They find it difficult to own and express their own reality and needs and take responsibility for them. They want others to make life better for them. Co-dependence is a defense against feeling. Rather than deal with their own pain, they focus on rescuing or merging with others. In the process, they stay in a relationship in which neither person can ever really grow up and be successful, it's more about "give my life meaning by allowing me to take care of you." If the other party refuses and does not revert back to the old behaviour, enmeshment, the more damaged partner will often experience and express their feelings in an inappropriate manner, with lots of emotion, tears, anger and even threats of harming the other, stalking and going as far as threatening suicide and sometimes actually killing themselves.

Your journey

- In your own behaviour do you see signs of codependency?
- What forms does it take?
- Do you insist on others accompanying you or sharing your views, even when they don't want to?

SINS OF THE PARENTS

Often the roots of codependency go back over a number of generations. If your grandmother was subjected to an abusive childhood and her needs weren't honored, how would she know how to treat your mother? The same pattern of behaviour would be passed down to you. Now you have the chance to break the cycle, but many may not have the opportunity to learn and so the unhealthy behaviour goes on, affecting generation after generation.

The sins of the father are passed to the sons. The abusive use of power and control leads to shaming and children feeling defective and unworthy, engage in codependent or other dysfunctional behaviour. They in turn pass that same behaviour down to their children. Most people using abusive behaviour, have usually been abused themselves as children. It becomes a family's norm and it is dysfunction. If all we have ever known is abuse, how do we recognise that there might be another way? Why should we even think about it? With no healthy role model the cycle can only perpetuate. It is only after people are a considerable way down the road of recovery that they can really see how destructive their behaviour was. Abusers act out of deep seated shame and feelings of inadequacy, and although often they are not conscious of this, unconsciously they feel very uncomfortable, and one way of feeling a bit better is to try and feel powerful at someone else's expense. This is yet another example of our unconscious, alive, well and running our lives without our awareness.

> **Your journey**
>
> ▪ In your family can you identify any patterns that have come through the generations? For example, grandfather drank heavily as did father and now you are following their footsteps? Or grandmother always wanted company to do anything, as did mother and now you also want to be accompanied in most of what you do?

BOUNDARIES

Another characteristic of the unhealthy relationship is when others do not respect your boundaries. Boundaries are the limits that you place around yourself, like a symbolic barrier, giving you a sense of self. Boundaries stop people coming into our space and abusing us. They also stop us from abusing others. Children have to be taught boundaries. Teaching them not to touch a hot stove is teaching them boundaries. Not allowing the infant to stick his finger up your nose, or teaching the toddler not to push or stand on the baby is another boundary. Boundaries are not just physical limitations, they are a way of protecting children against abuse by others. They are taught by confronting the youngster, explaining that is not appropriate behaviour and at the same time, protecting him or her against others who try to hurt. The same thing applies to adults. We need to explain to another when their behaviour to us does not feel appropriate.

We all have our own physical boundaries and you are probably well aware of when people come into your space, when a stranger sits too close to you on the train or bus, or tries to hug you at a party. There is a sense of shrinking or contracting your energy so that it does not connect unless you want it to.

- Do you have a strong sense of your personal physical boundary?

When you take responsibility for your feelings, not blaming others for what is going on for you, you are exercising another boundary. You do the same when you don't take responsibility for another's thoughts and feelings and don't allow them to manipulate or control you.

People who have no boundaries have no conception of the boundaries of others and without knowing it, could be insensitive or abusive.

- In your difficult relational dilemma does the other person encroach on your boundaries; or
- Are you aware of what your emotional boundaries are?
- How far do you let people go if they want to blame you?
- Do you tolerate people walking all over you, in an emotional sense?
- Can you stop them and defend yourself?
- Or, have you learned to put up rigid boundaries to keep yourself safe because deep down, you have a fear of being used or abused?

Ideally boundaries are flexible, depending on the situation and the choices we make. Developing boundaries enables us to be truthful and open with others, they open the way to true intimacy. They also give us faith that if anything hurtful comes our way that we can deal with it by talking about the situation honestly.

ADDICTIONS

Another type of unhealthy relationship often occurs if we live with an addict. The situation is usually abusive because of the emotional volatility associated with addiction. Addiction lends itself to highly reactive and dramatic relationships. Addicts don't usually make a choice to become addicts. They just find that life under the influence of whatever the drug they use, is easier to deal with. They are generally doing the best they can, given the emotional and psychological issues they face. Addictions are in part a coping mechanism to deal with feelings by masking them. Unfortunately the sad irony is, that by pushing feelings down with alcohol or drugs it becomes much more difficult to work through the issues causing those feelings. A vicious cycle is set up, that then becomes a downward spiral. As a generalisation most addicts use in order to swallow, or stuff down feelings of shame, anger, isolation, fear, sadness and loss, usually caused by abuse or sometimes much simpler situations that have arisen in childhood, that the child has not had the resources to deal with, but have caused a deep anxiety. The abusive cycle can then become habitual. When an addict can kick his or her habit and become clean and sober, life tends to become much more stable. (More on how to deal with addictions in Chapter 12.)

Your journey
- Do you use drugs on a regular basis?
- If so have you any idea of why you do?
- What underlies the need to make your life easier by using?
- What emotions do you think you could be keeping in check?

HEIGHTENED EMOTIONAL RESPONSES

If we are living with an addict, to some extent we become like addicts ourselves because to sustain and survive an abusive relationship, we need to become used to the drama and the adrenaline rushes of coping with the next upheaval. So like the addict, we are waiting for his or her next fix. By comparison, a healthy relationship could be considered unsatisfying, bland and uninteresting, compared to the dramatic highs and lows of a tension-filled relationship, mashed potato instead of chili crab. The adrenaline rush of surviving can become a physical addiction, as the adrenal chemicals flood the brain making people feel more alert and alive. If dramas happen regularly in life, they become the norm and people become de-sensitised. It is only when big, dramatic things happen that life feels interesting and exciting again. These people have learned to go relatively numb to survive and find it difficult to feel the small subtle feelings, they are more used to the extremes, fear or terror versus ecstasy. The calm peace of a healthy relationship is too comfortable and it might mean some of their suppressed emotions would surface. Without being consciously aware that the suppressed emotions could be very scary, people in this type of relationship will often revert back to having more dramas so paradoxically they feel safer.

- Does this in any way resemble what happens in your life? It may not be about living with an addict, it may be about instantly responding to the demands of an unpredictable boss, or partner.

SUBTLY UNHEALTHY

Unhealthy abusive relationships can be quite subtle. In the questions below, would you term the behaviour healthy or unhealthy:

- Would you consider somebody who is sexually cheating on their partner abusive?
- If someone is having an affair with a person in the office, do you think they could be avoiding trying to sort out what is going on with their relationship at home?
- Would that be respectful to their partner?
- Is there a sense of power in being able to deceive another?
- Is the affair indicative of the relationship you have with yourself or maybe the lack thereof?
- If a partner is secretly drinking or looking at porn on the net frequently, is that abusive?
- Having sex with someone without telling them you have an STI (sexually transmitted infection)?

Although it may be difficult to gauge exactly what an abusive behaviour is, none of the above is indicative of a healthy respectful relationship, and can provide some telling pointers.

The sad thing is that unhealthy associations generally tend to get worse over time. Emotional and verbal abuse often deteriorates into more overt threats or physical abuse, particularly in times of stress. We know abusers are needy, controlling people and if they feel their relationship is threatened they may escalate the abuse in the hope of frightening the other person into staying.

Your journey

- How safe do you feel in a relationship with a secretive person or someone who is not truthful, or someone who only tells you what they think you can handle or need to know?
- Do you do this and if you do, what are you afraid of another knowing?
- If this is some of your behaviour would you like to be in relationship with yourself?
- How could you change it?
- How would you like others to treat you?
- What reactions are you having right now as you read this? Either you will be feeling quite comfortable or decidedly uncomfortable.
- Is this who you want to be? You may well be the product of your difficult background, but when do you decide enough is enough? You may have come from an abusive controlling background, but now decide that is not who I choose to be.

CHARACTERISTICS OF HEALTHY RELATIONSHIPS

It seems strange that the characteristics of a healthy relationship can be encompassed in just a few lines, where whole books can and are written about unhealthy behaviour. Unhealthy behaviour is often what fuels the soap operas we see on TV. If they were based on characters modeling healthy actions there wouldn't be much of a story. The dramas would be short-lived and quickly resolved.

Healthy relationships are invariably based on respect, so here we are again, coming back to this vital glue that holds interactions together. Respecting another, means respecting their boundaries, ideas and attitudes even when they differ from ours. In a healthy relationship people share responsibility for decision-making and have respect for all the people in the relationship, including the children. A healthy relationship is one in which all parties feel safe to be able to express themselves honestly and be listened to. It will be a relationship which is emotionally affirming and understanding, where everyone's opinions are valued. Perhaps difficult for some parents, it will be a relationship where each member of the family is respected for their right to have their own feelings, friends, activities and opinions. Those people we find difficult to be around will generally not have the same feelings and opinions as us and this is where trouble usually lies. In one sense, it is inevitable that at least some of their opinions and feelings will differ from ours; after all, they were brought up differently.

> *In a healthy relationship everyone feels safe to be able to express themselves honestly and to be listened to.*

A healthy relationship will be honest and accountable, with each member accepting responsibility for themselves. Again, inevitably, we won't all think the same way and at times we will encounter anger when we disagree with others. However, healthy anger is not to be feared. It is very different from rage. Healthy anger involves confrontation of what makes you or another angry. It is important to pinpoint what is causing the anger and draw it to the other's attention. Often in the resolution of a situation, boundaries need to be set: i.e. when you do _____I feel _____ and to protect myself I will_____.

In order to have a healthy relationship we need to acknowledge the past use of violence or emotionally abusive behaviour and undertake to change that behaviour. We have all been guilty of abusive behaviour, we wouldn't be human if we weren't. Before reading this, and confronting the true issues we may have made an excuse for it. Unfortunately now that we know what disrespectful behaviour looks like, we no longer have an excuse. That said, we don't need to be unkind and harsh with ourselves either. We did what we did most of the time because we felt vulnerable and threatened. Now we can be respectful and considerate of ourselves, apologising to others where possible and resolving to do better next time.

Whilst striving for relationship health, we can apologise and admit mistakes when it is appropriate, even if the other party cannot do the same. People who want a good rapport will be able to communicate openly and truthfully, acknowledging past abuse, and if necessary seek help for abusive relationship patterns. Ideally, if we are parents we will share parental responsibilities and be a positive, non-violent role model for children, sharing family decisions with all concerned.

We recognise that each of us has a legitimate need to be noticed, taken seriously and respected. Healthy people do not have to make a constant effort to earn admiration. They don't have to do anything to impress and they generally feel confident. Their self-respect is not dependent on qualities, functions and achievements that can suddenly fail. A healthy relationship, with respect as its cornerstone is the fast track to easier living. If we could all follow these simple guide lines, ultimately we would never need police, prison services and armed forces.

> *Each of us has a legitimate need to be noticed, taken seriously and respected.*

As you come to see what underlies your own behaviour you can slowly bring about that change. You only need to change yourself and the rest will surely follow. Instinctively you know what healthy behaviour feels and looks like. It feels comfortable and situations do not become highly reactive and drama driven. It feels calm because no one is battling the other for control. A healthy relationship is when both people feel connected while maintaining a strong sense of individuality and independence, with a marked lack of emphasis on power and control. There are few power struggles and when they arise the issues are dealt with quickly. Power is not used to manipulate. We recognise that power does not bring growth or long-term happiness.

TRUST

Trust obviously plays a huge part in healthy relationships. Each person trusts that the other has their best interests at heart. Each also trusts that the other is doing what is right for them. It becomes difficult when we see the other doing something we do not agree with, such as drinking too much, but after voicing our calm respectful comments, we stay respectful, understanding that he or she is choosing to go a different way. (Obviously this does not apply if we are responsible for children.) When we can put this trust into practice, there is a spiritual unfolding of relationships. However, to get to this point requires us to know that we can take care of ourselves at all times, and in all circumstances, even when we feel quite certain that the other is going in the wrong direction by drinking too much, or doing whatever they are doing that we don't approve of. This is so easy to say, but so difficult to do.

Many of us have not been encouraged to trust in ourselves and have rarely seen healthy modelling of trusting another. We learn to trust by becoming more self-aware, examining what is really going on for us when another doesn't do what we want them to do.

Your journey

- If others aren't doing what you would like them to do, is your concern really about them or is it really about you?
- What level of trust do you have in yourself?
- How trusting are you of others?
- What broke your trust in the relationship you have with that impossible other?

With each step we take the next becomes easier. (More about this in Chapter 14.)

If we have a somewhat jaundiced view of life and see others as dangerous or not trustworthy, that is our choice of how we choose to see them. Those are the lenses in front of our eyes. At times it is essential to be cautious, but if we look at everyone suspiciously, it has more to do with us than them. Perhaps at times we may have been betrayed, but not everyone will have betrayed us.

- Do you feel you have been betrayed?
- When and by whom?

If betrayal is a theme in your life, it could possibly come back to a life script, adopted as a child, which said life was dangerous, don't trust anyone. That now manifests itself in mistrust and generally a need to control in order to feel safe.

- Did you have a life script that implied that life was dangerous?
- Were your parents suspicious people?
- When did you learn to mistrust, how old were you and what happened?

If childhood trust had been broken at an early age we probably learned it was safer not to trust. We most likely absorbed that the world was a dangerous place and was, to some extent, characterised by hostility or a need to survive, perhaps by competing. Consciously or unconsciously we may have learned to be wary and quick to fight or defend. Our default programming may be to be suspicious of others, we might even have become a rebel. To feel safe we could have learned that we needed to be stronger than others, particularly if you are male. Females often protect themselves by having a sharp cutting tongue. Obviously, there are degrees of how we use this essentially hostile behaviour. Some people may be extremely violent and view everything competitively, while others anger quickly if they feel threatened in any way. This would be the opposite way that "people pleasers" would tend to relate.

So, if our conflictual relationship is with someone who has learned to please and we are naturally more aggressive, there is a strong likelihood that the pleaser will often compromise their behaviour and needs in order to keep the peace, but the resentment and feelings of revenge would eventually start to surface.

Your journey

- Is this what is happening, or is it the other way round, with you being the pleaser and your anger percolating through?

PEOPLE PLEASERS

These people will often take undue responsibility for others.

- Do you have a life script which says, others are more important than you?

If you do you could be trying to meet the needs of people who are quite capable of meeting their own needs. If you are always there to help, you are in fact doing them a grave disservice. You are not helping them learn that it is far healthier to be able to take care of themselves, rather than rely on others to be there to pick them up after every mishap. Many women fall into this category, having been taught, "You must be there for others," but it is by no means a feminine preserve, many men will also fall into the same category of "people pleasers."

Brent and Janice, (pages 53, 64 and 233) are a good example of this. Janice tends toward being obliging, while Brent expects to take what he wants with seemingly little consideration. This seems selfish to Janice but it highlights a secret self or disowned aspect of her. She learnt early to be compliant, earning the approval of others in order to feel safe. It has underpinned her life to date but is now no longer working so well, the simmering resentment is working its way closer and closer to the surface. She is a people pleaser.

- Do you fit that category of compliance and obedience?

THE BEHAVIOURAL SECURITY FOR PEOPLE PLEASERS

Whilst it is very laudable to want to help others, there is a return for that behaviour. The return, generally speaking, is, "I will be liked by those I help." If we look further you'll probably find reasoning that will go something like this, "If I'm liked I will be safe. If I'm safe, I won't be rejected or abandoned." Bottom line of our behaviour is the unconscious need to keep ourselves loved, and safe. The down side of being too helpful, too rescuing, is that it keeps the other person in a weakened situation. If we never have the opportunity of pulling ourselves out of a hole, because someone is always there to help pull us out, how do we know we can get out unaided? What we do for ourselves empowers and builds us.

There is a Buddhist saying that after you have purified yourself of your vices, then purify yourself of your virtues. This way we can sort out what is self-serving behaviour.

Always helping others puts us in a more powerful position than the other person, we effectively set ourselves up in a one-up position. The return for helping others is that it makes us feel more important. Obviously again there is a balance to be achieved here, we all need a helping hand at times, but often what we need more is someone to really listen to us. We don't need advice, because if we are heard, really heard, we can usually then make our own decisions. The primary job of a counsellor is to listen. Clients are usually able to make their own decisions and when they do, they come away feeling empowered.

Your journey

- Are you consciously aware of being a "people pleaser"?
- Do you have an understanding about why this behaviour is important to you?
- Is being super helpful something you were taught as a child or something you consciously decide to do?
- Do you get resentful if you have worked hard to provide other's needs and have not been recognised for your work?

SAFETY IN DISTANCING

Not all of us went down the same road and became "pleasers." If we did not get emotional security by doing what we were told, we may have unconsciously decided that it was too difficult to get others' approval and love, so we distanced ourselves. As children, our feelings were not validated or respected and we learned to put emotional distance between ourselves and others. We learned to feel safe being alone, so we become loners, supposedly not needing others, becoming self-sufficient. We are probably not aware on a conscious level that this is what happened, we just tell ourselves we prefer the peace of being somewhat withdrawn. Tom (latest references pages 147 and 193) had such tendencies, preferring to keep to himself. However, his psyche had a great need for connection, hence his attraction to Cherie. Cherie's primary need was to please others, in this case her four children's needs came first, followed by Tom's. Tom's self-sufficiency also manifested itself in a sense of superiority and feelings of uniqueness and specialness.

This detachment was a predominant characteristic in Sue, Barbara's daughter-in-law, (last referred to on page 213). This made it particularly difficult for Barbara, a people pleaser, to relate to Sue. Sue's apparent indifference was threatening to Barbara. Normally Barbara would never have verbalised her feelings, keeping them to herself, in case she was seen as not nice, however, because her only son was involved and she wanted him to be happy (in the way she thought best) she was quite outspoken. This irritation with Sue, allowed Barbara to channel her resentments with other relationships into this one, making it a good vehicle for her projections.

Daniel (page 210) is quite an aggressive person. He was an only child and both his parents worked full time, so he spent much of his time alone. Often they were too tired when they were home to pay much attention to Daniel and he became an angry, quite aggressive child, his own pursuits became the most important focus in his life. We can now see how his attitude to Neil starts to make sense. He had rarely received praise and validation for his own efforts, so why should he give it to Neil, who tended more to being a people pleaser and felt victimised a great deal of the time. Daniel regarded him as weak while Neil saw Daniel as a bully, whom he disliked.

In Patrick and Rachael's relationship (pages 68 and 206), Patrick was the more aggressive while Rachael's conditioning had led her to be more detached. Her self-sufficiency played on Patrick's sense of not being able to control her and roused his anger, which only exacerbated the situation between them. Likewise in Branson and Terry's relationship (page 256),

Branson was the aggressive one and Terry was detached, which was partly why the situation had hit stalemate. Branson's natural inclination was to force the situation and that was scary for Terry, so he withdrew more and more.

DEFAULT BEHAVIOUR

Your journey

- If you are not particularly a "people pleaser" which category of behaviour do you default to feel safe, detached or quick to attack?

It is quite possible that your behaviour will not always fall into any one particular band, but there will probably be a marked tendency toward one. The more psychologically healthy we are the more we will be able to use all three styles of relating. We need to be friendly, we also need to be able to withdraw and where necessary, able to fight. You will have gleaned some clues by looking at your triggers. Remember that what triggers a strong reaction is indicative of the secret self aspects of you, and possibly of what you project onto others. If we have survived by being a fighter and quite aggressive, a calm passive non-combative person would probably annoy us, but what we would need to learn, is be less aggressive and more trusting of others. For the loner the social butterfly would probably seem superficial and intensely irritating. Ideally, we would need to become more social and to experience the joy of being with others.

If our need for compliance and obedience is strong, it is hardly surprising that when it comes to thinking about what we need for ourselves that we might well hesitate. If we are very compliant and obliging we need to learn to be more assertive, and feel confident doing what we want to do, not just what others want us to do. This is changing a pattern of behaviour that we may have had for decades and it is not easy. We need to reinforce our behaviour with logical self-talk as encouragement to back up our resolve for change. This might sound something like, "It is OK for me to do what I need to do for myself, at this point in time. I deserve to give myself what I need."

Likewise, if you prefer to spend most of your time alone, your self-talk, to help you lead a more balanced life may sound like this, "It is safe for me to be with others to find closeness and spontaneity and I may find I enjoy it if I give myself the chance."

If we survived by being aggressive and trying to take what we want, the ideal would be to balance that with trust, gentleness, and vulnerability. It sounds easy reading it here, but putting this new type of behaviour into practice will take time, courage and perseverance. Ideally as responsible thinking adults we need balance in our behaviour, and to be in a position to actively choose a course of action, rather than react as a default setting.

- What sort of self talk would be the most useful for you to adopt?

BALANCE

We all know balance is one of the most important tools in life. However, let's face it, it is a perfectionistic ideal, rarely achieved, and if momentarily grasped never stays for long, being ephemeral and fleeting. So getting it right is usually a life long juggle. Perhaps the best way of achieving it is to feel the pull of the opposites, acknowledge them and stay with the feeling. Acknowledging the tension in relationships is a healthy sign.

It is also difficult for us to objectively and realistically appraise ourselves. To see our personal characteristics objectively, and then decide if they need to be moderated or strengthened to give us the ideal balance and the best chance at happiness, is a continually changing process.

This is where awareness of the secret self and projection comes in and gives us useful tools for determining what characteristics we do or don't have, and in what measure. How do we know if the balance is right? Generally, life works much better. We feel better about ourselves and our relationships work better. What is certain is, that if we maintain flexibility and communication, we go a long way towards getting it relatively right.

Seeking feedback from others, i.e. asking them if they think you are being inflexible or difficult, whilst sometimes scary because you may feel exposed, is an excellent way to check if you are finding a good balance. To follow this through, will mean being able to sit with possible criticism, without loosing your cool. We need to remember a certain amount of what others say will be their own secret self and projections talking.

We can then balance the feedback with our own feelings and in this way come to some sort of compromise. It is also about observing what others are doing and keeping ourselves open to change. Usually, rigidity is the greatest enemy.

12 WHAT OUR DIFFICULT RELATIONSHIPS COST US

- How do you gauge the cost of your difficult relationships?
- What yardsticks can you use?
- How do you know if you have given enough, if you have tried hard enough?
- When is it OK to finally walk away from the impossible other?
- What does the impossible other want from you and what do you expect of him or her?
- Do you walk around on eggshells when you are with the monster?
- Just how do you modify your behaviour when you are with him or her?
- Can you talk and feel heard by the ogre?

Before trying to answer some of these questions let's think about what we are powerless to change in this inhuman being.

WHAT WE CANNOT CHANGE

Most of us spend too much time trying to change the unchangeable. This is where a small part of the Serenity Prayer below can be useful, although there are times when it doesn't matter how many times it is said, it does not soothe the troubled soul.

> Lord, grant me the courage to change what I can,
>
> To accept what I can't,
>
> And the wisdom to know the difference.

We can't change your history or theirs. David Jansen and Margaret Newman in their book *Really Relating* say, what's happened has gone and is now part of who you and they are. No amount of wishing will change what's gone. Nor can either party change their basic physiology. You were born with the genes you have and they will dictate your physical characteristics to a large extent. Of course you can gain and lose weight, change your hair colour, straighten your teeth and do some minor surgical reconstructions, but your level of intelligence and the way your brain works is largely predetermined, so is theirs. However as we know experiences can and do change and enhance our brain. But unfortunately you won't become another Einstein, Beethoven, or Picasso just by trying, and neither can they, which might give you some comfort. There would be nothing worse if the person you are having such problems with suddenly became a famous genius.

It would be too much to take. So these are the things we can't change. You can change your culture, your religion, your primary language and you can modify the impact of some of your life experiences, such as the rules you were taught as a child, but you can't change who you came from, those relationships are fixed. You can of course choose not to have relationships with them.

Your journey

- Are any of the above factors causing problems in your trying relationship?

In considering this question of "otherness" or difference, it seems we perceive that the differences between us all outweigh the similarities. After all we have different personalities, different genetics, different bodies, different aspirations and so on, the differences can be almost endless.

In recognising the differences we may be able to avoid making some fundamental mistakes. Mistakes we hear so often are things like, "Of course you can do it—" which minimises a person's concerns, "Of course she knew how that would hurt me when she said it," and so on. Maybe we are making assumptions based on our own understanding and ability, but not necessarily respecting the differences between us.

Your journey

- In that irritating relationship are you respecting the "otherness" of each other?

Part of assessing the cost of your relationship will be to factor in all the unchangeable fundamental differences.

THE NEED TO BE RIGHT

Another key question is:

- Do I have a need to be right or blameless?
- Do you want to make the ogre wrong?

Chances are they would love you to be wrong. This one is a killer. Problem is while you want to be right, it automatically makes the other person wrong. This can be satisfying in the short term, but five minutes later they are determined to prove you are wrong, at fault and you have to be continually on your guard not to be caught with your trousers down, so to speak, which is trying.

Most of us hate to be wrong, it's hard to admit a mistake. The desire to be right is a very human reaction, it links directly back to the unconscious and keeping safe. If we're right, we have a better chance of being safe because the other person is wrong. Being right also links directly back to our secret self, proving others are wrong gives us the upper hand. Rather than outwardly coming out and saying we know best, we do it only slightly more subtly by proving the other wrong. This is a hard question and one well worth asking:

Your journey

- How much of the time do I need to be right?
- If the answer is uncomfortably often, why do you think you may have this need?
- What does being right give you?

STAYING IN AN ABUSIVE RELATIONSHIP

Most people really want their relationships to work and are willing to hang in there waiting, believing the promises and hoping things will improve. They may think this is what love is, praying for things to get better, but not really taking concrete steps to facilitate change. They may believe there is enough "good" in the relationship to counterbalance the bad. They may have been taught that if you really love someone you will put up with their behaviour. People with children may reason that it is better to stay with the father or mother of their kids even if he or she is destructive, rather than becoming single parent families. Perhaps we fear that if we leave we will be financially destitute and it is better to put up with some rough stuff, rather than be a financial burden or poverty-stricken. This is a common situation for mothers with children. However, the effect of staying in an abusive family environment is very destructive to the children, who then believe this to be a normal way of behaving. This is how violence and abuse is passed on through the generations and the intergenerational pattern continues unchecked.

People can become stuck in unhealthy relationships if they are emotionally blackmailed by threats of suicide or harming themselves: "If you leave me I will kill myself." Often the most common fear that keeps us trapped in an unhealthy association is: "If I leave who will be there for me? At least this way I have somebody." It is true that staying may allow us to kid ourselves that we have somebody, but that somebody is not truly caring. If they genuinely had our well-being at heart, they would not be abusive. It is possible that they didn't know they were being abusive but once told, a continuation of the same abusive behaviour is not acceptable. So are we really better off being with somebody who is abusive or with nobody for a period of time?

Sometimes pressure from family, friends and even our religious beliefs can keep us locked into an unhealthy situation. Marriage vows can also play an important part in keeping people trapped in destructive circumstances. Most religions strongly discourage divorce or the break up of the family. The ideals are admirable, but if they cause long-term suffering they are ultimately counter-productive to society. People with very strong religious convictions can feel enormous guilt if they break up relationships. Maybe we are tied to an old blueprint, learned as children, that says we should be loyal, regardless of the personal cost, and telling the truth about abusive behaviour is not acceptable or loyal.

Many people do not even realise that they may be in an abusive relationship, or if they do realise, do not really want to believe it or even think about it. This denial mechanism is very common.

Your journey

- If you have come from an abusive background do you even know what it feels like to be treated with respect?

- Do you find ways of justifying the lack of respect or mistreatment, whether emotional or physical?

- Do you feel that it is no big deal and you can handle it?

Eventually however, abuse escalates and finally, people feel trapped and have to get out. If you are being abused, you are irresponsible to stay. You are allowing an unhealthy situation to persist. This is serious. The best way an abused person can help another is to learn how to model healthy boundaries. It doesn't mean the relationship has to come to an end, but it certainly means it has to change very dramatically. By changing yourself and not tolerating disrespectful behaviour, you are doing the best thing for yourself and for the other. You are respecting yourself and the other.

Healthy boundaries are an important key to good relationships.

In fact, if you are allowing yourself to be continually abused, you are also being self-abusive. This may shock you but if you do not take action to stop the abuse, not only are you being self-abusive, but you are also inflicting abuse on the person doing the abusing in the first place. The abuser can only grow psychologically if he or she changes their behaviour. It is your responsibility to yourself to stop this dynamic and hopefully stop the cycle continuing. We are not being responsible, respectful human beings when we allow abusive behaviour to continue. An obvious example is if we know someone is a murderer, do we allow him or her to keep on killing innocent people, or do we step in and make a stand? It is the same story with abuse.

Martin loves his Romanian wife Hannah, who is a slim petite pretty woman, but their marriage has hit serious problems. When Hannah first arrived in Australia she only knew Martin and felt very isolated and uncertain in a culturally different country. Martin had his family and friends around him which only emphasised Hannah's loneliness. When he joined his mates for a drink, Hannah would get very angry and accuse Martin of not caring for her. Her anger, which unbeknown to her, was covering her feelings of isolation, would flare up and she would physically attack Martin, who was a big strong guy. At the beginning he rather enjoyed his wife's passionate nature but in due course it was no longer a laughing matter. She wanted to have children and Martin was now thoroughly alarmed at her unpredictable violent temper and was not prepared to risk having a child. His refusal only aggravated the situation because Hannah felt utterly rejected. He still loved her and it didn't matter what he did to try and appease Hannah, it failed miserably because the core issue of Hannah's feelings of rejection were not being addressed. Despite the escalating level of violence Martin did nothing to protect himself. During one violent incident he called the police, but a few days later when Hannah said she wanted him back, back he went, for the whole cycle to start afresh.

Hannah and Martin were enmeshed in each other's dramas. They both lacked a sense of self and were codependent, which is why the situation persisted. Hannah had always felt a sense of rejection but in her teens and early twenties had covered it with a very active social life. With her social network stripped away by coming to Australia, the feelings of rejection started to surface. At a conscious level, she was unaware that her blaming Martin for not loving her enough to want to have children with her was a way of avoiding facing her sense of rejection. It was much easier to blame all of her discomfort on Martin and until she did some therapy, she was consciously unaware of her deep sense of rejection. Meanwhile, Martin had learned to survive and thrive in his family of origin by being a pleaser, compliant and obedient, always wanting to help others. The issue of bringing a child into an unpredictable violent relationship was serious enough for Martin to lay down a clear boundary, which Hannah understandably took very personally. Martin explained: "When you can control your temper we can think again about children," but Hannah's sense of self was so precarious that all she could hear was more rejection, and the whole cycle would start again. Martin felt a huge sense of responsibility for Hannah as he had been the one to bring her to Australia and he felt guilty that she was not happy. Although she could tell Martin why she was unhappy, she could not see what was motivating her feelings and did not want to look. It was easier to project and blame.

The cost to both of them staying in the relationship was huge, although the gain for the behaviour was that each somehow got some measure of validation by being the bane of the other's life; negative attention is always better than no attention. If they had understood how to do it differently no doubt they would have. For their personal growth to start the situation had to change. They separated to do their individual work of exploring childhood issues to improve their sense of self and create clear boundaries. The relationship has enough passion and love to grow and strengthen through such a huge learning curve, but it remains to be seen whether they will meet the challenge.

RESOLVING THE UNCONSCIOUS NEEDS

Hannah's father had walked out on the family to pursue a love affair when Hannah was small and she had always resented him, as his leaving had embittered her mother and left the family in extremely straitened circumstances. In some way, Hannah was projecting her own childhood bitterness onto Martin when he refused to have children with her. It was a second abandonment.

Some of us will have heard stories of how the daughters of alcoholic fathers say they would never marry an alcoholic, but often marry men who do become alcoholics. Or, how daughters of abusive fathers, brought up in a dysfunctional family say they will never marry a violent man, yet do. This is our unconscious at work. Remember how unconsciously we want to resolve the issues that gave us pain as children and how we look for resolution to those unsatisfactory childhood experiences, often through other relationships, well these are prime examples. Unconsciously, we want to recreate the situation of when we were powerless, so that this time we can get our happy ending. The daughter of a drunk marries a drunk, with the unconscious hope that this time it will be different. This time we can change things, this time we will be powerful. Unfortunately, the only way we get the happy ending is to become aware of the pattern and give up our need for things to be different. We cannot change others, we can only change ourselves. It is our own need that we want things to be different.

Unconsciously we want to recreate situations when we felt powerless in order to get an opportunity to do it differently now.

ADDICTIONS AND MENTAL DISABILITIES

People with a low sense of self often find they are living with someone who has an addiction.

> **Your journey**
>
> - If this is you and the person you are living with has no desire to control his or her addiction and doesn't want to make changes to save the relationship, what do you achieve by staying with them?
>
> - What are you gaining or losing?
>
> - Why are you with someone who is emotionally unable to cope without the prop of an addiction to make life bearable?

If someone is genuinely mentally disabled with a major personality disorder, then again, it becomes a different situation. You may choose to make the necessary sacrifices to help them, if those in charge of their medical situation feel that is appropriate. For people involved with others who have mental disorders, Paul Mason and Randi Kreger have excellent advice in their book *Stop Walking on Eggshells*. Although they are specifically taking about Borderline Personality Disorder their advice holds true for personality disorders generally. They say, "Remember the three Cs and the three Gs:

> I didn't cause it.
>
> I can't control it.
>
> I can't cure it.
>
> Get off their back.
>
> Get out of their way.
>
> Get on with your own life."

Similar advice is given to families affected by alcohol and drug users. We learn that individuals are not responsible for another person's disease or recovery from it. We need to let go of our obsession with another's behaviour and then we begin to lead happier and more manageable lives, with dignity and rights. As Mason and Kreger put it:

> "Not to suffer because of the actions or reactions of other people.
>
> Not to allow ourselves to be used or abused by others in the interest of another's recovery.
>
> Not to do for others what they could do for themselves.
>
> Not to create a crisis.
>
> Not to prevent a crisis if it is in the natural course of events."

THE IMPACT OF LOW SELF WORTH OR FEAR

Your journey

- Is low self-worth or fear why you stay?
- If you are struggling to make an abusive relationship work, what do you think that says about who you are?

You are probably a very caring person and are working desperately hard to make it all work, but you do not have a very clear idea about your own self worth.

- Do you feel you are the one responsible for making the relationship work?
- If so, why are you taking the bulk of the responsibility?

As said before it takes two to tango, and each partner in any relationship is responsible for fifty percent of whatever dynamic they create. We are not mind readers. Each of us is responsible for *showing* the other person how we want to be treated. However, if we have a very flimsy idea of our self-worth, this fact often seems to get forgotten, there is just a feeling of needing to make it all work because the alternative is you have to cope on your own and face your own issues, which may be much harder than coping with someone else's mess.

FEAR OR LOVE

The common denominator of why people stay in situations that make them fundamentally unhappy is fear. Fear for themselves, or fear of hurting the other person. Fear, easy to say, a single word; but it is one of only two key motivators for every type of behaviour in our life. All our actions ultimately come down to two choices. Either we do things out of **love** or **fear**. This is where the unconscious comes in again. Its job is to enable us to survive. Anything that is fearful to us is a threat to our survival.

There are only two key motivations in life, fear or love.

In gauging the cost of your difficult relationship, it is important to see if there is any projective identification, as it is very common. (Projective identification is when you come to believe what others are saying about you. You have heard it so often that it is an ingrained truth for you.) For example, a mother who continually feels inadequate, may start telling her five year old daughter that she is no good and isn't a nice person to be around because she won't do what she is told. The daughter absorbs that and because she believes it, it becomes a self-fulfilling prophecy. Etched into her very being is the fact that she is not worth much, she's pretty worthless. But is it really true? Was that little girl worthless?

Your journey

- If you think you are fundamentally flawed or worthless how can you believe in yourself or take the steps to protect yourself?

- Spend a little time thinking about what those difficult people have said about you.

- What have you been blamed for?

Your journey

- What is the most commonly voiced criticism you have heard about yourself?

- How much of it is true if you look at it realistically and objectively? Perhaps you could ask someone you trust to give you their opinion. Perhaps there is some truth in what others say, but is it all correct?

- How much have you allowed what others have said about you or expect of you, to mould who you are and what you are capable of doing?

A common example is when parents are disappointed with a child's academic performance. They really want a clever child who is an asset to them. When the child does not get good grades at school, the parents, perhaps in an effort to make him or her work harder, say things like "You are stupid, you can do better than that, that isn't good enough, you are dumb." If the message is repeated often enough, the child truly believes he or she is dumb and that message then becomes a self-fulfilling prophesy. If we believe we are dumb, why try to do anything about it? The acceptance of someone else's label is very damaging and unless really thought about and challenged, may easily become a life script. It is safer to accept that we are dumb and that's just the way it is, just like some people are tall and others short, rather than run the risk of trying to prove them wrong.

> Zac came to Australia from Vietnam and his parents put great pressure on him to perform academically. They saw Zac's potential academic achievement as their way out of a low standard of living and he would look after them in old age. Zac worked hard and did well but his parents didn't praise him, which was something he greatly resented. As revenge, he would steal the family car at night, drive it around then later put it back unmarked. His behaviour extended to shoplifting, skipping school and eventually not even sitting his final leaving exams, all without telling his parents. In that way he felt he had power over his parents. They were expecting him to go to university and when he refused because, of course, he did not have the qualifications, he left home and refused to have contact with his family for many years. They still do not know that he never took the exams. The pressure of trying to conform to his parents' expectations was too much for Zac. His rebellion was covert, it became a power struggle in which everyone lost. Each party was coming from a place of fear. His parents were fearful for their financial survival in old age and Zac could not risk taking the exams in case his results did not match their expectations.

Others may react in the opposite way. They have also heard it said umpteen times that they are stupid, but are determined to prove those people wrong. Anita has three degrees, one majoring in psychology, a Masters of Business Studies and a PhD, yet still feels she is "not enough." Her continual quest for more and more qualifications was coming from an unconscious need to have her father validate her for her achievements. She was desperately seeking his approval.

Without realising what underlay her behaviour, she had undertaken to type up his memoirs and was working long and hard into each night because he wanted to take them overseas to his relatives. This was despite working hard at her full time job. Anita had little sense of her own needs, she just felt driven to achieve what her father had asked. Once she realised the cost to her physical health and the underlying motivation, Anita was able to pace herself more realistically.

WHAT'S THE MOTIVATION

We know that underlying each and every interaction in a relationship there is a motivation, a need trying to be met. The secret is to determine what the need is and then where it comes from. When we look at the need, we can ascertain if it is appropriate or if it is driven from the unconscious.

- In the relationship with that person you are trying to get along with can you identify the need, where it is coming from and what is driving it?

- Can you determine if your course of action is appropriate? What motivation underlies your interactions with the impossible other?

Anita's motivation, at one level was trying to please her father, but at a far deeper level, she was trying to keep herself safe, by getting his approval. The fact that she was a fifty-year-old mature woman with her own children made absolutely no difference. The driver was just as strong as it had been when she was a small girl.

What is the cost for "people pleasers" who are nice and obliging? As previously said "people pleasers" definitely have an agenda, albeit one that perhaps is unconscious. They please others so they will be cared for. When cared for, we are safer, much less likely to be abandoned or rejected. However, there is a big trap here. In order to be accepted and cared for we probably overextend ourselves too much at the beginning of the relationship. We are too kind, too thoughtful, too giving. We are not aware that our giving has an unconscious price tag attached. The price tag is that we must get back, in some form or another. This creates huge problems in that later, down the track, if the pay-back is not forthcoming we feel exploited, rejected, lonely and abandoned. Perhaps we feel like the victim. The irony is that our need to be accepted and cared for, is our need, and a need that we eventually have to face, otherwise it drives our behaviour unconsciously. We are back to what Jung said about our secret self, what we avoid or hide from, will eventually come back to us so we have to face it.

In a situation like the above when we have given to the best of our ability and then nothing is forthcoming in exchange, we usually become angry, resentful and bitter. We become the innocent victim of that "user" and the relationship goes sour. If only we could realise that we had an unconscious agenda at the very beginning. The fact that it has all gone sour has more to do with us than the other party, who could consider themselves trapped or manipulated into something they were totally unaware of, a sobering thought.

THE COST OF STAYING CAN BE OUR OWN EMOTIONAL ABANDONMENT

Although one of the themes of this book is that the difficulties in relationships have much more to do with you than the other person, there does come a time when the cost of staying in a relationship is too high. We know and accept that we have no right to change others and if we cannot accept a situation as it is, we need to walk away for our own health and well-being. To stay would mean we are emotionally abandoning ourselves.

We are emotionally abandoning ourselves when we stay in a relationship that we know does not work.

There is an expression: "Life is as much to do with holding on as letting go." To improve your sense of self you know that you need to trust yourself to do the right thing for yourself. Some of those seemingly impossible situations we have with others will require us to take care of ourselves and walk away. It is easier to see what needs to be done in an abusive situation, but how do we determine the cost of staying in associations where there is no abuse but there are major stumbling blocks?

> Skye and Miguel had recently married. Miguel was a strict Catholic and did not want to live with Skye before marriage. Skye had reservations but she recognised that Miguel was a good man and she loved him, if not with the depth of passion that she would have liked. Although she did not share his religion, she was deeply spiritual. The first upset came when Skye did not want to share his weekly religious service. Miguel had assumed that given time he would be

able to show her that his way was the purest and best. When Skye challenged him he would just say, "Let it be," so the issue never got satisfactorily resolved. This is what happened to many different issues, they weren't discussed. When Skye pressed him to talk things through Miguel would change the subject or deflect the conversation. He had a great fear of confrontation and wanted everything to be smooth and peaceful. Over time Skye realised that there were issues that were no go areas as Miguel was not prepared to rock the boat by discussing sensitive matters. Little by little, with each invitation to discuss things declined, the boat was sinking. Although Skye still loved him, she learned that she would never be able to have the relationship she desired. Whilst he kept blocking and cutting off the communication, they were losing intimacy. They were also losing trust in each other. Skye couldn't trust that as issues came up they would be resolved so the relationship started to feel unsafe. Skye came to realise that while she did feel safe enough to stay in the relationship, the cost was a loss of communication and intimacy, which was too high. To accept the cost was an emotional abandonment of what she wanted in a close and loving partnership.

Although Miguel had many fine qualities, Skye came to understand that she would be sacrificing a vital part of herself that wanted to grow in a relationship if she stayed. The marriage ended. Miguel felt Skye was at fault and could not understand why it hadn't worked. He was not able, at that point in time, to look at the part he played in the dynamic they had set up. He chose to stay a victim. Skye realised that if she did not value and honor her own needs eventually they would turn to resentment and bitterness. If one party is not prepared to talk and be flexible, the other party is left with little choice. This dynamic is common when one party is more self aware and psychologically healthier than the other. Skye had the stronger sense of self and Miguel was not willing to do the work of looking at his fear of confrontation and thus becoming more self-aware.

A similar situation happened with Richard and Paul.

They had fallen in love and been together for a number of years but slowly Paul was becoming more exasperated with Richard's procrastination. He would say he would arrive at a certain time, but always managed to be held up at work. He had a high-powered job, which seemed to consume his life. Paul found that his own life was continually on hold while he waited for Richard. He didn't want to always do things by himself and wondered about the point of the relationship. It seemed to be a few snatched hours here and there, with fine promises that never eventuated. Although there was still deep affection, Paul's irritation outweighed his love, until eventually the partnership came adrift. Richard's excuses that he was working so hard to provide a better life for them both, no longer had any pulling power for Paul. In fact, Richard was a workaholic with a procrastination problem, but he did not want to look at what underlay his need to spend most of his waking time in the office.

In both these relationships, the person that left had a higher self-esteem than the person who was too uncertain of themselves to risk looking at what was really going on at a much deeper level. Yet both felt they had been the victim of a partner that was not willing to compromise, without wanting to acknowledge that it takes two to set up the dynamic.

Your journey

- Do you feel you are compromising the core of who you wish to be by staying in relationship with the difficult other?

- How much responsibility do you take for setting up the dynamic you have?

- The answer cannot be less than 50%.

You may not have had your eyes open when you started but you certainly have now, as well as the ability to do something about it. It is extremely likely that it will cause some conflict but conflict and pain is usually the path to personal growth. Unfortunately, without it you stay stuck and in the "stuckness" lose some of who you are. You lose life force and joy. It is not about blaming others, it is about clearly seeing your motivations and underlying fears. It is about taking responsibility for your part:

Your journey

- If you try to put on another's glasses and see the world as they see it, does it make any difference?

- If your mother-in-law is your "bête noir" because she is so fearful and suspicious, try putting on her glasses and imagine seeing the world as a frightening suspicious place. Is she really getting at you, or is it the way she looks at everything?

- Does it just happen to really annoy you because it is catching on part of your secret self?

> - Your boss always seems to be on your back. Put on his glasses and maybe you'll notice his boss is on his back, clamouring for progress and results. Is it really about you, or more about the image he has of himself as boss?
>
> - Are you a victim here or just part of the way he thinks he should be?
>
> - If you could practice some detachment would those difficult people become more bearable?
>
> - Can you discipline yourself enough to detach and observe, rather than immediately jump into victim mentality?

Your journey

However, if the relationship is a long-term abusive one, it is a totally different story. It is unrealistic to expect that all relationships will never be abusive at the odd time. We all get mad, and call someone a bitch or a bastard, or worse, that's part of being human. Abuse that can come from someone with an addiction, a mental disorder or an inability to control how they act, that wears away at the very fabric of who we are by using ongoing physical, verbal or emotion battering, ongoing belittlement, humiliation and criticism is unacceptable. Furthermore, it is irresponsible to continue to expose ourselves to that situation. We are allowing an abusive cycle to perpetuate. If we continue to let others abuse us we are staying, either in victim or martyr

If we continue to let others abuse us we become self-abusive.

mode and it becomes important to look at why we do this. Is it helpful to the perpetrator to allow him or her to continue their actions, do we allow the bully to keep on bullying, or do we take a stand and try and teach that his or her behaviour is unacceptable? The ultimate cost to the bully is that he eventually becomes isolated. Is allowing that to happen real love? We need to detach in order to be helpful.

Obviously, in assessing the cost of our relationships we need to weigh up the positive versus the negative. The negatives cover a lot of paper, while the positives of relationships fit into just a page or two. However, if there is not a very large percentage of those positive attributes, including respect, trust, nurturing, friendship, fun, support, joy and happiness in the relationship, then the ultimate question has to be, what do I gain from being a victim or a martyr?

13 CHOICES

> A man sitting in a crowded New York subway train had his seven children with him, who were yelling, screaming and climbing over other passengers. The children's behaviour was so bad that it was upsetting a number of people in the train. Eventually one traveller said to the father, "Can't you get your kids under control, they are behaving appallingly. What sort of father are you anyway, to let your kids go on in such a way?" To which the father replied, "We have just come from the hospital where my wife has just died, and I don't know how I am going to cope." Instantly the passengers turned from being very angry to being very concerned and caring about the father and the children.

The point of the story is that within seconds we can completely change how we think about things. The paradigm shifted completely. Everything you think about is a thought in your mind. You have unlimited power in the way you look at things. Difficult, impossible situations become that way because that is how you choose to look at them. The behaviour of the children in the train was offensive one minute but the next

You have unlimited power in the way you look at things.

minute our thinking about them had completely changed. Now, instead of probably feeling the same irritation as the train passengers, we feel sorry for those children.

Let's work through the following example. Imagine the stock market has crashed and everything you own has gone, years and years of hard work with nothing to show for it, except your grey hair. You are destitute.

Your journey

- How will you choose to look at the situation you find yourself in? No doubt there will be a period of grieving and of feeling victimised, that is a normal human reaction. Then you have some choices to make:

- Do I sign out now and commit suicide?

- Will I complain for the rest of my life?

- Do I think there must be a purpose in all this, something to learn, and try to work out what it is?

- Do I think this certainly is a huge challenge, this time what will I do differently?

The choice boils down to two very simple options: am I going to be a victim or am I going to use this situation as a growth opportunity? As we look back through history, we see such wonderful stories of people's heroism and ability to come back from dire circumstances. You have that strength of backbone, it is a matter of whether you choose to use it, or choose to let the circumstances defeat you. These are the moments that define who you are and what strength of character you have. It is all a matter of choice, your choice.

AS YOU THINK SO SHALL YOU BE

The Bible tells us, "As you think, so shall you be". If you choose to see somebody as the bane of your life, that is what you will experience. We can choose to shift the paradigm. It is much easier if it happens as it did for the passengers in the train, but usually we have to create the shift ourselves. We could speculate about what the circumstances are like for the person that drives us mad.

- What do you think he or she is experiencing or has experienced?
- Could it explain the attitude that you find so difficult?
- How would you cope with a similar situation if you swapped places?
- Can you trace it back to any particular event in your life where you felt unsafe?
- Does the person remind you of anyone else in your life that you feel anxious around?
- For example, if you feel that your aged aunt is always so critical of you, is it because she reminds you of your father, (her brother)?

As Rachael (page 68) thought about why she was so unhappy with Patrick, she understood that somehow there was a connection, albeit tenuous, with Patrick's ambition and with her father's treatment of her. Was Patrick's drive to succeed at work going to come before his relationship with her, in the same way as whatever was going on in her father's life that caused him to leave, came before her?

The renowned psychotherapist, Dr. Carl Whitaker once said, "The only you that I know is me." We can really only see another through our own lenses. Our mind, our eyes, and our belief systems predetermine everything that we see out there. We cannot actually experience another person, we can only experience them through our mind and our perceptions, all of which have been shaped, as we have already seen, by our programming, which started when we were children. Dr. Wayne Dyer in his book *Real Magic* says, "All of the other people in your life are simply thoughts in your mind. Not physical beings to you, but thoughts. Your relationships are all in how you think about the other people of your life. Your experience of all of those people is only in your mind. Your feelings about your lovers come from your thoughts. For example, they may in fact behave in ways that you find offensive. However, your relationship to them when they behave offensively is not determined by their behaviour, it is determined only by how you choose to relate to that behaviour."

THE MORE WE THINK ABOUT SOMETHING THE BIGGER IT GETS

It's difficult to change your paradigm when you have a certain view of something. There is a certain satisfaction in chewing over the bone, a certain security in staying stuck. Perhaps if you can't change your thinking completely, what you can do is not to feed it too much energy, that means not to think overly much about it. The more energy you invest in something the bigger it grows. Dyer also says, "What you think about expands." The more you dwell on that painful irritating person the more space they take up in your mind. The more we feed it energy the more it is kept alive and the bigger it becomes. Your thoughts are the food that feeds a situation. Eventually if you keep thinking about something it becomes obsessive thinking, or as it is also known in psychotherapy terms, stinky thinking. Women tend to be good at going over and over a particular situation in their minds and often find it difficult to let thoughts go, while many men seem to have an ability to switch off when they don't want to think of some issues, as many of us women will know to our cost.

Your thoughts feed a situation. The more you think about it the bigger it gets.

The flipside of being able to obsess about a problem is that if this energy is used creatively it allows us to create with energy, focus and excitement and will lift us up so that we can envisage and dream. However, if this same energy comes from fear, it will spiral us down and what we will be obsessing over will become some huge catastrophe. The obvious solution to the problem is to think about it so we can work out our plan of action but not over think it. The trouble for many of us is that the more we say I won't think about something the more our mind keeps returning to niggle away at it, giving it attention and energy. We may be able to have great mind control and be able to compartmentalise a problem and not think about it much at all, unfortunately, this isn't the answer either. The downside to that course of that action is if we do it with every problem, it is called denial, and while it may work in the short term it can all blow up later.

Another solution is to accept what is. The more we can accept something the more it loses energy and its hold on us. To do this, we need to acknowledge the situation but not judge it as right or wrong, it just is. This won't happen overnight, but the more we refuse to feed into it, the quicker it will go away. So, as the negative self-talk starts up, we become aware of it, acknowledge it's there and then shut it down, or change it. The step of acknowledging how we feel is very important. If we don't acknowledge it, it then becomes an issue of denial and slowly sinks into the unconscious to wreak its havoc. There is a certain peace in neither accepting, nor rejecting, just staying in that place in the middle. Imagine a situation where you think your friend is being a bitch. Your mind keeps saying, "She's such a bitch doing___. And each time it says this, you simply acknowledge it. "I know you are feeling she's such a bitch" Try it with a repetitive thought, just keep acknowledging without hooking into justification or blaming, simply acknowledging. Quite soon the thought loses its energy. It has been heard.

> Sue was finally able to do this with Barbara (latest references pages 213 and 286). Every time Barbara crossed her mind, she just acknowledged that she wasn't the daughter-in-law Barbara wanted, but that was the way it was and she didn't want to change who she was to please Barbara who, she felt, would never be pleased anyway. Little by little, Sue accepted that Barbara didn't like her and she couldn't do anything about it. She was able to detach emotionally while still being polite when they had contact for Mark's sake, although he knew exactly how she felt. A bit further down the track she was able to say to Barbara, "I'm sorry I am not the daughter-in-law that you wanted, I find your criticism of me hurtful and I would really appreciate it if you wouldn't criticise me to my face, so we can have a polite relationship for the sake of Mark and your grandchildren." She felt immensely better after she had finally said it and the relationship, although always somewhat strained, was quite affable. Eventually Barbara accepted Sue as she was, without trying to change her.

JUDGING

The judging of others is what causes us the greatest angst. It is in the judgement that we come to the conclusion that we are unhappy with that other person. Yet, the judgement is really about us. It defines where we are at when we look at a certain person or situation. It probably has nothing to do with the other person. They are defined by their own thoughts and actions. The Buddhists teach us that it is our own thoughts that cause our suffering. If we could allow others to be as they are, we would not continue to inflict ourselves with all this pain and anxiety. This teaching has been around for centuries, yet we still find it so incredibly difficult to do. The reason for this is, is that it links straight back into our own fears and our need to control. We think that if we can control, we can alleviate those fears. When we understand our fears and where they have come from, we have a much greater chance of letting go of our judgement of others. In judging others, you are judging yourself, and it is much easier to project your feelings rather than accept that, at this point in time, this is how you feel. It doesn't mean that those feelings won't change in due course. It is in that acceptance that you have already moved forward.

If we could accept others as they are and not judge them we would greatly reduce our own pain and suffering.

You are on your own path right now and we are not all at the same place at the same time. If we have a problem with another's eating, drinking, or smoking habits that is where they are at. We can reassure ourselves that others like us are doing the best they can, right now, with the tools they have got. As we each get more tools we can make different decisions and attain different outcomes. We don't have to process or judge negatively. We can say, they are doing the best they can right now, just as we are doing the best we can in judging this situation.

It is comforting to know that when you realise what you are doing, you already have more tools. Now you have a choice. In the case of the other person eating, drinking or smoking, you can ask yourself, Are they really doing it to annoy me, or are they doing the best they can? Am I judging their self-control and what does this tell me about my judgement and my self-control, what aspects of my secret self is this throwing up? Caroline Myss in her book *Sacred Contracts*, makes the point that, "If I don't know why I am acting in a negative fashion then it is easier to excuse my behaviour or blame someone else. But if I am aware both emotionally and intellectually that I am harming another being, I not only have to hold myself accountable, I must also admit that I consciously choose to be negative."

Maybe you feel you are being loving and caring telling others how to be and if you didn't tell them, you would be neglecting your duty. Remember that is how we were taught as children. Over and over again we were told what to do, until it was engrained and then we did not have to be told. Parents might tell us every night for years, brush your teeth, and then as we become older they may ask, "Have you brushed your teeth?" Eventually they stop asking because they know beyond doubt that we know that is what we should do. However, that happened when we were children, but we have learned so well that we think we need to continue that nagging behaviour all through our lives and all the while, under the delusion that what we are doing is showing love. Love would respectfully ask the other if our behaviour was helpful, or if they would prefer us to stop reminding them. *Happiness in a Nutshell* puts it beautifully when Andrew Matthews says, "Loving people means giving them the freedom to be who they choose to be and where they choose to be. Loving is allowing people to be in your life out of choice."

THE FAMILY SCENARIO

The above words are inspiring but where do they fit in a typical scenario such as this one?

> It is Saturday morning. Brian is going off to play golf, and Mum, Harriet, is taking the kids to sport. Brian gets up in the morning, doesn't offer to help make the bed, has his breakfast, leaving his dirty dishes on the bench-top, gets his golf gear, jumps into the car, and as goes he shouts, "See you later at lunch time, have a nice morning."
>
> Meanwhile, Harriet is seething. Not only does she have to clean up the breakfast stuff, but also make sure that James has both his soccer boots. She is also in charge of getting the oranges for the soccer team this morning. Jane has ballet, so Harriet drops her off first before getting James to his game, then sits and watches the nine-year-olds, all running this way and that after the soccer ball. Harriet realises that the game is running late because the coach insists on giving the team a pep talk and she will be late to pick up Jane.
>
> Harriet's stress and tension level is growing alarmingly. The Saturday morning traffic further exacerbates her lateness. Jane is really upset, and in picking her up, she berates her Mum, "Why can't James wait for a change, just because he is a nine-year-old baby? You are always going to James's game and never watching me and you are always late to pick me up. How do you think I feel waiting on the street corner, when all the other parents have gone? You don't even care." In an attempt to calm things down, and to appease James's appetite and thirst, Harriet stops at McDonalds on the way home. Arriving home, she sits down to read the paper, and Brian walks in. The first thing he wants is lunch, but the family has had McDonalds and

Harriet hasn't prepared the usual meal. Nor has she picked up his magazine at the newsagent on her way home as she promised. Tempers explode.

Brian has been working hard all week. He has had a trying week. His boss is particularly difficult because he is unhappy with Brian's performance. So Brian is really looking forward to his weekend at home with the family. He loves his golf on Saturday morning. Then, after a leisurely lunch he will sit down and read his golfing magazine, relax, swim in the pool with the kids and generally unwind. However, on arrival home there is no lunch, which Brian feels is unfair. His game of golf didn't go so well and he lost two balls in the water hazard, which really put him behind. Then Harriet hadn't even remembered to buy his magazine on her way home. This day is not turning out as he had hoped. He is mad and loses his temper.

Harriet tells him, "You are so selfish, you do exactly what you want when you want, and then expect me to pick up your stuff after you and run around cleaning up. You are forever pleasing yourself, never thinking of anyone else and the load I am carrying. You don't do your fair share with the kid's activities, yet expect them to be able to choose whatever activities they want, leaving me to do the fetching and carrying. You think I am some kind of servant or something, you have absolutely no idea of who I am, or that I might have needs and wants. You just expect me to do it all never complaining, and then get irritated when I'm tired and not interested in sex. Then you ask in that patronising way, what's wrong with me, implying that I am enough to try any man's patience, and lucky you are such a good natured sort of guy to put up with me. You have no idea how much I do and you've got it all wrong when you just say my life is easy. I'd like to see you do it."

> "Yeah well, I do think you do have it easy. You don't go out and work your guts out all week for some weirdo, who doesn't have a life except for work. It's not that difficult looking after two children, doing the house and the shopping. You at least can go out play tennis and have coffee with your friends. Imagine me doing that during the week. I only have two days off on the weekend, and most of the time I have to do jobs around the house. Yeah, I think you have it easy. You should see what the real world is like—". And so it goes on.

A MYRIAD OF CHOICES

It is easy to see both points of view. Harriet and Brian seem locked into their own judgements, but they could make a lot of different choices when looking at this scenario. Do they choose to try and talk about it so they can improve the situation? Or do they choose to ignore the whole incident, sulk for a while and then pretend it hasn't happened. Both can choose to deny the other's feelings, which is what many of us do and is disrespectful. We do not have a right to deny people their feelings, or to tell them they shouldn't have those feelings. Both can choose to listen to each other and hear what each says, or they can choose to walk away. If they decide to listen to each other, they can choose to hear how their behaviour is impacting on the other. They can choose to think about how they might modify their individual behaviour, or they can

We do not have a right to deny people their feelings or tell them that they shouldn't have those feelings.

choose to ignore it and say, it has nothing to do with me, it's your problem. We could surmise that Harriet's lack of sexual interest could be an unconscious using of one of her power cards. One partner may decide they have had enough and not want to talk, which will have a negative effect on the relationship. If enough such incidents occur that are never satisfactorily resolved, the relationship will inevitably sour and therein will come another choice. So, from a familiar incident for many people, there are a number of choices to be made and they all have an impact on what happens next. All choices have outcomes, results, consequences. The choices we make today determine how our lives will look tomorrow and the day after.

Now let's come back to deciding where those wonderful words about love being about allowing others to be as they are, fit into the scheme of things when we are trying to run busy lives and raise families.

Your journey

- Does any of this sound familiar to you?

- How would you deal with the above situation?

This book is primarily about choice. It is such a vitally important step in the journey of you becoming and being who you choose to be. You have choice every minute of every day and about everything, choice about what you think, how you think it and when you think it. Even if the choice is between a rock and a hard place, it is still a choice, and being able to choose which way to go is empowering. Usually, the harder the choice you have to make the greater the learning that eventuates. Even the negative thoughts you could welcome, instead of fighting or railing against them. You could choose to see them as gifts, opportunities to learn about yourself. In learning about yourself you are becoming aware, paying attention, and you grow more vibrant and alive.

Sometimes the concept of choice can be overwhelming.

- Can I trust myself to make the right choice?

- If you don't feel comfortable about making choices how much does that tell you about your level of self-esteem or self-worth?

Awareness and focus on choice is like setting goals. When you are aware of what you choose to think, or do, you are being creative and taking every opportunity to empower yourself.

THE STRUGGLE BETWEEN EMPOWERMENT AND DISEMPOWERMENT

Scott Peck, in *The Road Less Travelled*, talks about the feeling of impotency we experience when we give our power away. He says that sooner or later, if we are to be healed, we must learn that the entirety of one's adult life is a series of personal choices and decisions. If we can accept this totally, then we become free people. To the extent that we do not accept this, we will forever feel ourselves to be victims. The secret self side of victim or helplessness is empowerment. But empowerment can be scary. Where will it take you? What responsibilities will it entail? Nelson Mandela said in his inaugural speech,

> "Our deepest fear is not that we are inadequate,
>
> Our deepest fear is that we are powerful beyond measure,
>
> It is our light, not our darkness, that most frightens us.
>
> We ask ourselves, "Who am I to be brilliant?"
>
> Actually, who are we Not to be?
>
> You are a child of God.
>
> Your playing small doesn't serve the world.
>
> There's nothing enlightened about shrinking
>
> So that other people won't feel insecure around you
>
> We were born to make manifest the glory of God that is within us.
>
> It is not just in some of us: it's in everyone.
>
> And as we let our own light shine,
>
> We unconsciously give other people permission to do the same,
>
> As we are liberated from our own fear,
>
> Our presence automatically liberates others."

Your journey

- Do these lines feel uncomfortable to you?
- What would your life look like if you did not shrink?
- What specific areas in your life would change?
- Who would criticise you if you were fully yourself?

If they do, that is your unconscious at work. It wants to keep you safe, and to do that, we often need to play small. To be brilliant is too "out there," so it is disowned and often we go out of our way to cut down the tall poppies. Yet you can probably recognise the truth in "your playing small does not serve the world." And so your unconscious and your secret self is alive and well. Now with greater awareness and more tools at hand you have choice. You can make conscious choices, rather than having your unconscious make decisions based on your programming as a child, to be who you chose to be, right now.

The difference when making conscious choices, is that you are in the driver's seat of your life, not trapped as a blind passenger strapped in and powerless. Choices are always creative, they are thoughts and, as you know, thoughts create. The difference between you making conscious choices or letting life just happen, is the difference between a tram having to follow a predetermined track, over and over, and you being in a car and having the ability to choose and direct where you are going. You may still choose to use the same route as the tram, but you are not locked in.

A DIFFERENT CHOICE: SAFETY OR GROWTH

> Michele and Zola have been close friends for many years. They called themselves spiritual sisters. They felt they had lived past lives together as mother and daughter. Michele had been Zola's mother and in the relationship today, there were some vestiges of her taking care of Zola's emotional needs. Zola would at times lash out and make very patronising comments, which would hurt Michele deeply, but she chose to ignore them, thinking that if she said what she really thought it would have a shocking impact on Zola's emotional well being. She also felt, because of her spiritual knowledge, that she could handle Zola's temper tantrums. Inevitably, as time went on the resentment and hurt about these comments started to bubble to the surface and again Michele choose to ignore her discomfort, but she noticed that she was distancing herself from the relationship. Zola sensed this and angrily challenged her about it. Michele just shut down. Zola's anger was so powerful that she was speechless. Michele's silence enflamed Zola still more. She shouted, "It's always me doing the giving in this relationship and now things are going wrong you can't say a bloody word, well goodbye." Michele was devastated and deeply sad the relationship was over.

Here was her choice point. She could walk away, which after grieving would have been easier, or go back to Zola and try and get the relationship onto a different footing. The relationship as it was, had finished. She realised that in caretaking Zola's emotions, she had been protecting herself against Zola's anger. She also realised, that she had set herself up in a top dog position by assuming she was taking care of Zola. In many ways, Zola had every reason to be angry she was feeling devalued and diminished in some subtle unexplainable way. Michele was not respecting her ability to take care of herself, but neither of them were conscious of this at the time. Michele made the difficult decision, she decided to write to Zola and offer her hand in forming a new friendship. She had made an important choice and Zola still had a choice to make. If she could hear and accept Michele's apology and realise her part in the dynamic they set up, they would both learn, even if the relationship did not continue.

We make choices all the time without even realising it and those choices then make us who and what we are. As we judge situations or people to be good or bad, we are really making a statement about ourselves. Our judgement is about us, not the other person. It defines where we are. The other is defined by his or her thoughts and feelings. How you choose to see situations gives them the flavour they tend to have. If you look at them negatively, that's how you'll see them. If you look at them as opportunities to learn about yourself, a window into how you react, you will become more aware,

> We make choices all the time and those choices then make us who and what we are.

more vibrant and alive, the more difficult the choice, the greater the learning opportunity. But sometimes the concept of choice can be overwhelming. There is a weight of responsibility to make the right choice. Often we opt for safety rather than growth, as it is less scary. The greater your self-confidence and self-worth the more you will trust yourself to make the right choice. Our secret self, wanting safety often means there is a struggle between empowerment and disempowerment. We may like to think of ourselves as competent powerful people, but the fear of being seen and judged as too smart, too clever or a tall poppy is often enough to deter us from choosing to be who we really can be and are.

14 SELF-ACCEPTANCE

Self-esteem and self-acceptance are signs of personal growth, development, and maturity, but today it seems that many of us seem to suffer from a lack of both. In the past, psychological development seemed simpler. People had specific roles which they tended to stick to, a blacksmith was a blacksmith, he didn't change careers, the housewife largely stayed as a housewife throughout her life, and a farmer remained a farmer and for the greater part they seemed content. Although they were only using part of their potential, it seemed that there was no pressure to be more than they were. They had their place and were content to stay in it. Today we have the opportunity to use so much more of our potential, which leads to a richer but more complex life.

> *Self-esteem and self-acceptance are indicators of personal growth, development and maturity.*

Psychologically it is much more challenging as we struggle for balance and fulfillment. In many ways our self-esteem and self-acceptance seem much more fragile than a hundred or even fifty years ago, as we demand so much more of ourselves. Continual exposure to advertisements on how we can be better, more successful people adds to the pressure to be more than we already are.

Today personal growth and development comes when we feel confident about feeling what we feel and can make choices based on that information. This gives us a feeling of empowerment. Our self-awareness or inner consciousness is an extremely powerful force and its influence is present in every aspect of our life. It largely determines your happiness or unhappiness in life. It is an energetic force that we bring to bear when we imagine, or visualise attaining something, or conversely fear that we will not be able to achieve. Our faith and confidence are not only attitudes, but vibrations of energy. When we have confidence, the energy we emit pulls others along, it's like a motor boat going through the water, it leaves behind it a wake which rocks everything behind it. If we imagine ourselves as the motor boat, emitting a negative "I can't do it attitude", that is what our wake will be transmitting and people will sense. That's why self-fulfilling prophesies come true and are so self-destructive when they are negative, when a belief comes from the unconscious, this is what usually happens. It can stem from avoiding looking at what's uncomfortable or has become a repetitive pattern in your life.

With awareness comes introspection regarding our unconscious promptings and motivations. As we take responsibility for our feelings, thoughts and actions, we become aware of our responses to all those tiny day-to-day reactions and interactions. The greater our awareness of those responses, the greater the understanding of the "hows" and "whys" of our unconscious, the greater our ability becomes to respect and accept ourselves as we are, imperfect with warts and all. The imperfections are all a very necessary part of the process of our personal evolvement and need to be accepted.

They are part of the path we each walk and as we progress, we can look back and say, I have changed, I no longer look at this or that, in the same way. Without the "warts, " how would we know that we had made progress? We only know who we are, by knowing who we are not. Does that sound confusing? How do you know you are honest? You know, because you do not lie or steal.

ACCEPTANCE OF OUR SECRET SELF

Acceptance of self means acceptance of our secret self, which as we already know doesn't mean that we act out of our secret self characteristics. In fact, just like above, it is by not acting on it that we know who we are. We know we have the potential to kill but we choose not to become killers. We can say, "I am not a killer," yet if the worst came to the worst, we have the ability to kill if we needed to defend ourselves, which is a comforting thought. Likewise, with theft, we have all no doubt felt the temptation to shop lift, but by choosing not to engage in it, we know we are not thieves, yet if we were starving, we know we could steal a loaf of bread to survive. There is something reassuring in knowing we have the ability to do the "bad" as well as the "good." Sometimes the bad becomes good if we have to kill to survive, or steal to live. It comes back to the relativity of life, as we know it. There is no day unless we have night. There is no good without the contrast of bad.

> *Our imperfections are a necessary part of our personal evolvement and need to be accepted. Once accepted they will evolve and change.*

A vital part of self-acceptance is accepting where we are right now. Put another way, when we enroll our children in kindergarten we do not expect them to be at university entrance level, within the year. Yet that is so often what we expect of ourselves. We learn something new, which shifts our way of looking at things and then instantly expect that our behaviour, the result of decades of programming, will immediately change. When we are hard on ourselves we are not self accepting at all, we are judging harshly and finding ourselves wanting.

Whether consciously or unconsciously, we are all trying to improve ourselves, it is an innate human drive. So one way or another we will grow. When it is our clear intention we will grow faster and our personal work progresses. The clearer our intent the easier it is for the brain to get the message. The path of personal growth is always upwards, but it is a lifetimes work, and for many of the world's religions, many lifetimes. Accepting that, and accepting that the pace of our own growth, perhaps with two steps forward and at other times with a step backwards, is all part of the process and is reasonable. When we can accept where we are at, we can accept others for where they are at, and be respectful of where they are. They are learning different things in their journey toward becoming whole, just as we are learning what we need to become whole. Self-acceptance means respecting our own pace. There is an old Chinese saying that, "you cannot pull up the grass, it grows in its own time at its own pace." The same applies to each of us.

In our world of instant gratification this is hard. We do the self-help course and immediately expect to be fixed. This is our unconscious and our secret self telling us that we are not acceptable as we are, we are not safe. This is old programming. Our need to be "fixed" is our secret self not allowing for our imperfection. We come back to that question of balance, sitting in that place of tension between perfection and imperfection. It is reasonable to sit there in fact it is positively healthy. When our core motivation is toward growth and evolvement, perfection will come, not today, not tomorrow necessarily, but it will get closer as we become more and more self aware in the choices we make.

> *The more we respect and honor ourselves the more we will respect and honor others.*

The more we respect and honor ourselves, it stands to reason the more we respect and honor others. Mistreatment of others comes from mistreatment of ourselves, because we do not know another way of being. Until now your background has largely dictated how you "should" be. It is an interesting thought, that those people torturing others in jail will have a very low self-esteem, they will not value themselves much at all, if they did, they would not choose to do what they do. (Of course that is presupposing that they have choice in what they do.)

As we become more confident of our motivations and our intent, we will be able to call things as we see them. All we need to do is to tell the truth as we see and feel it. The trick is to preface what you want to say with, "I, " I feel, I believe, I see... because it is our perception of the story, it is not the whole story, but only a part of it. Furthermore, we are totally entitled to our opinions, just like everyone else is entitled to theirs. After hearing what each of us wants, we then have the freedom to make a choice as to what we want to do about it. Hopefully, the choices that we make are for the highest good of all including ourselves. If however, our choices are formed by our unconscious, reacting out of insecurity and defensiveness, they will not be made for the highest good of all. When we are unaware of our secret self, we can't be clear and true. We are well on the way to personal empowerment and personal fulfillment when we are aware that we want the highest good for all.

REVERSING THE PROGRAMMING

To truly accept ourselves is an enormous step. It is a complete change of the programming of decades. Since we were tiny toddlers we have been taught to look to others for our validation. After all, we knew we were acceptable when we were approved and loved. Now we need to largely reverse that indoctrination and start to give ourselves respect and approval, for who and what we are. The paradox is that while we crave the validation it makes us vulnerable to the criticisms of others, it undermines our sense of self. Validating ourselves makes us strong. That does not mean we don't listen to other's criticisms, but we don't allow ourselves to get overwhelmed by them. We listen and evaluate the truth in their words, we practice discernment between what others believe and who we believe we are and who we choose to be. Only we can truly validate ourselves, particularly as we make our mistakes. No one deliberately sets out to make mistakes. Mistakes happen because we don't know better, or don't think. Every day, as we gain more experience that scenario changes. When we clearly see the patterns underlying our mistakes we tend to do things differently. We know we may be far from perfect but we are trying, like small children on the way to adulthood.

This story illustrates how a seemingly insignificant incident actually contains major issues revealing that both Marie and Claus lacked trust in themselves.

> Marie picked up the camera in its bag that Claus had left on the floor, thinking this needed to be safely put away. She placed it on a high shelf but it seemed unstable. She gave it another shove and it stayed put. Walking away, she heard it crash to the floor. With sinking heart, Marie picked it up. She knew how precious Claus's camera was to him. The filter had smashed and there was glass everywhere. She emptied it in the bin, and wondered how she was going to tell Claus the bad news. Fortunately, the camera itself seemed intact. Marie decided she would lie to Claus and tell him the camera had tumbled from a very low shelf. He was annoyed about the incident but found the story incongruent. How had the metal filter ring got so badly bent after such a tiny fall? Marie then told a half-truth. She said she initially put the camera on a high shelf but she had caught it. It had slipped from her hands and hit the floor.

Why had Marie lied? Accidents happen. Marie was fearful that Claus would think that she didn't think and was careless, which was a frequently levelled criticism from her childhood; that she could not be trusted. Rationally, it does not make sense that because you have an accident, you are not trustworthy. But this touched an unconscious belief that Marie absorbed as a child, that she couldn't be trusted. Any implication that she has been careless and can't be trusted must be minimised at all costs, so if she lies it won't seem like she's been careless. We can see fear plays a big part in this incident. Fear of being found untrustworthy and at a deeper level inadequate. Even though Marie is a middle-aged adult, this belief formed in early childhood, is still at work. At some level, she believes herself to be untrustworthy, inadequate, and perhaps unlovable which could lead to rejection. That deep belief is dictating her actions, and she is acting like a child. If she was confident of herself, she would not need to lie, and although Claus would inevitably get angry she could tolerate that, knowing it would pass. She would also be able to accept that she could be more careful at times and would endeavour to do so without berating herself.

The change won't happen overnight just because she realises where it comes from. If she is persistent in monitoring her self-talk and making conscious choices it will come.

What does this incident reveal about Claus? His camera is precious to him. Leaving it on the floor was not an issue for him. He felt it was safe in its bag. What really irritated him was that Marie obviously lied to him about how it happened. The metal ring could not have become so badly bent in such a tiny fall. Why did she lie, why didn't she admit she made a mistake? He felt that Marie always found it extremely difficult to take criticism. She would never just admit she had made a mistake. She always had some excuse. She was careless, particularly when she knew his camera meant a lot to him. She had not thought when trying to put it on the high shelf where there was insufficient room.

Claus's anger came from his powerlessness to look after his possession, which in some way represents himself. When Marie doesn't look after his camera it raises the possibility that perhaps she hasn't got his best interests at heart. So two issues come up, not only did he feel out of control but also, at a much deeper level, probably largely unconscious, was a fear that maybe she didn't care enough about him to look after his possessions. Perhaps he couldn't trust her to do the right thing. Somewhere in Claus's conditioning he had learned it was not safe to trust, he needed to be in control, otherwise life was scary. It is probably an exaggeration to say that Claus could not trust, it is all a matter of degree, but even in such a small incident we can get an idea of the deeper conditioning at play.

Marie and Claus were mirroring similar core issues, although the routes down to them were slightly different. Both, at a very deep level could not quite trust the other, yet this was a deeply committed, happy marriage of over thirty years. The growth and learning this incident could give this couple is to see that they both need to learn to trust themselves. To realise they are acceptable and lovable as they are, without needing others to validate them. It wasn't about Marie getting her feeling of being trustworthy from Claus, because that would have been forever conditional on Claus's continual presence. It was about her knowing, in a deep part of herself, that when she made mistakes or when others criticised her that she could acknowledge it, without feeling she was inadequate or unlovable in any way. Nor was it in Marie's power to give Claus the control he needed so that he could trust others, his learning is that he can trust himself to handle whatever happens.

It is so important that we can validate ourselves and that we have the confidence to accept ourselves as we are. Then we don't need to resort to lies and subterfuge. Self-acceptance also allows us to withdraw projections and better still, not to project.

EMOTIONAL JAIL

A necessary part of the process of self-acceptance is to get out of emotional jail. What is emotional jail? It is the place many of us are in before we start uncovering and deconstructing the implanted beliefs we have about ourselves. In order to fully give ourselves the freedom to be who we choose to be, we need to give ourselves "a get out of gaol card." Virginia Satir talking about emotional gaol said, "We try to get out of it by begging, threatening or pleasing other people, trying to get them to do it for us… Most people lose their battles on the outside because they waste their energy on the inside. Our inner life and our outer coping are linked. One feeds into the other. As children, most of us were taught how to conform and to be obedient. Until we learned otherwise, that was all we knew. Whatever pain we had to endure to continue life, we took inside, believing that was how life was and thus began building the walls of our emotional gaol."

Unfortunately, there seems to be no short cut to the process of getting out of your own emotional jail. If you deny that you are in an emotional jail because it doesn't feel like that to you, your unconscious and secret self are in all probability still running your show. Getting out of emotional jail is not done overnight, but little by little. The doorway is to be aware of your uncomfortable, sad and unhappy emotions, then go back to when you first felt that similar type of pain. Thinking about that situation will give you the key to the belief you held about yourself, when the pain first happened. Screaming, shouting, fighting and resenting what happened, what belief you held about yourself, while being a necessary part of the process for a time, will change nothing. We can stay in that place of feeling those feelings, but ultimately they keep us trapped. The great energy depleters are hopelessness, helplessness, powerlessness, no possibility, no change and no choice, says Satir.

> "We betray ourselves in belittling our deepest hopes, values, ambitions and our story. We become less."

It seems that if we take this option of staying in the pain, we are compounding the original betrayal by our caregivers, with self-betrayal. As Jean Houston says in her book, *Search for the Beloved*, "We betray ourselves in belittling our deepest hopes, values, ambitions and our story. We become less." And that betrayal was then, not now. Yes, we were a victim of the mistaken belief we were given about ourselves, but now we are in a very different place. Rather than being powerless we are in a place of choice and self-empowerment. Because someone once mistakenly taught us that we were less than we are, doesn't mean that we continue to live our life based on that erroneous assumption. Perhaps now that we have more knowledge and understanding, that will change.

TRUSTING OURSELVES

Within betrayal there is always trust. Confusing though it may sound, out of betrayal trust can emerge. Trust that we can take care of ourselves and not allow the same things to happen again. We may fear that we'll fall into the same trap again and suffer betrayal in the same way, but the fear may be ungrounded, or we'll spot the warning signs earlier. It is in the acceptance that we move forward, knowing that we have learned, we have changed and we have gained wisdom. The scar is still there, it will never go away, but a scar is often a very strong part of our tissue. Having gone through our time in emotional jail, we are stronger and far better equipped than we were. Now we have choice. Our choice brings us the energy providers as Satir calls them, which are hopefulness, helpfulness, powerfulness, new possibilities, change and choice.

> Norma's sons love to climb, be it rock climbing or snow and ice, the more dangerous the better they liked it. Watching a movie about a mountain climbing adventurer who had a terrible accident, Norma could feel herself getting more and more annoyed. How selfish the boys are to do this ridiculous sport she fumed, they could kill themselves and then how would the rest of the family feel, and what about me, I've spent so many years getting them to this stage and all they want to do is risk their lives. It is just incredible selfishness. On reflection, Norma realised that her anger was covering her fear that they could get hurt and at a deeper level, her fear of how she would feel if one of them got killed. She suddenly understood that her wanting to

> stop them pursuing such a dangerous sport, was as selfish as their desire to climb. It had equal power. She chose not to reproach the boys for their sport, trusting that whatever happened she would be able to handle it, that she had the inner strength to cope, and that felt comforting. She liked the choice she had made.

EXTERNAL VALIDATION

While we look for validation from others we will always think we are not good enough. This is partly because we are still the focus for others projections, and may well fall short of their expectations. If others are projecting and expecting us to provide what they want, without communicating their needs, we are always on the alert. There is an expectation hanging over us that may not be verbalised, but is energetically communicated and we feel it. We may feel our boss's anxiety, or a friend's displeasure, yet because the need is covert, we may sit with a discomfort knowing that something is not quite right, but not sure what it is about. This discomfort, which is effectively anxiety, then eats away at our self-esteem. Our self-talk may go, "What's going on, have I done something wrong? I wonder if they are upset with me for something." A self-accepting healthy person may feel the energetic pull, but be confident enough to be able to detach, or check out with the other person if what they are sensing is correct. This way projection diminishes and is replaced with clear communication. Unless we have that strong sense of self, we will always run the risk of being someone else's puppet on a string. When our own self-respect and self-esteem is somewhat tenuous we take others' attacks as being valid and true, when they might just be projections.

The challenge is that only you can do the work of accepting yourself and thereby building your self-esteem. While you judge yourself against others, you will probably always fall short, because no matter where you look, there are always others out there that seem to be doing better than you.

There is another factor here too, that the more we change, often the more uncomfortable others feel around us, and the more they project this discomfort onto us in an unconscious attempt to get us to change back to how we were. At least how we were was comfortable to be around because it was familiar.

> Myra had a drinking problem which she was dealing with by attending AA (Alcoholics Anonymous). Her partner Edna always said she would be there to look after Myra (codependency), but when Myra started to change and become who she chose to be, she founded Edna's attentions restricting and irritating. For her part Edna felt rejected that Myra didn't love her anymore and she longed for the old Myra even with the drinking problem, because at least she was loved.

THE STEP IN FAITH

It seems that to fully accept and like ourselves as we are, we have to take a step in faith. We take a step in faith if we decide that there is a God, albeit called Buddha, Allah, Mohammed, Shiva, Christ and so on. We commit to the idea. In self-accepting we take a step in faith to honor and respect ourselves for where we are now. We consciously choose to think we are valuable people, in spite of what we may have been told in the past. This opens up choice, a choice to be who we choose to be. And who we choose to be, is made up of the minute-by-minute choices we make each day.

As said before, this path to true self-acceptance involves acknowledgement of the power of our unconscious and an acknowledgement and awareness of our secret self. Irvin Yalom says in his book, *The Theory and Practice of Group Psychotherapy*, "When we deny or stifle parts of ourselves, we pay a heavy price: we feel a deep, amorphous sense of restriction; we are on guard; we are often troubled and puzzled by inner, yet alien, impulses demanding expression. When we can reclaim those split-off parts, we experience a wholeness and a deep sense of liberation." We are no longer trying to hide anything from ourselves.

It really is all so beautiful, so simple and yet so complex. The greater the trigger, the greater the energy that resonates within us. The distaste, dislike, judgement or whatever the feeling, is exactly equal to the disowned secret self part of us. The greater the judgement around an issue, the exact same proportion is to be found in the disowned part of you. It is a closed loop. The extraordinary thing is, is that there is a gain for us in being harsh on ourselves. We are unconsciously giving ourselves permission to judge others and in that way, we displace our own anxiety about ourselves.

Judgement of others can be a projection of our own anxiety onto them. When we finally come to grips with that, we can let go of the judgement around the other person and look fairly and squarely at the problem within ourselves, understanding where it comes from. Even in the silent acknowledgement of it, the situation changes. With the release of judgement comes acceptance, which brings with it major personal growth and evolvement.

Self-acceptance is embracing the secret self, accepting the negative thoughts, not fighting them or trying to make them change, but loving them so that they can change. We can look at our negative thoughts with compassion, because really they are only fearful thoughts. Deep down they come from the unconscious child within us, needing reassurance and love. Low self-esteem comes from judging ourselves as inadequate, often because of what others have told us, as well as our own unrealistic expectations. It is all fear based. If you can reassure yourself, accept this is where you are at and nurture yourself, you will change your critical thoughts. You will recognise them for what they are, essentially fear, and using your respect and love for yourself, you will slowly transform.

Low self-esteem comes from judging ourselves as inadequate, often as a result of what others have told us.

Sanaya Roman says in *Spiritual Growth*, "Love all your thoughts, even those that are limited or fearful. Think of them as small children needing your love and reassurance. If you catch a negative thought, don't make yourself wrong for having it. Love all your negative thoughts and they will have far less power over you." This is then allowing the secret self aspects to emerge into the light, which makes them much easier to deal with, to come to terms with, and to accept. Negativity and the secret self, are not running your life, they are in balance, complimenting the positive and the light. You need both, the light and the dark, in order to highlight love and light. Acknowledge and embrace those negative thoughts and they lose their repetitive strident voice. Likewise, when we acknowledge that we have negative thoughts and love ourselves regardless, we are far less likely to project out the negative aspects onto others.

A low sense of self-worth keeps us locked into the blaming, judging and shaming cycle. When we realise we are worthwhile, but have made mistakes, we can start to move out of that negative destructive pattern that makes good connections with people more difficult.

Compassion is the key. When we can find the compassion for ourselves, we can forgive ourselves and move on. If we had known a better way, we would have used it. In understanding and reclaiming our secret self with compassion, we recover our lost parts, our riches, our gold. With that, not only do we become more whole and more healed, but we become more loving compassionate individuals. The moment we own both sides of ourselves we become true and authentic. As Jung says, "No tree can grow into heaven unless its roots also descend into hell."

SELF-ACCEPTANCE IN CONFLICT

There will always be periods when there is conflict in our lives, it is a basic condition of mankind as we wrestle between our instinctual drives for satisfaction and safety, and the forbidding environment of family and society. For most of us our innate desire is to avoid conflict, it triggers into our childhood fears. If there was conflict, we might be isolated, helpless and alone in a hostile world, our conditioning and our unconscious taught us to avoid it. Even in adulthood, we can go to great lengths to avoid the huge anxiety fights generate and in this way, we suppress our anxiety to make ourselves feel safe. However, for some others, conflict was an accepted way of life, but their challenge was to be stronger than their opponent because if they weren't, their anxiety would be triggered and they might be isolated and rejected. The core fears are the same but the paths are different.

> *Conflict is an opportunity for change and growth.*

Conflict is an opportunity for growth. Avoiding conflict is like denying ourselves the possibility of growth and self-development. Opposition is often crucial to the formation of our identity. Self-esteem and self-respect grow as we choose how we will handle a conflictual situation. We may choose to look at the argument as someone's projection, or it may be about us insisting on meeting our own needs. Conflict is always a power struggle. Are we trying to force others to do what we want or, are they trying to force us to do what they want? We will always have different needs from each other, how could we not, after all we are all different people. If we can accept those basic differences in each other, the conflictual situation can start to be resolved. Dr. Wayne Dyer once said, "Everything we fight only weakens us and hinders our ability to see the opportunity in the obstacle."

Our conflicts come usually when we insist that an issue be viewed one way, our way. When we can get out of our own way and try to see a win/win situation for all parties, then we greatly enhance our own sense of self-esteem. Conflict comes because we feel threatened, our security is the issue here and fear steps in. We do not trust ourselves to be able to handle a situation as it arises and safeguard our own interests, while looking for a good solution for the other person as well. If our attitude is to "get" the other person, we are again operating out of deep fear. Fear that we will be inadequate, and we need to get rid of this threat, before it gets rid of us.

If we can look fairly and squarely at the fear, we increase our self-esteem and self-worth, we trust ourselves to be able to take care of ourselves. We see choices and opportunity instead of negativity. We trust ourselves to be able to follow our own road map, which is forever changing as we gain more information and become more empowered. This self-acknowledgement is essential to growth. The solutions to our problems lie within the problems themselves. It is the way we look at them. If we are capable of recognising our own problems, we are capable of solving them. We need to trust ourselves to do that.

WE ARE ROSES

The famous US poet, essayist and lecturer Ralph Waldo Emerson once said, "These roses under my window make no reference to former roses or better ones; they are for what they are; they exist with God today." We are those roses, who and where we are today, right now, is exactly who and where we need to be in this journey of ours. As we grow and understand more, our blooms open up more, we can reveal more of our true colours, and release more of our perfume into the air. Thus we evolve into who we want to be. The more we accept ourselves and honor ourselves, the safer we feel to do this. We recognise that we are different from others, but that we are interdependent as human beings. We respect ourselves and others while respecting the differences between us. We cannot do this unless we have the confidence in ourselves and in our fundamental right, to be who we choose to be, at any given time. The paradox is that the more we honor and respect ourselves, the more others honor and respect us. Polarity and ambiguity seem inherent in life, and these are key ingredients in this process of self-acceptance. Instead of external validation, we need internal validation, and in honoring and respecting ourselves, others will follow suit. We teach others how we want to be treated.

RECLAIMING YOURSELF

When you embrace all the parts of yourself fully and all of you is waiting to be embraced this very second, you can live with anyone you choose. You will be strong enough to stand in your own truth, being able to hear what others say about you without reactivity and be able to decide how you want to react in that situation. With a strong sense of self you will enjoy greater intimacy, as you will be confident that you will not get submerged or subsumed by another. You will have reclaimed yourself.

When you can challenge yourself to truly know what you desire or need, when you can ask the questions that most of us avoid asking because the answers may mean changing your life, you are reclaiming yourself.

When you choose to look at everybody that you find difficult in your life, without moaning and becoming a victim, but as people who each have something to offer, you become empowered, which changes your life dramatically. This is the beginning of spiritual maturity.

We start life as the picture on the jigsaw; beautiful and complete. Then we become fragments or pieces as our social programming comes into play, combined with our own natural characteristics as we meet challenges and oppositions. When we embark on our personal growth we spend the rest of our life reassembling the jigsaw, getting to know ourselves intimately, hopefully to end up with a clear picture again. Yet we could never know how amazing and complex we really are, unless we had split into lots of pieces. The beauty of it is that as we recognise our own abilities and complexities we also see the same in others. We must fall from innocence, so that we can return to it on a more sophisticated and less childish level. The picture on our jigsaw is ever evolving reflecting who we are.

We need to trust in ourselves because we will be challenged. We may not get it right the first time but we will get it right, and our actions will reflect who we choose to be. It is already embedded within us, we only have to recognise the old programming and clear it out of the way. It's like cleaning out all the old junk that has been dumped into a room in the house over decades and suddenly finding that the room has lovely proportions, but we never saw it before because it was always such a dumping ground. Now we can throw out the junk and use the room to its best advantage.

15 THE SPIRITUALITY OF OUR RELATIONSHIPS

All through this book the journey has been about you. Learning how you live with yourself, learning the cost of the difficult relationships, learning about your secret self, learning how your unconscious was programmed, what effects its programming has had on you, how you can recognise and harness its power, what you need in order to have healthy respectful relationships and finally, how the awareness of all this information can dramatically impact your relationships. We've understood that because we are naturally egocentric, we bring everything back to ourselves. Now contrary to what we have been doing up to this point, instead of it all being about you, let's think of the other person in this trying dynamic. Unlike you, he or she probably thinks the problems are all your fault. In all probability, the difficult other doesn't have the awareness and the knowledge that you now possess about the power of the unconscious, they are still in the blaming stage and quite possibly projecting their irritation onto you. Instead of a knee jerk response, you now have a much greater understanding of what is probably going on for them, and can stand back and not be hooked into the friction so easily. Instead of the issue being all about you, it becomes all about them.

It seems a crazy contradiction that before you do the self-work it is all about you but when you have the self-confidence, self-esteem and critically important, the self-awareness to be able to stand back, you realise that the remarks others make about you may have much more to do with them, than with you. Because we are the center of our own universe, we automatically tend to bring comments, gestures, disparaging looks and so on back to ourselves and take offense. Having done all the work that you've done, you can see that the comments that others make about you, has probably as much to do with them, as they ever had to do with you and hopefully, you can be less reactive and more able to stand back and evaluate their comments. There is probably always a vestige of truth in what they say, remember the expression if you spot it you've got it, at least a modicum of it, but largely people will be coming from their own perspective, which means it is more about them than it is about you. This all seems paradoxical compared to the first page of the book when I said it is all about you, not them. It's almost impossible for us not to make it about ourselves, but when we don't immediately jump to conclusions, we are much more able to detach and observe with compassion and understanding.

> *With self-awareness you realise that remarks others make about you often have more to do with them than you.*

We can probably now see that there is always something of value, usually great value, for us in those difficult, painful, tortuous relationships. The greater the angst and irritation, the greater the rewards and sense of connection when we finally understand and accept each other. Sometimes it seems we need a miracle to even look at that most exasperating loathsome other and see anything of value in them at all. What we really long to do is walk away as quickly as possible, to forget that we ever had contact with them, to wish we could erase all memory of them. The strength of our emotions is the key to how much there is for us to learn. The trick is to be able to see what lies beneath that feeling, to identify if it is a lesson, a submerged grief or perhaps some other unidentified emotion, maybe a joy yet to emerge. But know that beneath the cover of anger, exasperation and irritation there is nearly always ground that can be recovered, as long as the other person is willing to participate in the exploration. Sometimes that is not possible, but unfailingly there is valuable information there about you, understanding how and why you are triggered. If you have spent sufficient time exploring your reactions, you will have a very good idea of what it is about.

With the knowledge you now have, you can change your frame of reference and imagine how the monstrous other's life has been, and try to walk a mile in their moccasins, as the expression goes. If you choose, you can find something they do or did, that is admirable. It is easy to dwell on the bad; but can you focus on what they have done right? You know you needed to go through this period of conflict, blaming, judging, hating and maybe shaming to learn about yourself. Now you understand that your judgement of others is equal to the judgement that you unconsciously direct toward yourself, but may project out. Usually it keeps you quite stuck, damaging your health, eroding your vitality and life force, until you forgive yourself, recognise your secret self, and take responsibility for your actions. In this different place, the energy feels somehow cleaner and fresher, as if the wind had blown through and cleansed the hurt and frustration, maybe leaving a sense of peace and perhaps stirrings of hope that it is not too late, things can change.

> *Your judgement of others is equal to the judgement you unconsciously direct towards yourself.*

When you stop blaming yourself and others, you become receptive and reflective. You can question what underlies this conflict. You can let go of your need to be right. Reflection is a gateway to psychological health and spiritual maturity. It takes the energy out of blame, it allows you to transcend it, and in the acceptance and understanding, the growth has already happened.

WE ALL SPEAK DIFFERENT LANGUAGES

Every relationship is an opportunity for growth. There is always a challenge for us. Inevitably, we see material in others that we don't like, even in those that we love most dearly. Everything we see in others we can see in ourselves to some degree, even if we are determined to do the opposite because we hate it so much. For example, you hate your mother's advice giving, because you feel she doesn't think you can do it by yourself. Consequently, you are determined not to give others advice in case they think the same thing. This is a trigger for you and so you spend considerable energy guarding against giving advice. While you are intent on not giving advice, there is negativity at play. It is as if each time you desist from giving advice you are criticising your mother's behaviour. Yet your mother's advice giving may be her way of saying, "I care and therefore I want to help you by giving you this advice." If you could ask her if she thinks you are incapable because that is how her advice giving makes you feel, what do you think her response would be?

Our wishing another would change, holds us stuck in negativity and resentment. When we can move past it to a place of deciding that maybe it's her way of saying she cares or, she is doing the best she can with the tools she has at this very moment, we are showing her respect and giving ourselves the gift of moving on, freeing ourselves from stuckness, loosening rigidity. When we feel angry or threatened a lot of the time, we know we are not living as we wish to. Every time we can give ourselves the gift of moving on, knowing that we can't change others, only ourselves, we are giving the world a gift, we are freeing up trapped negativity allowing it to escape and transform.

The world becomes just a little bit more peaceful.

We each have a different way of communicating the simple message, I care for you and your well-being, as Ruth Ostrow says in one of her articles in *The Australian* newspaper. Some may give advice, some may cook a magnificent meal, or maybe not magnificent, but ensures there is always food in the house and cooks simple meals almost every day of the year. What's that action really saying? Others may check the oil in your car, which you could interpret as you are not capable of looking after your own car and they have to do it for you, but equally it may be their way of saying, I care and I'm trying to show you that in practical ways. Your clothes may always be washed, or you may be reminded of your dental appointments or to do this or that.

Your journey

- What ways do you use to show people that you love them?

Some of us may feel these type of actions are interfering. They may feel others are treating them as children and in some way defective, unable to look after themselves properly. Other people will talk about the latest sports results and that may be their way of trying to establish contact. Watching football games or other sporting events, there is a great sense of connection between people when they are barracking for the same side. They are communicating with each other at a different level, which allows some sense of intimacy, yet does not get gooey or sentimental. The emotional connection is covered by the oohs and aahs of the game.

Many people are too vulnerable to show their loving emotions toward others openly, so the language they use may not be words but actions. Unfortunately when the relationships are tense, these actions can be interpreted as controlling, manipulative, interfering, everything they are not designed to be. We ascribe our own meanings to the actions and they may not be what the other intended. Many of us can only see others through our own eyes, our particular lenses, and that is how we interpret what we see and hear. It all starts with you, which can really complicate intimacy.

> **Your journey**
>
> - When you reflect on that trying other is it possible that what most turns you off is perhaps their way of communicating that you matter to them?
> - Is it just that you both talk different languages?
> - If you put yourself in the difficult other's moccasins what would they say about you?
> - How do they interpret your particular language or code of giving and caring?

Perhaps there was an element of that in Barbara, (page 321) the mother in law from hell, who was fearful that Sue might end up in the divorce court if she didn't take care of Mark properly, and she didn't want that for either her son or daughter-in-law, so her way of coping with that anxiety was to find fault with Sue. Tom's need to control the activities of his household, was a way of containing his anxiety and his need to keep his family safe (page 193), but his language of caring somehow became distorted. If you can eliminate or suspend your own suspicion, which gives us a guarded judgmental approach to life, until you can check it out, can you view their actions differently?

> Early in the morning, Carmen was lying in bed looking out at her garden when suddenly a crowd of sulphur-crested cockatoos decided to attack her tubs of geraniums. She charged out of bed, nightie flapping, rushed past the bottle recycling bin, grabbed two large plastic bottles and proceeded to bang them together with great energy, to make the loudest noise she could at a moments notice. She was desperately trying to frighten the cockatoos away from her geraniums, which they were decimating at alarming speed. No sooner was one new young tender shoot broken off, but another immediately followed. Within moments the ground was littered with succulent young twigs, and months of valiant work by the geraniums, forced to endure drought one week or flooded the next, was wasted.

The paradox is that nature produces such seemingly willful destruction combined with such painstaking slow work, and it all makes up the whole. Like the volcano erupting destroying centuries of vegetation. Yet before Carmen had reflected, she made the judgement that the cockatoo's behaviour was unacceptable, and in that judgement assumed that destruction is not OK. Yet paradoxically, re-growth does not come without destruction, as we see so clearly with bushfires in Australia. As Carmen works toward her integration, she has had to destroy the foundations of much of her old thinking. Survival strategies that served her well, are slowly discarded replaced with strong new growth, the cockatoos gave her a gift of realisation, in the ruthless indiscriminate pruning of her geraniums. Sometimes it might behoove us to look at those teeth grinding relationships and decide to prune the outdated beliefs or, look carefully to see what language the difficult others are using. Are we limiting our opportunity for connection because we have already predetermined the outcome?

BLAMING OTHERS INDICATES A LACK OF SELF-WORK

This sounds harsh but unfortunately, it is largely true. The degree to which we blame others is the degree of self-work that we have not done, i.e. the more we blame others, the less work we've done on ourselves. That can be a somewhat scary thought. Change is not an easy matter. As Scott Peck says, "Integrity is never painless and reformation is not an easy matter. It is a matter of discipline." The discipline is being aware that we have choice and don't immediately blame or find fault. When you are feeling reactive and about to blow your stack, a useful exercise is to think of a set of traffic lights. When you are mad and just want to react, the lights are red, so that instead of reacting, you try and force yourself to stop. The orange light is about thinking what is really going on here. The green light is OK, you are aware of your choices so now you can make an informed decision, as to how you will react. However, if we think that in each and every obstacle or circumstance there is an opportunity for growth, then we might choose to view it differently and it becomes a challenge. Instead of looking at things negatively, it is a challenge to see the trying situation or person in a positive way. A way that can teach us things about ourselves and a way that we could choose to see as an opportunity for our spiritual development.

DETACHMENT

We know that our suffering comes from our preferences, our wanting to have things our way and not allowing others to be, just as they are. Unconsciously, we continually want people to be as we want them to be in order to redress our childhood wants. Are we like the monkeys in the following story?

For centuries the Indians have used an ingenious trick to snare their prey. They hollow out a coconut shell and carve a hole in the center with sharp teeth around the opening. They secure the shell to the ground, fill the coconut with some delicious bait for the monkey and wait. The monkey arrives, puts his hand into the shell, seizes the bait but cannot withdraw his hand because the sharp teeth cut into him. The monkey could release the bait and then he would be free, but he doesn't. He will sit, screeching with pain and rage, beating at the shell, but he will not let go of the bait. Eventually the monkey catchers come and take his skin. In many ways, we are similar to the monkey. We are often desperate to get others to change and go to great lengths to get resolution, but on our terms. It is not then surprising that we get angry and frustrated, letting go of our wanting is an important aspect of growth.

> *Unconsciously, we continually want people to be as we want them to be in order to redress our childhood wants.*

Many spiritual masters have said that the key to genuine happiness is to be detached in the midst of action. The detachment is practiced by observation, without being fixated or preoccupied with the outcome. We need to let go of the outcome. If despite our good efforts, the most difficult person in our life doesn't want a bar of us, or the changes we want them to make, we need to accept that and let it be. We need to console ourselves with the fact that we have tried, but not get caught up in the struggle, we walk away. It is highly likely, that in the disengaging of the power struggle, the dynamics of the relationship change and, that might be the prompt that starts change in the other. On the other hand, it may not and that is, as it is.

Total respect for somebody's opinion or their viewpoint, is actually spirituality in its truest form. When we can recognise and accept another person's truth, that is spirituality. If we don't like that truth, we have the right to question it or ask for clarification, not in an aggressive way but gently, so we can seek understanding for ourselves. Their truth may be very different from ours, but that is OK because it is not about us.

COMMUNICATION, CURIOSITY, COMPASSION, AND INTEGRITY

Honest communication combined with curiosity and compassion, is the most common way to resolve problems. Curiosity is always a useful tool, and particularly helpful in opening the box on the difficult relationship. Inquiring into why others are thinking the way they do, is automatically communicating that you are emotionally engaged. True curiosity, allows for the momentary suspension of our judgement and enables a sense of sharing, a sense of connectedness. The compassion comes because by this time, you are hopefully able to be compassionate toward yourself. Unless there is honest communication, there is little hope of evolving past conflict

Curiosity is a useful tool for opening up difficult relationships.

and there is no personal or spiritual growth. Our tools for spiritual growth are physical, emotional, energetic and verbal communication. Energetic communication includes body language which tells us a lot about what is going on, even when the words are telling us a different story, or particularly when the words are not matching the message we are receiving. Social scientists tell us that some 70% of the messages transmitted in face-to-face communication, is nonverbal. Therapists are taught to pay attention to how they are feeling about their client, because that will give them an indication of what feelings the client elicits from others, and how he or she operates in the world. It is in being able to express our feelings honestly and with integrity, ask others for clarification if we are not sure what they mean, that we then start to be able to lead authentic lives. Integrity demands that we experience the tensions of competing demands and conflicting ideas. Integrity doesn't allow us to compartmentalise.

When we feel stress, pain, friction or tension, we may tend to compartmentalise. We may want to stick the difficult situation into a box and try to shut the lid. This way we can get on with our lives and try not to think about it. But as we have learned, sooner or later the lid starts to come off the box and all those uncomfortable feelings seep out, which gradually contaminates our being and our interactions. In becoming aware we try to avoid compartmentalising and learn to live with integrity, which means facing and dealing with the secret self. We know to do that, we need to have a healthy sense of self-confidence and self-esteem, which many of us, up to now, have lacked. Most of us have probably been secretly terrified of admitting that we like ourselves, in case others think we are "up" ourselves, Yet, I'm sure I'm not wrong in saying that, we all secretly crave to have others tell us that they can see our goodness, love and compassion. Many Easterners look at this concept of lack of self-worth and find it difficult to understand. It does not underpin their religious traditions in the same way. In Buddhism, there is an unshakeable belief in one's own goodness, love and compassion.

SPIRITUAL MATURITY

Spiritual maturity seems to be a natural byproduct of self-esteem and self-acceptance. When we can truly respect and love ourselves for where we are at, we have more respect and love for others. The two inevitably go hand in hand. The Dalai Lama puts the concept of self-love in an interesting way. He says in his book, *The Art of Happiness* that if we think that the most exalted form of love for another, "is the utter, absolute and unqualified wish for the other's happiness regardless of whether he does something to injure us or even whether we like him. Now, deep in our hearts, there's no question that every one of us wants to be happy. So, if our definition of love is based on a genuine wish for some one's happiness, then each of us does in fact love himself or herself – everyone of us sincerely wishes for his or her own happiness."

He also talks about how gifted we are as human beings, with a wonderful intelligence and by reflecting on our opportunities and potentials, we will be able to increase our sense of worth and confidence. Furthermore, we have the capacity to be very determined and can direct that strong sense of determination in whatever direction we want.

Inspiring words that bring us back to the choice we have of how we look at things. All our relationships reflect back to us a mirror of how we conduct ourselves. Spiritual relationships do not judge and blame. They are co-creative experiences in which each person takes responsibility for their choices and decisions. Each expresses his or her desires, says what they choose to say, be whom they choose to be and gives the other the freedom to do exactly the same thing. In this way, all choices are made very consciously. This full consciousness or awareness, as well as bringing freedom, is like a psychological immunisation or inoculation. There are no victims or martyrs, and relationships offer us a wonderful opportunity to express and fulfill who we really are. These are true and wonderful concepts but not easy to put into practice.

INTIMACY

Intimacy may be the last thing you think you want from the ghastly other but the greater the reactivity, the greater the potential for reconciliation and yes, even perhaps intimacy. After all, it would be logical to assume that at some deep level, you wanted resolution and some degree of connection, otherwise why did you buy this book? Presumably, you hoped it might enable you to find some answers.

Connection and intimacy brings aliveness, but can be dangerous and messy, and let's face it, love and connection with each other is messy. No relationship is ever totally straight forward, as you well know. It will inevitably have its ups and downs and the deeper and more intimate it becomes, the bigger the mess we can get into. However, to put a positive spin on this, the bigger the mess the greater the rewards.

Intimacy comes after knowing how you feel and what you need, and being able to drop your defenses and tell your truth. This leaves you exposed, but if at the same time you can hear another's truth, that's when connection happens. To gain intimacy you risk loss, you risk exposing your inner secret self and that may be used against you, the greater the risk the greater the gain. True intimacy comes when we don't expect to get anything from the other person, we don't expect them to keep our secret or safeguard us in any way. We are telling them how we feel because that is what we wish to do, not with any reciprocal expectation. We can trust ourselves to be able to handle any back firing that may occur due to our openness. We can trust ourselves to be able to look after ourselves even if the other person misuses our intimate disclosure. That is where they are at and is no reflection on us. Intimacy is the expression of a spiritual connection, we are giving out of the best part of ourselves. We are not giving to get, which would then make it conditional.

> *Intimacy comes when you know how you feel and what you need, and then being able to drop your defenses and tell your truth.*

UNCONDITIONAL LOVE

Many of us have been brought up with conditional love. If you do the right thing by me, I will give you love and acceptance. As children, we generally experienced love by getting approval and we couldn't differentiate between the two. Many of us in our adult lives still confuse conditional love with conditional approval. We receive unconditional love when others have respect for us, even if they don't agree with what we are doing and may say so, but nevertheless respect our need to do what we choose. We may not get unconditional approval, but we could easily have love and maybe not recognise it for what it is.

When we give unconditional love we can clearly see the flaws of the other, but accept them as part and parcel of who they are, we are not fearful of risking intimacy. When people can be loved for who they are, they can then feel less fearful of changing aspects of themselves. None of this happens overnight, just as we may not necessarily be able to accept and love unconditionally overnight.

Mature love is able to tolerate the personality differences we all have. Mature love can see the soul beneath the flotsam and jetsam of our personalities. It can see the essence of love that we all are, and can if we choose, transform the interpersonal difficulties and differences that we have. We can accept that we are different because somebody does not agree with us, it doesn't necessarily mean that is about us, it could be about the other person. One of the problems is, that we are naturally egocentric, so we bring things back to ourselves and feel that comments that people make are somehow directed at us, when in all probability the truth is different. Just as we've learned how and why we bring everything back to us, we can now apply this learning to others. The comment that stung you is probably reflecting something about the person that delivered it, and we now have the choice of either taking it personally, checking out what the other meant, or think, "hang on this probably has nothing to do with me." This is a huge leap to make because our egocentricity seems to be hard-wired into us and we automatically bring everything back to us, when in fact, it may have little to do with us, except that in some way we act as a trigger for the other.

Part of our spiritual maturity is to turn our need for love and approval, into a desire to give love with an awareness of our capabilities. Therefore, we keep the glass full and give from a place of being filled ourselves. The stronger we become within ourselves, the more we start to view others with curiosity and a desire to find about who they truly are. As you uncover who they are, they will reflect aspects of you back to yourself, and lives become richer. Relationships are the raw material that after a long process of sorting, shaping, transmuting and transforming, can be turned into gold. We tread a fine line between excitement, danger, fear or peace and fulfillment in our relationships. It is only in this continual juggling of choosing to be who we are, that we grow in love and self acceptance. It is in our interdependency and the challenges that we present to each other, that allow us the opportunity to evolve.

PSYCHOLOGICAL HEALTH IS THE GREATEST GIFT WE CAN GIVE THE PLANET

An Indian holy man once said, the greatest gift we can give the planet is a healthy you, this is undoubtedly true. What is psychological health? Dr Abraham Maslow, the twentieth century father of humanistic psychology, says in his book *Toward a Psychology of Being*, that a psychologically healthy person is naturally motivated to achieve a state of self-actualisation, "An ongoing actualisation of potential, capacities, talents as fulfillment of a mission (or call, fate or vocation) and….as an increasing trend toward unity, integration, or synergy within the person." He goes on to say, "A musician must make music, an artist must paint, a poet must write if he is to be at peace with himself. What a man can be, he must be. This is the need we may call self-actualisation...It refers to man's desire for fulfillment, namely to the tendency for him to become actually in what he is potentially: to become everything that one is capable of becoming..." There is considerable overlap between this and the survey by the American Psychological Association (page 198).

When you are integrated you acknowledge and embrace your secret self, are able to take responsibility for yourself and your actions, can communicate honestly, are aware of your projections, and strong in your belief and respect for yourself, you are psychologically healthy. You can stand with your own integrity, aware of your needs, aware of how much you can ask of others and hold the tensions of competing demands and conflicting ideas with some composure, knowing that you are trying to do the best you can. You can, if you choose, live with anyone. What a gift you are to the world.

As a rule, if we are psychologically healthy, our biology generally follows suite.

RELATIONSHIPS ARE A SPIRITUAL PATH

We know that if we want to follow a spiritual path, our relationships are the one sure way of doing that. In ancient times, people went into monasteries and nunneries and took vows to follow a mystical path. In that spiritual environment, they tried to become more loving, more compassionate people.

Today, we do it in coping with our busy, stressful lives and making our relationships work. It is by far the greater test of our spiritual faith. We do not have the discipline of the monastic life behind us, so it is so much more difficult to stay focused on who and what we aim to be, and to be conscious of the choices we make. Those of us making those choices "are modern day mystics without monasteries" as Caroline Myss says in her book, *Sacred Contracts, Awakening the Divine*.

VITAL TOOLS FOR THE MODERN DAY MYSTIC

The vital tools for modern day mystics are respect, compassion, self-honesty, awareness or consciousness, and the greatest tool of all, choice. Although relationships are our vehicle for spiritual growth, it all starts with us and our compassion and respect for ourselves. From this springs everything else.

When we can respect other's differences, without trying to change them, we truly have respect and our spiritual evolvement can progress in leaps and bounds. When we make others wrong, we are not showing spirituality, in fact we make ourselves less, because we're right and they are wrong. Sometimes when we have been deeply hurt, it is easier to cope with our hurt by making others wrong. It allows us to cover our pain with righteous indignation. We will each have suffered, felt wronged, ignored, or denied at some time and if we dwell on the injustice, it allows us to safely ignore the part that we have played in setting up this dynamic in the first place. If we can feel the compassion, both for ourselves and for others, if we could forgive ourselves for being wrong, we would find it so much easier to forgive others.

REJOICE IN THE DIFFERENCES

There is a saying that, "There are as many gates to paradise as there are human hearts." If we think of the differences that those human hearts represent, it makes for a hugely diversified universe. In fact, if we rejoice in the differences, they make up the excitement and the joy of life. Imagine if we were all dressed the same, walking down the street, or we all drove exactly the same car, or thought exactly the same thoughts, how utterly dull that would be. The differences stimulate us and prompt us to find our own style and be our own person, not merely clones of one. Seeking to understand the differences is one of the core tenets of spirituality.

There is a paradox in knowing that all our basic needs are exactly the same; to be loved, accepted, validated, and yet at the same time marveling at the differences within everyone, and how we all manifest our need for those things in such a diversity of different ways. The more you see, the more you understand and the more that is revealed, the more you can give back. It is in the giving back that we find true fulfillment. It is in the doing for others, with a very real regard for meeting our own needs first that we gain. If we expect others to meet our needs at the same time as we are giving, we are not truly giving in the purest sense of the word. True giving is giving with no attachment to gratitude, appreciation or pay back. It is not, if you scratch my back I will scratch yours, which is how much of the world gives. When we give with no thought of pay back we are also giving to ourselves. We give ourselves the gift of knowing we are giving in a true spiritual sense.

It is in the acceptance of ourselves and others that spirituality comes. Maybe the words spirituality and respect could be used interchangeably. Perhaps they are one and the same thing. In this acceptance is the evolvement of the soul. On our soul journey we are all going to the same place of compassion and understanding. Some of us are further along the track than others, just as people are chronologically older or younger than us, but where we are at along the track, doesn't matter. We will all get there in our own good time. It is as inevitable as the fact that we were all born and we will all face death.

The paradox to come to terms with again, is our interdependency and our separation. We all need others and at the same time we must accept that we are fundamentally alone. There is a continual interplay of dependency and independence in our lives. It is the existential struggle of aloneness, yet the dependency of the spirit. Again, it is the juggle of the two polarities, which is all part of the whole. The mystics tell us that it is the same with us humans, we are separate and yet together, and at another level again we are all one and the same.

> "*Enlightenment is taking responsibility for your actions.*"

Spirituality is also about seeing the divine in others. Sometimes it is easier to see the divine in others rather than ourselves. Buddha urged us, "to see our original face" and in that original face see the hand of God. That has nothing to do with deserving or working to deserve, it is how we have been created, it is who we are. If we are children of God, as all the religions teach, then each and every one of us is surely magnificent. By denying that, we do ourselves and others a grave injustice. It seems it is like denying that a Rolls Royce is a special car or that a diamond, is no more valuable than a piece of glass. We can trust that we are enough, because like everyone else, we are special. Somehow, in acknowledging the powerfulness of who we are, we acknowledge the responsibility that accompanies it. The one is part and parcel of the other. The greater the acknowledgment of our divinity, the more we have to take full responsibility for ourselves.

"Enlightenment is taking responsibility for your actions," says Wayne Dyer. There is a Zen saying that goes, "Before enlightenment, carry water chop wood, after enlightenment carry water, chop wood." So, if enlightenment is to take responsibility for our actions then we will need commitment, discipline and the courage to take the necessary steps to change and grow, for they are a life time's work. The more we can accept others the more others will be able to accept yet more people, and the outward ripples of this acceptance get bigger and bigger. That is part of "the continuous circulation of spiritual energy into the world", to coin Joseph Campbell's phrase.

The greatest gift you can give yourself is an unconditional belief in yourself, and the greatest gift we can give the world is to become self-aware and take responsibility for our feelings and actions. So your greatest gift to humanity, is a healthy you. In becoming aware, we know if we are operating out of love or fear. When we transcend the fear and our unconscious reactions and choose to operate out of a paradigm of love, we are being spiritual. I pray that you will agree and we can all work together on this vision toward respect, love and acceptance.

APPENDIX

SOME COMMON PERSONALITY DISORDERS

It is important to emphasise that the following descriptions are very sketchy. As mentioned on page 59 if you feel either you or the difficult other may fit a particular disorder it will be important to seek professional help, which is readily available.

Eileen continually needs her husband to make all her decisions for her. At the beginning of the relationship this made him feel important and he wanted to make all the decisions. But a few years down the track he feels shackled by the enormous weight he carries and completely frustrated that even the simplest things turn into decision-making dramas. Eileen suffers from a Dependent Personality Disorder, which is a pervasive and excessive need to be taken care of. It leads to submissive, clinging behaviour and sufferers have a fear of separation. This is one of the most frequently reported personality disorders encountered in mental health clinics.

These people have a need for others to assume responsibility for them that goes beyond appropriate age and situational requests for assistance from others, for example, the specific needs of children, elderly or handicapped people.

All of us at times can display histrionic behaviours when life does not go our way and we throw a tantrum. However, people with this disorder feel uncomfortable or unappreciated when they are not the center of attention. With this disorder they are prone to self-dramatisation, theatricality and exaggerated expression of emotion, such as sobbing uncontrollably on minor sentimental occasions, or having temper tantrums, all of which can be turned on or off very quickly. This behaviour can sometimes be displayed by famous performers.

A common personality disorder is the Borderline. Natalie's behaviour is a typical example. Jason and Natalie had been together for five years and during that time Jason, has been turning himself inside out to maintain the relationship. Sometimes Natalie was delightful, loving, and thoughtful, then she could turn very vindictive, accusing him of all sorts of things including not loving her and infidelity. When she was having one of her "off" days, she would threaten to kill herself, or sometimes disappear for hours without telling anyone where she was going. If Jason spent any time with his mates after football practice, he would often face a raging tornado when he got home. He stopped playing football, the tantrums weren't worth it. Natalie was threatening suicide more often and then drove her car into a tree. Jason was beside himself, but it didn't matter what he said or did, it was never enough to reassure her. Unfortunately, she did commit suicide. In her fear of real or imagined abandonment, she was self-destructive, angry, unstable, and impossible to live with. Part of Jason carries guilt and responsibility for Natalie's suicide, even though she had a mental problem, which manifested as a Borderline Personality Disorder.

An Antisocial Personality Disorder is much the same as the name suggests, a disregarding of the rights of others. They can be aggressive to animals and people, destructive of property, deceitful, or seriously violate rules. They are frequently dishonest and manipulative in order to gain personal profit or pleasure. Often criminals will have these characteristics.

Someone with an Avoidant Disorder will be incredibly socially inhibited. This comes from feelings of inadequacy or hypersensitivity to criticism. People may avoid work or school activities because of a fear of disapproval or rejection. They will be extremely sensitive to some even slightly disapproving or critical comments and believe themselves to be socially inept, personally unappealing, or inferior to others.

We have all heard of the Paranoid Personality Disorder, which is a pervasive distrust and suspiciousness of others whose actions are interpreted as malevolent. People with this believe others are out to exploit, harm or deceive them even if no evidence exists to support this expectation. Many people, as they get older and frailer start to develop tendencies toward this disorder. As they lose confidence in their own ability to take care of themselves they can feel more vulnerable to being taken advantage of and become more suspicious.

Someone with a Schizoid Personality Disorder, detaches from social relationships and has a restricted range of emotional expression. Suffers lack a desire for intimacy and seem indifferent to developing close relationships, nor are they particularly interested in being part of a family or social group. They prefer to be loners, and seem indifferent to others' approval or criticism.

People with a Schizotypal Disorder, which is similar to a Schizoid Disorder, will often be very uncomfortable in close relationships. Their thinking can be quite distorted and their behaviour eccentric. They may be superstitious or preoccupied with paranormal phenomena. They may also believe they have magical or special powers. People with this disorder can often be suspicious or paranoid. The film *A Brilliant Mind*, the true story of the famous mathematician John Nash, illustrates this condition beautifully.

We have all heard of people who continually wash their hands, or who will check and recheck umpteen times whether they've locked the house, or like Jack Nicholson in the film *As Good as it Gets,* will not walk on the cracks in the footpath and always brought his own cutlery to restaurants in case he was exposed to germs. These and similar symptoms are indicators of Obsessive-Compulsive Disorders. These folk are preoccupied with orderliness, perfectionism and control at the expense of flexibility, openness and efficiency. They try to maintain control through painstaking attention to rules, trivial details and procedure, which defeat the object of the activity. They are excessively careful and pay extraordinary attention to detail and checking for possible mistakes. While it may be funny in the movies these disorders cause their sufferers a great deal of distress and anxiety.

BIBLIOGRAPHY

Berne, Eric. *Games People Play*. 1964. Cox & Wyman. Great Britain
Bradshaw, John. *Healing The Shame That Binds You*. 1988. Health Communications Inc. Florida
Campbell, Joseph. *The Hero with a Thousand Faces*. 1968 (2nd edition) Princeton NJ: Princeton University Press (37–38)
Dallos, Sally., Dallos, Rudi., *Couples, Sex and Power The politics of Desire*, 1997 Open University Press, Buckingham
Dalai Lama, Cutler H. Howard., *The Art of Happiness, A Handbook for Living* 1999, Hodder & Stoughton, Australia. (p.283)
Dyer, Wayne. Real Magic, *Creating Miracles in Everyday Life*. 1992 Harper Collins, Australia
Erikson, Milton, Rossi, E., and Rossi, S. *Hypnotic Realities*. 1976. Irvington, N.Y.
Freud, Sigmund. *The Ego and the Id* 1923. W W Norton & Company Inc, N.Y.
Hendrix, Harville. *Getting The Love You Want – A Guide for Couples*. 1988. Schwartz & Wilkinson, Australia
Houston, Jean. *The Search For The Beloved – Journeys in Sacred Psychology*. 1987. J.P. Tarcher Inc. California
Jansen, David; Newman, Margaret & Carmichael, Claire. *Really Relating, How to build an enduring relationship*. 2003 Random House, Australia
Jung, Carl Gustav. *The Practice of Psychotherapy : essays on the psychology of the transference and other subjects*. 1946. 2nd edition and augm., 3rd print
Kehoe, John. *Mind Power*. 1987 Zoetic Inc. British Columbia
Keller, Jeff. *Attitude is Everything*. INTI Publishing & Resource Books

Mason, Paul T & Kreger, Randi. *Stop Walking On Eggshells – Taking your life back when someone you care about has Borderline Personality Disorder.* 1998. New Harbinger Publications, California

Maslow, Abraham H., 1987. *Motivation and Personality, 3rd ed.* New York: Harper & Row.

Matthews, Andrew. *Happiness in a Nutshell.* 2002 Seashell Publishers, Queensland, Australia

McGraw, Phillip. *Relationship Rescue Don't Make Excuses! Start repairing your relationship today.* 2000. Vermilion Random House, London

Myss, Caroline. *Sacred Contracts – Awakening Your Divine Potential.* 2001. Harmony Books, New York

Miller, Alison. *The Drama Of Being A Child.* 1995. Basic Books Inc, Great Britain

Milligram, Stanley. *Obedience to Authority: An Experimental View.* 1974

Ostrow, Ruth. "I just cooked to say I love you". Article printed in *The Weekend Australian,* June 23–24 2001

Peck, Scott. *The Road Less Travelled.* 1990. Arrow Books, London

Piaget, Jean. *Handbook of child psychology.* 1970. Vol.1. New York: Wiley, 1983.

Siegel J. Daniel & Hartzell, Mary. *Parenting from the Inside Out, How a deeper self-understanding can help you raise children who thrive.* 2003 Tarcher/Penquin

Siegel J. Daniel. *The Developing Mind. How relationships and the brain interact to shape who we are.* 1999. Guildford Press

Spinelli, Ernesto. *The Mirror And The Hammer – Challenges to therapeutic orthodoxy.* 2001. Continuum, London

Richardson, Ronald. *Family Ties That Bind – A self-help guide to change through Family of Origin therap.* 1996. Self-Counsel Press, Vancouver and Bellingham WA

Sanaya, Roman. *Spiritual Growth – Being Your Higher Self.* 1989. H.J. Kramer Inc. California

Satir, Virginia. *Your Many Faces.* 1975. Celestial Arts. Millabrae CA

Schiraldi, Glenn R. *The Self-Esteem Workbook.* 2001. New Harbinger Publications, Inc.

Tucker-Ladd, Clayton E. *Psychological Self-Help.* 1996. Mental Health Net.

Yalom, D. Irvin. *The Theory and Practice of Group Psychotherapy.* 1995 Basic Books, USA
Wilson, Timothy. *Strangers to Ourselves, Discovering the Adaptive Unconscious 2002* Belknap Harvard

This book forms the basis of a programme I have written called the Awareness Advantage. This programme aims to improve relationships within organisations and groups by enabling people to understand why they think the way they do and how that impacts on their behaviour.

The workshop is designed to empower and facilitate self awareness, choice and responsibility. It leads to empowered successful relationships.

For further information see www.awarenessadvantage.com

www.ingramcontent.com/pod-product-compliance
Lightning Source LLC
Chambersburg PA
CBHW051812090426
42736CB00011B/1444